OTHER BOOKS BY
Roger E. Herman

The Process of Excelling
(in English and Portuguese)

Turbulence! Challenges and Opportunities in the World of Work
(in English and Spanish)

Signs of the Times

Lean & Meaningful: A New Culture for Corporate America
co-authored with Joyce L. Gioia, CMC

How to Become an Employer of Choice
co-authored with Joyce L. Gioia, CMC

How to Choose Your Next Employer
co-authored with Joyce L. Gioia, CMC

Work Force Stability
co-authored with Joyce L. Gioia, CMC

Impending Crisis
co-authored with Tom Olivo and Joyce L. Gioia, CMC

Keeping Good People was first published in hardcover by Oakhill Press in 1990. McGraw-Hill published the work in hardcover and trade paperback editions from 1991-1994. The book was featured by the *Business Week* Book Club and The Newbridge Executive Book Club. ***Keeping Good People*** has been a consistent best-seller for the Society for Human Resource Management for years.

Keeping Good People has been published in Spanish, German, and Portuguese and is distributed internationally. The content continues to serve as the foundation of the author's speeches, seminars, and workshops on the topic in the U.S. and around the world. Employee retention is a global problem.

Other learning tools on this topic include a six-cassette audiotape album (not a reading of the book's text), a video-based training package designed for small businesses and segments of larger organizations, and a video tape designed for corporate training. These products are available from The Herman Group at www.hermangroup.com.

Roger Herman is available for consultations and speaking engagements.

The Herman Group
3400 Willow Grove Court
Greensboro, North Carolina 27410-8600
(800) 227-3566
(336) 282-9370

Keeping Good People

Strategies for Solving the #1 Problem Facing Businesses Today

Roger E. Herman

Oakhill Press
Winchester, VA

10 9 8 7 6 5 4

Library of Congress Cataloging in Publication Data

Herman, Roger E.,

Keeping good people : strategies for solving the #1 problem facing businesses today / Roger E. Herman

p. cm.

Includes index.

ISBN 1-886939-26-8 (pbk. : alk. paper)

1. Incentives in industry — United States. 2. Career development. — United States. 3. Compensation management — United States. I. Title.

HF5549.5.I5H467 1999

658.3, 14—dc21 99-11120

CIP

Dedication

If we're lucky, there comes a time when we become energized. Someone enters our life and somehow kindles a long-forgotten flame . . . or even a spark that has never burst into brightness before.

That special person may be a teacher, a mentor, or some distant hero who inspires, cares, and serves as a role model. As we begin to grow, to blossom, a new excitement stimulates a whole new dedication to life . . . to making a difference. We dare to dream—big dreams—and suddenly find ways to live those dreams.

Sometimes that special person brings knowledge and understanding from the outside, but really helps us discover even more of what's inside. The new energy and enthusiasm create an almost indescribable kind of power that makes a person feel that anything is possible.

Over our lifetimes, we encounter a number of people who influence us . . . some a lot, some a little. It all adds up. I dedicate this book to those people who have made a difference in my life—who have inspired and encouraged and shared with me.

Most especially, I dedicate this book to my wife, Joyce. Thank you for enriching my life beyond anything I expected. You are truly a partner in every sense of the word.

Table of Contents

Section 1

Section 2

Section 3

Appendices

Foreword

In 1996, our company was faced with a dangerous employee turnover problem. Because we were not able to hold on to people long enough, we had serious difficulties serving our current customers. Our expansion plans were stalled because we did simply didn't have the stability to support our growth. The market was there, but we just didn't have the people to get the job done.

When we measured 300% turnover, we decided we'd had enough. Turnover was costing hundreds of thousands of dollars—right off our bottom line. Something had to be done. As we started looking around for answers and advice, we discovered ***Keeping Good People***. The book was filled with ideas and approaches for us to put to work.

We experienced such great results applying what we read in the book, we called the author, Roger Herman, for more in-depth support. We wanted to lead our industry in employee retention. Roger sent his partner, Joyce Gioia, CMC, to work with us. Joyce pointed out some specific strategies in ***Keeping Good People*** and told us about some others that would appear in the new edition. Result: our turnover dropped from 300% to 25% within five months! Details can be found in the January 1998 issue of *Inc.* Magazine in the feature article about our success, "How Ya Gonna Keep 'Em Down in the Firm?"

This new, expanded edition of Roger Herman's best-selling book is even better than the one that started us on our exciting journey to leadership in our field. I commend this guide to you. As you move through the pages, you'll learn a lot from the man who literally "wrote the book" on employee retention. I learn from him every time I hear him speak or talk with him about our success . . . and our continuing challenge.

The campaign to keep good people never stops. Your mission is to apply all these great ideas in your company, continually. You'll see a difference on *your* bottom line, too.

Eric Rabinowitz, President
I-H-S Helpdesk Service
New York

Acknowledgements

In thinking about who has contributed to my work in employee retention—to make this expansion and revision possible, I first acknowledge my valued clients who have taught me so much over the years. They have provided me with rich platforms for learning. Each of them has contributed to my background, understanding, and experience. I trust I have also contributed to their growth and progress.

My colleagues, especially those who are Fellows of The Workforce Stability Institute, have contributed insights, critiques, and support to keep me focused. They have challenged me to keep looking deeper and to continue sharing what we have learned. Other Certified Management Consultants, particularly some who serve with me on the board of directors of the Institute of Management Consultants, have helped me see things from different perspectives. They have helped this book become even more readable, relevant, and constructive. A special thanks to Wayne Outlaw, CSP, CMC, who keeps me challenged intellectually in the work that we do.

The fine team at The Herman Group deserves public appreciation for all they have done to strengthen my work, to challenge me, and to encourage me to produce our books, tapes, and other tools to help employers keep their good people and keep them productive.

A salute to the professionalism, support, and harassment from Paula Gould and Ed Helvey at Oakhill Press. I now have a better understanding of deadlines, though I may still miss them! Craig Hines continues to do his fine work as a member of the Oakhill Press team.

Last, and certainly not least, is my family. My wife and partner, Joyce L. Gioia, CMC, makes it all worthwhile. The challenge, support, and energy I receive from her is cherished. Her contribution, through our editing and critical review process has been instrumental in making this book what it is. Her involvement is invaluable since, as my partner, she has shared with me the consulting and speaking experiences that have enriched the re-write of this book. Thanks to my children, Scott and Jennifer, and my stepchildren, Bruce, Jeff, Belinda, Melissa, and Samantha for their support and for the insight they have given me to their generations.

Introduction

Running a business, institution, non-profit organization, or government agency is certainly different today from what it was a generation or two ago. The world has changed; the rules have changed. What we took for granted in the past isn't necessarily true anymore today

Resources are not as plentiful as they once were. When we gather the resources we need, we must make more creative uses of them to maximize our return on investment. The risk of losing those resources, even though we thought we had them well in hand, hangs over us like a Sword of Damocles.

Success is described in many different ways. Each of us subscribes to our own formula of achievement and satisfaction. However we define it, success rarely comes easily. Accomplishment takes time and hard work. In order to get things done in our lives, we have to marshal the necessary resources and apply them well.

For most of us, success is not achieved alone. Sure, we like to think we were responsible for what we've done and what we've become. We are—in part. We provide the impetus, the leadership, the inspiration, the drive to make things happen. But, other people are part of our success, too. Other people play a number of motivating and supporting roles to enable us to make a difference. In our complex society, we have become significantly interdependent. Particularly in organizational settings. Everything we do is connected with things other people do.

Since I was in the ninth grade back in the 1950s, I have worked in business organizations, interacting with other people in one way or another. I've learned a few things. I've discovered what works . . . and what doesn't work. I won't say I have all the answers. No one really does.

In this book, as in my consulting and speaking work, I enjoy sharing answers, approaches, and ideas that I have found to be successful. Some of these ideas and techniques I have learned and practiced personally. Other insights have come to me through other people—directly, through observation, and from reading what they have written. We learn from each other.

As you read through the pages that follow, you will benefit from the knowledge and experience I have gained from my colleagues in The Workforce Stability Institute, other consultants and researchers, our clients, and countless others who have shared with us over the years.

In my work as a corporate consultant, focusing on the application and development of human resources, I have found it quite helpful to raise issues, to ask questions, to get people thinking in ways they had not been thinking before. A great deal of organizational success results from people looking critically and/or creatively at their circumstances, then designing better ways to do things.

I don't claim to have any great secrets that will change the world. You can't turn to a certain page in this book, recite some incantation, and watch amazed as a flash of lightning reveals the secrets of the universe! The power comes from relating the concepts in books like this one to what's happening in *your* organization, then applying what you learn toward making a difference.

Keeping Good People, like my other books, is an extension of my life's work. Through these writings, I aim to stimulate your thinking. If your awareness is raised, if you can see things you hadn't seen before, if you can see familiar things differently, then you will have the power of insight.

I can but share perspectives, approaches, ideas. Their value rests in what you do with the knowledge you gain from reading these words. I hope some of what you discover in this book will serve as an inspiration for you to take actions to make a difference for your organization and for your people.

You're a Leader of Good People

Most of the men and women who read this book will be leaders and managers of various kinds of organizations. Those organizations will include for-profit businesses of all types, not-for-profit organizations and agencies, educational institutions, local governments, and associations. While the purpose and technology of these entities may be quite different, all share the need to produce the greatest possible return on their investment in human resources.

Our human resources, our people, are at once the most valuable, the most costly, and the most volatile of all the resources we use to accomplish the organization's work. We need good people to get things done. Our biggest challenge in management today is to attract, optimize, and keep our good people.

"Good" can be defined any way you wish. For some, the descriptor will apply to someone's technical expertise. For others, it will refer to dedication, productivity, drive and determination, high achievement, creative capacity, experience, educational level, position in the industry or field, or any combination of these and other factors. I will leave the definition to you, based on what qualities are most important to accomplish your goals.

If your people are not what you would describe as "good," you have other problems to address. To manage a successful organization, you must establish minimum standards describing the competencies and performance of people. Don't hire applicants who fail to meet those standards; you're simply asking for trouble. If current employees don't meet your standards, you have only two choices: work with them so that they grow to meet your standards or give them a creative career redirection opportunity.

Design of this Book

In structuring ***Keeping Good People***, I designed the first section of the book to provide a foundation for the balance of the text. The more we understand about a problem, any problem, the better we are equipped to respond to it. The background information provided for you will help you develop that all-important "big picture."

Following the discussion of current and future conditions, we will consider a variety of strategic approaches to keeping good people. Our assumption is that you have hired good people to begin with; recruiting and hiring won't be discussed in this book. There is an abundance of material already written about those aspects of human resource management (see: Suggested Reading). Other books focusing on various aspects of building a stable workforce will be published in cooperation with The Workforce Stability Institute. Watch the Institute's Web site, www.employee.org, for announcements.

People leave their jobs because of internal drives to improve their position in life. They also leave because their working conditions are not comfortable for them. Many people move to another job, another company, simply because they feel they've been in one place long enough. There are other reasons, too, like a spouse's transfer to another section of the country, but this book can't possibly deal with all those situations.

Therefore, we're stating up front that this book is not complete. It can't be. The world is changing too rapidly to assert that all the answers on any topic can be locked into one volume. That's why we encourage you to be alert to everything you can learn about this topic.

What we will share in the following pages are strategies and techniques that have worked, in one situation or another, for people and organizations just like yours. You should have already thought about, and applied, some of what you are about to read. Some of the material in these pages should not be new for you. When you read something that seems familiar—you know that already, challenge yourself. Is your company practicing the technique, or just giving it "lip service"?

As a manager and a leader for most of my career, I have personally applied many of the strategies presented in this book. Most of the time they worked. As a management consultant serving a wide variety of organizations since 1980, I have observed and recommended many more approaches. Most of them worked.

No, not everything you try will work just the way you expect it to. It's not a perfect world. Some things are beyond our control, and some situations are a lot more complicated than we know. Simply put, you just have to gain all the information you can, then apply the strategies that seem to make the most sense at the time. Monitor your results, then make modifications as appropriate.

If you've done your best, be happy with yourself. If your plan worked, great! If it didn't, try something else. Life will have its setbacks. Just because you've perhaps lost one member of your team who was really important to you does not mean your entire organization is falling apart. There are probably many other good people around you; they need you and your enthusiastic leadership!

No Stories about Specific Companies

This book is not simply a recitation of success stories of specific companies that have kept good people on their teams. Many companies are doing wonderful things, with gratifying results. I have not cited these countless examples for several reasons:

First, just because a company is successful today in a particular endeavor does not mean that the company will be as successful in the future. Companies that are successful in one aspect of their activity may not be worthy of note in other aspects.

Second, it is counterproductive to compare yourself to others. Each of us works with a unique set of circumstances. What makes sense for Company A may be totally wrong for Company B. And, if Company A's executives were asked, they'd probably tell you not to try their way in your situation.

Third, from my experience as a manager and as a consultant, I encourage every reader to think for himself or herself. Engage in a careful examination of your environment, of your challenges, of your people. Then, with good intentions and knowledge gained from this book and other sources, do what you feel is best for your organization.

You have to take calculated risks to determine what is most appropriate for you and your people. You can't simply "go by the book" when leading a team of people and managing a company. You must apply your instincts, your "gut feelings," to achieve your desired results.

Keeping Good People offers ideas, food for thought. It is up to you to decide which approaches would be most effective for you.

Let's Move Forward Together

As you continue with your reading, please consider me as your personal consultant. I'll be talking directly with you. It will be like having someone right there in the same room with you, sharing ideas, raising issues, encouraging, pointing out problem areas for you to consider.

Reading this book will be a "cafeteria" experience for you. Some of what is offered you will hungrily and eagerly consume. Other things may not be what you are looking for. You may already be doing some of the things suggested, or they simply may not fit in your situation. You pick and choose, cafeteria-style. If you find but one good idea that makes a significant difference for you, our investment in each other will have been worthwhile.

You will find ***Keeping Good People*** a worthwhile book to read from start to finish. You'll also find value in using the book as a reference tool to re-visit from time to time. Many companies have used the first edition as a training text, arranging for teams of managers to read assigned portions, then discuss the application of the book's ideas in their companies.

There is so much that needs to be done in this field, I know I've missed some things. It's a human foible and a frustration for all writers and speakers. After we've delivered our message, we think of something else we could have said. Or we discover something we didn't know before; and the book went to press or we delivered the speech or seminar. We all continue to learn and grow, discovering new things we didn't know before.

This revised, expanded, and enriched edition includes valuable information, ideas, and insights that I've learned since ***Keeping Good People*** was first published in 1990. The labor shortage and market churning I predicted to start around mid-decade happened as forecast. This condition will prevail for at least another ten years. Since the problem won't go away, we might as well approach it head-on.

If you have some ideas that I haven't covered in this book, please let me know. If there are techniques or approaches that have worked for you, I'd like to learn about them. We'll share them in our weekly electronic newsletter, *Trend Alert,* and in *Workforce Stability Alert,* the monthly newsletter published by The Workforce Stability Institute. For information on the Institute and subscriptions to the newsletter, call (336) 282-1480 or e-mail executive director James G. deWindt at jimd@employee.org. Subscribe to *Trend Alert* by e-mailing alert@herman.net, typing "subscribe" in the subject box.

So . . . read, learn, apply, and enjoy!

1

Good People and Their Value

For any kind of an organization to run successfully, several human elements are essential. One need is good leadership at the top and, for best results, throughout the organization. A second need is for good management. Third, there must be a team of people with the knowledge, skills, aptitudes, and attitudes to perform at a sufficiently high level of production to accomplish the organization's mission.

The same requirements are there, whether you are running a manufacturing company, a service business, a professional firm, a non-profit organization, an educational institution, a social service agency, a volunteer group, or any other kind of entity. The need is universal.

When we use the term, "good people," we're talking about your employees who have the capability, and use that capability to accomplish the work of the organization in a high-achieving manner. These are the kinds of people who are sought by managers and human resource professionals. When the recruiting effort is successful, the next objective is to enable the new team member to be as productive as possible . . . and to keep that person on the team.

What makes these people "good"? There are a number of factors that distinguish what we describe as good people from others. It's a quality issue. The ones who are good are the top performers we would prefer not to lose. They are the people who get the job done.

We find good people in every occupation. There are good people in management, in research and development, in the production area, in sales and marketing, in administrative services, and in the custodial ranks. They're everywhere! Each kind of organization has its categories of employee titles and roles, and there are good people in all these places.

Being good does not require any particular level of education or professional credentials. Experience does not automatically make someone a better employee. The difference is how the education and experience are applied. And the organization's culture and leadership significantly influence that application. Encouragement and reinforcement make a difference when you have good people to make it all work.

The speed with which someone works does not necessarily make that person a good employee. Quality is just as important, if not more important, in measuring actual results. Hours worked are not, by themselves, a performance indicator. We're looking for results, not merely levels of activity.

Some people are good because they're so creative, but in another occupation creativity may not be as strong a factor in considering a person's value. Some are good because they can stick with a project and see it through to completion. Others are highly valued because of their ability to solve problems or initiate new projects.

Some people are valuable to organizations because of their ability to communicate, to work well with coworkers, customers, or suppliers. Collaboration can make a major difference in organizational success. Other people are equally valued because of their ability to work independently to get their jobs done. Each person brings different strengths to the group.

The assessment of an employee as "good" is a value judgment made by the organization's leadership and others on the team. In making such a determination, they recognize that this good employee is one of the more important members of the team, for whatever reason(s). This is one of the people most responsible for the organization accomplishing its goals.

Ideally, all the employees will be good. Working together as a high performance team, they get results. We would not want to lose any of them. If we have hired, trained, and managed well, each of our people will be good—highly valued—for one reason or another.

It is these good people we want to keep on our team. They make the difference for us. They enable us to do what we are expected to do (or even to exceed those expectations). If these people are not working on our team, they could be just as successful on some other organization's team.

The Value of Good People

Those we describe as "good people" often set the pace on their work teams. As pacesetters, they inspire and motivate others by their example and by their enthusiasm. Those around them strive more diligently. In some cases, the entire work team is more energetic, more supportive, and more productive. Good people inspire others directly and indirectly toward high achievement.

Research, development, production, and service people are more motivated when working with someone who has demonstrated expertise. Everyone around such a person feels more confident because of the high level of competence shown by this one dedicated employee. Quality and accuracy are measurably higher when good technical people are involved.

Sales and marketing efforts are considerably more effective when undertaken by conscientious professionals. Such good people can assure a company an abundance of solid, profitable business that can be sustained over a long period of time.

Creativity and innovation are in high demand in many organizations today. Those who can solve the puzzles, who can aggressively meet the challenges with new and different approaches, can make a significant difference in overall success. We need adaptable people with problem-solving skills.

Persistence is valued in many organizations today. The perseverance to stick with a project or task until it is finished is vital. To get things done, methodically following through on routine and special assignments with reliability is important. Practically every team needs good people who can be depended upon.

Accuracy, attention to detail, quality control, careful research and analysis are required in the effective functioning of most organizations. Good people who can perform this kind of work are vital to their continued success.

Good people don't necessarily stand out in the crowd. Our definition includes those who don't do anything dramatic, but you can depend on them to get their jobs done. These unsung heroes show up for work every day, they're dependable and reliable, and they aren't looking for recognition. They are still highly valued members of our team, deserving of our appreciation and support.

Each of our good people brings something unique to the work team. Each becomes even more valuable when led by other good people who mold them into highly productive teams. As these good people work cooperatively together, the work gets done, people enjoy what they are doing, and the desired results are achieved.

2

The Employer's Predicament

As we move from the 1990s into the 2000s, employers face a predicament few might have predicted. The economy is strong, technology is expanding our capacity, global markets beckon, but we don't have enough qualified people to get the work done. Many business owners and executives feel like they're poised at the starting line for a high-purse Grand Prix, in a car with a power plant that can outrun anything in the field. Just as the flag comes down, the car runs out of gas. The crippled capacity to compete is frustrating, irritating, and difficult to comprehend.

Let's explore the history that brought us to this place, the trends that will influence our future situation, and the strategies we can use to re-position ourselves for success in the years ahead. As we consider the "big picture," we can better understand and appreciate the conditions and the challenges of the world around us . . . the world in which we each live today and the world in which we will live tomorrow.

While the problem of plentiful jobs and a volatile workforce is not a simple one, some of the potential solutions are not that difficult. A clear vision of the overall predicament is helpful to better appreciate the importance of the strategic solutions. Understanding the challenge of attracting, optimizing, and keeping good people will enable you, as an employer and/or organizational leader, to better manage the achievement of desired results.

A Brief Historical Perspective

For decades, we had plenty of good jobs and plentiful talent available to fill them. Although many work functions were labor-intensive, there were plenty of people available to fill them. Employers had choices of who they would hire. The jobs to be done were not that complicated. If we lost a worker, it wasn't difficult to find a replacement.

Workers tended to stay with one employer for many years. The societal trend was to work for a company for a long time. The scenario of someone retiring with 30 to 40 years of service was relatively common. Earning the gold watch was an honorable experience. Being a "company man" was highly regarded.

But all was not rosy. There was discontent among a lot of those people. Many would have preferred to leave, but were discouraged by society from "job-hopping." Instead, they endured the existence of daily toil in jobs they didn't like. The psychological pain was palpable. These unhappy men (and the majority of workers were men in those days) usually resigned themselves to carrying their burden. That's what everyone else did—even with complaints; to move from one job to another was frowned upon. Instead, these sad people expressed their unhappiness to their sympathetic families in the privacy of their homes.

Their children listened. A generation of children vowed to find some sort of more satisfying career design for themselves. Although we began to see more movement, more people changing jobs several times during their career, the shift was gradual. While the interest in more frequent movement was growing, we still had more people than jobs. Workers seeking new opportunities approached the job search process aggressively, sending out resumes or personally applying to prospective employers. Across the land, personnel departments accumulated thick files of well-qualified people looking for greener pastures.

The search for a new position was not an easy endeavor. Looking for one's next job was described as being similar to working a regular job. Employers had plenty of choices of good candidates and, if someone didn't work out, there were plenty of applicants waiting for their opportunities.

Gradually, society accepted the concept of people working for several employers during a career. The norm was still to invest many years—a decade, perhaps—with one company before moving on to another job. This time investment was different even from past years, when the expectation was to work for one company for many years, if not your entire career.

Keeping good people was not a big concern for most employers, since job security was highly valued by workers. Civil service positions and jobs with companies that had unions were coveted because termination by management was more difficult. And if people did leave, their work was easily absorbed by others or assumed by fellow employees eager to move up the career ladder.

Some workers discovered they could improve their income and prospects for the future by moving more frequently from company to company. They would invest several years with an employer, gaining valuable experience and training, then seek an opportunity at another company. Selling their strength, achievements, and potential, these ambitious folks would negotiate higher compensation with each move. The sense among a growing segment of the population was that to better one's career destiny, it was wise—often necessary—to move from one company to another.

The stage was set. The trend was in place. Successive generations would enjoy more societal freedom to progress from one employer to another. Young people, still hearing stories of unsatisfactory job experiences from their parents, older friends, and relatives, vowed not to be trapped in unhappy employment. Other influences, such as television shows, endorsed the concept of quick solutions, frequent changes, and control over one's own destiny.

Corporate Loyalty Disintegrates

The employment commitment was changed forever in the early 1990s. Most employees felt secure with their employers during the late 1980s. The "cradle to grave" concept was firmly in place. Workers were loyal to their employers; in return, companies were loyal to their people. Most people weren't aggressively looking for their next job. It was comfortable to commit to one company for long periods of time. People felt secure that their company would take care of them.

During this era, employers were still almost paternalistic toward their dedicated employees. Extensive fringe benefit programs were in place to take care of workers and their families. In a mutually dependent environment, employers and employees were invested in each other for the long term.

Then the recession hit. The business downturn hit with the vengeance of an economic hurricane. And, as happens with many hurricanes, the downturn was not as serious as the media projected and reported. Still, the financial squeeze was devastating to many employers.

At the same time, companies were moving toward restructuring. Technology had already made it possible to produce with fewer people, or at least different people. Many employers had discovered they had fattened up by hiring too many people. Personnel departments, now enhanced and renamed "human resource" departments, realized that their companies had significant numbers of "redundant employees."

All these conditions came together with a resounding crash. Employers, sometimes panicking and sometimes thinking very carefully, began trimming their ranks. In seemingly dramatic moves that felt like massacres, these companies put thousands of people out in the street without their jobs. Whether people were laid off, removed through a "reduction in force," given early retirement, fired, or terminated due to plant closings, the result was the same. Suddenly, a generation of workers, who had placed their trust in their employers, experienced the emotional trauma of losing their employment security.

The shock was emotionally severe, aside from the economic challenges that people had to face. People who had placed their faith in their employers, who had put all their career eggs in one basket, were devastated. What happened to the loyalty? "We've given you our lives!" The agony was felt by employees at all levels—including those in the management ranks who had been forced to make the decisions.

Trust evaporated. Who would be terminated? (The word had an ominous sound.) Who would be left? And how long would they be around before the next wave of layoffs would come? Since the economic conditions reached practically all sectors of employment, few people were able to find other jobs. The mood was reminiscent of the depression of the early 1930s, though it was not as serious. People—families—who were affected felt the pain just the same.

Corporate loyalty died.

Never again would workers blindly trust their employers. Trust would have to be earned, and it wouldn't come easily. The generation of workers affected directly would be skeptical forever. Their children, the next resource of workers, would be cynical. They had watched in horror as their parents were emotionally destroyed—ripped away from relative security and thrown into uncertainty for which they were unprepared.

Yes, these words sound somewhat melodramatic today . . . years beyond the initial impact of the downsizings, rightsizings, and other euphemisms. But, when employers cut deeply into their ranks—many too deeply, history would show—the emotional jolt was far-reaching.

The next generation to enter the workforce, Generation X, heard the message loud and clear. Workers would henceforth be responsible for their own career destinies. No longer would they depend on—trust—employers to take care of their careers. The essential relationship between worker and employer had changed forever. Workers would no longer depend on employers to guide their careers, provide needed training and education, assure them a future.

Corporate Cocooning

The media picked up on the downsizing theme and spotlighted the tactic every time an announcement was made. The image of good people simply being discarded like unwanted garbage prevailed as the media reported every layoff or negative movement. The prevailing mood was that few, if any, decent jobs were available. The lines of the unemployed and homeless became longer.

Those people who had jobs counted themselves fortunate. So many of their friends, neighbors, and relatives were unemployed or had been forced to take early retirement. Their feeling was reinforced at work by supervisors who reminded them, often in a not-so-kind manner, "you're lucky to have a job." A general malaise set in, slowing employee turnover. People resigned themselves to their circumstances.

Most workers held onto the jobs they had. They did not

necessarily like the work they did, their bosses, their co-workers, the location, the pay, or even the company logo. But they stayed there, clinging to the continuity of the jobs they had. There was nowhere else to go. They remained within the safety, the security, of the job they had—much like staying in a cocoon, a corporate cocoon. The societal message was still validating being gainfully employed, avoiding breaks in employment.

The people who were fully employed in the mid-1990s worked hard. They put in long hours to get the work done and insure that they satisfied customers. Managers pushed people to produce, but many didn't show the gratitude that their employees would have appreciated. Productivity climbed to high levels; America was setting records again. But, at what expense? Many people spent a lot more time at work and a lot less time with their families than they wanted to. Stress levels were high.

These workers felt trapped. When things improve, they vowed, "I'm outta here." "I'm history." Pressure was building to jump ship. Staying on board was too much to bear . . . but there was no place to go. Employee turnover remained low.

Their situation was exacerbated by the allocation of work to be done. Companies were now operating with leaner staffs, but the workload had not decreased. In fact, in some cases, the workload increased as employers aggressively went after any piece of business they could find. Now all this work had to be spread among fewer workers. Working hours—and stress—increased. Efficiency dropped as people were pushed beyond their limits. Frustration increased.

Employers discovered, to their horror, that many of their employees had significant difficulty rising to the tasks to be done. Their lackadaisical hiring practices and whitewash performance evaluations had caught up with them. The more demanding situations revealed a disturbing lack of competence in the workforce.

Rebuilding

As the economy picked up, employers began hiring again. They were cautious; the drive was first to get more productivity out of the people they had.

As a number of corporate economists predicted (and I agreed with their forecasts), the economy began to heat up in the second half of the decade of the 1990s. Some leading edge economists suggested that the country was on the threshold of an unprecedented boom—one that would create more jobs. We saw the beginnings of an economic turnaround.

The growing economy stimulated more business for employers who had downsized "to the bone." Now they needed more people. Positions opened at every level of the organization . . . what I term "vertical job growth." And they needed much more than just "burger flippers" or other front-line hourly workers. Corporate America had gone on a crash diet, shedding fat all over its "body." Now it was gaining weight again—all over its body. Structures were changing; use of new technology was more widespread. People were placed into different kinds of roles—at all levels of the organization.

Recruiting began again, cautiously. Employers understandably hesitated to hire aggressively without more confidence that they would be able to sustain their higher level of activity to pay for the higher labor costs.

In spite of the careful hiring, enough new jobs were created to have a noticeable impact on the unemployment rate. Before long, the most competent people on the unemployment lines had been absorbed back into the economy. Employers began looking for people who could be trained to perform the work that needed to be done. Corporate investment in training and development increased substantially as some companies even hired directly from the homeless shelters. The race was on to attract good workers to meet the growing needs of customers.

Before most people realized what was happening (they were

still reading the newspapers proclaiming doom-and-gloom downsizing), growth in hiring had produced a labor shortage. A drop in the birth rate a generation before produced a 15.1 percent reduction in the flow of new (young) entrants into the workforce. More jobs began looking for fewer people.

Where might employers go next looking for the people they need? That's right, the ranks of the currently employed. Recruiting became more aggressive. People valued enough to be kept employed were favored by employers hungry for increased competence.

Churning Predicted

The secret was out! Jobs were available. All kinds of jobs. People started moving to the greener pastures . . . or at least new pastures. Many initial moves were more escape from current situations than seeking a particular new opportunity. In the early 1990s, I predicted that in the mid-1990s we'd see "an unprecedented churning in the labor marketplace," as the pent-up pressure released, enabling trapped workers to break loose of their cocoons.

The movement became noticeable in 1994. As I raised the churning issue in my speeches to groups of corporate executives around the country, I began to hear stories about pockets of churning—industrial and geographic pockets. Employers began reporting, anecdotally, that employees were dissatisfied, disenchanted. The workers were looking for something better, but didn't know what. I heard story after story about good employees, people who had been with their companies for years, leaving to try something different.

Employers were frustrated and confused. They had not expected this out-migration and did not know how to handle it. They asked me a lot of questions—should they offer more money, should departed employees be encouraged or even allowed to return, how could the drain on valuable personnel be stemmed? Many employers still ask these questions and are still confused. They're sitting in their offices contemplating the problem instead of getting out with their people to learn what's driving the exodus.

My advice? Whenever you are trying to solve a problem, be sure you are wrestling with the actual causes, not just the symptoms. Treating symptoms is only a temporary, Band-Aid® solution. Talk with people, conduct surveys, listen. Uncover the causes and deal with them. Take aggressive actions and you'll see results. Remember how cynical people can be after years of "lip service." Take action!

The Trend Continues

Workers will continue to seek better opportunities. They must manage their own careers now; they can no longer depend on their employers to provide "womb-to-tomb" job security. Each worker will take control of his/her own career destiny. This shift in career development attitude will encourage people to move as often as they have to in order to improve and maintain their own positions for career advancement. "Job Hopping" will no longer be a negative description. In fact, we may even look askance at workers who stay very long at one place; what's wrong with them?

Young people entering the world of work will not show high interest in long-term career opportunities. The multiple decades of service to earn a gold watch doesn't attract today's workers. Watching the trends, I expect people to work an average of about two to four years at any one job, then move on. The drive for self-preservation and ambition will stimulate people to continually seek better opportunities for themselves . . . as long as they are dissatisfied with their current situations. If they are comfortable where they are, and see that they can achieve their life objectives by staying with their current employers, they will remain.

Fighting the Trends

Keeping good people in the years ahead will be countertrend. The environment in the world of work will work against employers who are striving for workforce stability and continuity. A number of employees will move from job to job no matter what employers try to do to keep them. Greater insight into these trends is available in my book, ***Turbulence! Challenges and Opportunities in the World of Work.***

Some proportion of workers will seek more permanent positions. They will want to stay with you . . . or at least be willing to stick around for a while. By applying the strategies outlined in this book, and similar measures that will become clear to you, it is possible to manage your company's employee turnover. However, it will take more than mere "lip service." Employee retention requires concentrated, deliberate action.

Workers are now described as an asset for employers, not simply a "resource." More frequently, corporate leaders talk about capital assets (machinery, plant, funding) and human assets. Plant capital assets are relatively fixed; the people asset is volatile and requires a lot more care and attention to maintain. More than ever before in our history, our human resource is limited. We have more jobs than we have competent people to fill them. Employers must attract a high caliber of workers, train them, optimize them, and keep them.

Workforce stability is now a strategic issue.

3

The Competitive Environment

Competition is an accepted behavior in America. It's part of our national culture. We learn competitiveness as children, and it becomes a natural part of our existence.

Each of us competes against others in many aspects of our lives: in sports, in school work, in striving for a better place in line at the check-out counter, and vying for a more advantageous position in traffic as we race toward work—or home—each day. We compete with ourselves to do things better, faster, or cheaper than we did them previously.

So, it's quite normal for people to compete in the work environment, as well. We compete for the best parking spaces or office spaces. We compete for attention from the boss or favored customer. Promotions and special assignments are considered competitive arenas. The winners "earn" the benefits that come with winning. Losers, if the losing is perceived as bitter, may leave the playing field to look for another opportunity to win.

We compete, in the business world, for a wide range of resources to accomplish our objectives. Among these resources are capital, materials, space, time, and people. That's about all we really have to work with. Our productivity and profits come as a result of how we apply those resources.

Our competitive strengths come from efficient and effective use of resources by people. The way we utilize our human resource is really the last frontier of competition. We contribute strengths such as creativity, the development and application of technology, and task accomplishment focused on the achievement of results.

Essentially, then, to compete today we must earn the greatest possible return on our investment in human resources. The application of other resources is dependent on our having strong people on our team.

The Competition for Good People

It is an accepted fact in organizational growth, development, achievement, and stability, that we need to attract the best possible people to work productively as a smooth-functioning team.

Companies invest thousands of dollars in recruiting efforts to attract the quality of applicants they need. This investment is expected in the personnel marketplace. Employers must aggressively seek the people they want and need. No longer can we expect superior applicants to be knocking at our door. We have to go out and find them.

Good people can be found on college campuses, in high schools and vocational schools, working for other employers, and within our own organization. And here's where the competition starts. Other employers also know where those fine people are, and they want to hire them, too. There are only so many people available. For the balance of the decade of the 1990s and for the first 5 to 8 years of the next decade, labor will remain a seller's market.

Many companies compete for the eager, receptive college graduates ready to leap off the campus into job opportunities that are beyond their parents' wildest dreams. These often well-equipped and malleable young people are potentially strong assets for the companies that hire them. They have a great deal to offer.

College seniors are looking very carefully at the options available with employers hungry for their talent and energy. They respond to high salary offers that make them look successful in the eyes of their peers (there's that competitive nature again). But, they are even more concerned about the personal growth opportunity, the human quality of the company, and even the long-range potential. The criteria used by graduating college seniors to select their first post-college employers have changed. They're searching for meaningfulness more than money.

Good people who are well employed are still receptive to overtures from other interested employers. We have a natural tendency to better ourselves, so if we're not comfortable and bonded to the company where we are, we may switch to the new employer . . . at least until a better opportunity comes along.

Recruiting people already employed by other companies will be increasingly difficult as employers struggle to hold on to them. Recruiters will be challenged to show significant advantages to entice people to make career changes. Increasingly aggressive recruiting will make employers more alert to the constant competitive environment in which we will all operate in the late1990s and early 2000s.

In their efforts to find the best people, employers would be well advised to look inside their own organizations. Some of your employees may be targets of outside recruitment efforts, while you overlook their potential. Before looking outside, consider the value of your own team members. You may have some wonderful talent, eager to stay with you to make even more of a difference for their employer. And those current employees are already familiar with your company, your culture, your customers, and their coworkers.

A word of warning: don't take for granted that your best people will stay with you. Continue to reinforce their value, their opportunity, their mutually beneficial long-term relationship with you. When you begin taking them for granted, you open the door for the competition to come a-courting. Continually re-sell your good people on the wisdom of remaining with you.

How to Attract Good People

Part of keeping good people is attract and hire the right ones in the first place. The things you do to make your company more appealing for outsiders will also enhance the value of employment for those already on your team. So, there are multiple reasons for making yourself look good as an employer of choice. Create the right kind of image, and your recruitment efforts will be more successful.

There are numerous methods for spreading the positive word about employment at your company. Recruiters usually think first about displays and interviews at job fairs, on college campuses, at trade shows, and at vocational schools. Those are fine, for targeted efforts, but your company must have a positive image to support those sales pitches.

The values, shared by the majority of the good people you want to attract and keep, lean heavily toward employers being solid corporate citizens. It will become increasingly important for companies to demonstrate their civic responsibility by involvement in community activities, contributions to industry and trade associations, and caring about environmental and social issues.

Some of these efforts will offer opportunities to get your people involved. This involvement enables them to be a part of the good things their employer is doing, strengthening the bonds of long-term relationships. Some examples are support of walkathons for charitable causes, United Fund drives, management support of nonprofit organizations, and urban redevelopment programs. There are many other worthwhile endeavors in your local and global communities deserving of corporate—and employee—participation.

Your corporate image is enhanced by good publicity, advertising, and public relations. Whether you engage an outside publicist or manage your promotion program internally, strive to gain positive exposure in the media. Share with news representatives information about new products or services, achievements by your people, plans for expansion, and anything else that might earn you some news or feature coverage.

Don't concentrate only on the dramatic stories that make a big splash. A lot of little items will be as effective . . . or even more effective. Think of the power of spaced repetition the psychologists tell us about. Repeated positive exposure of your company name, even for such things as sponsorship of Little League or the high school play, will remind people of your positioning as a good employer.

Other opportunities for valuable exposure (which may also generate positive publicity) include talks to local civic groups, and seminars at conventions and conferences, testimony before legislative committees. Consider also sponsorship or support of educational programs such as Junior Achievement at the high school level and academic groups at colleges and universities.

Check out the needs of elementary and middle schools in your community; your help will be sincerely appreciated and may influence a parent or older sibling to consider joining you. Beyond mere financial support, share your expertise, your company's talent, expertise, and equipment. [That obsolete piece of equipment might be really appreciated by a vocational school or college in your community.] Earn a reputation as an employer supporting quality education.

Offer your company's expertise as a resource to news media such as metropolitan daily newspapers, business newspapers and magazines, trade journals, radio talk shows, and television news shows. Being recognized as a quotable authority never hurts, especially when one of your valued people represents you as an industry expert. Tapping your people for such service serves to recognize them personally, too.

When your people are involved in the ways described above, don't hesitate to share their contributions with others. Internally, you can express your pride through your company newsletter or bulletin board displays.

Consider ways you can brag, tastefully, about your people to your customers and prospective customers. For example, if someone is quoted in an industry magazine, you could reprint the article (with permission), highlight your company representative's comments, and send the marked article to interested customers.

Seek appropriate publicity for promotions, new appointments, discoveries, inventions, and significant accomplishments. If one of your people is elected or appointed to an office in a trade or professional association, recognize that achievement and dedication inside your company and to the public. Look for creative ways to spread the good word about what your people and your company are doing.

The same positive exposure you get in the "outside world" will strengthen your bonds internally with your people. Take advantage of every chance you can find to reinforce how important each one of your team members to your organization.

You can build employee loyalty by merely writing a letter to your involved team member expressing your appreciation, support, and admiration. These efforts will be well received by the concerned employee, and will also be noticed by others. People watch how others are treated; your actions should always generate good feelings.

Be Worthy of Good People

To attract and keep good people, you must have something to offer them. They must see joining you as being a positive career move. Your company must be perceived as a fine place to work, from the perspectives of being a comfortable environment, providing quality products and services, and being good for the reputation of the people who work there.

More and more, people are asking the all-important questions of "what's in it for me." If they don't see the positive aspects of working for you, on a short-term and on a long-term basis, don't expect to keep them.

As previously explained, we will not see the same level of employee loyalty to a particular employer in the coming decades that we have seen in the past. Any employer desiring that kind of dedication will have to earn it. Every day.

If you are not a solid, financially strong company, perhaps a start-up entrepreneurship or an older company in need of a shot of revitalization, make this clear to the good people you have and the ones you're trying to recruit. Your circumstances may call for some special kinds of folks; the cream will rise to the top and the talent you need will respond to the challenge.

Whatever your particular situation, be deliberate about what you are trying to do. People want to know there's someone at the helm, guiding their ship through the storm or through the racing channels. Knowing you are there, doing your job with a strong sense of purpose and focus, will help build confidence in you and in the organization. That level of confidence is vital if you want to attract and keep good people.

Take pride in your corporate achievements. Enable your people to do the same. Share with them every positive aspect you can think of. Empower them to stand tall—in your industry, in the community, in their families. As humans, we like to have pride in our affiliations, in our work, and in ourselves. We like to know that we're meeting the challenges of life and striving to make a positive difference.

Anything you can do to reinforce feelings of pride, satisfaction, and achievement will strengthen your position in reaching, hiring, and keeping the people who can lead your company into the years ahead.

Separate Yourself from the Crowd

What is unique about your company? Why should someone work for you instead of working for your competitor or a company in another industry? How can you establish your organization, and your opportunity, as being different from other alternatives in the employment marketplace?

Your better applicants are going to compare the offers they receive. As they make their choices they will look for "comfort factors." They will also look for "discomfort factors" that may inspire a negative decision.

In the area of comfort factors, it is valuable to consider all the things we've discussed in this chapter. Aggressively promote the positive aspects of your company, both internally and externally. Your external efforts will help attract the people you want, as well as support the image that will encourage people to stay with you because of the public perception of your company. Your internal efforts will generate positive feelings, reinforcing your current employees' decision to continue as part of your team.

When applicants visit your offices, they are judging your company by what they see. When you go to work tomorrow, look objectively at your neighborhood, grounds, building(s), reception area or lobby, and the offices an applicant is likely too visit. You may be surprised at what you see. Look critically; your applicants will.

One suggestion might be to have management and leadership books on display in your office. Of special importance will be those dealing with human resource issues. The books in your office send messages to visitors about your interests. Show them what is important to you. You might want to put this book, a copy of ***The Process of Excelling*** or ***Lean & Meaningful***, or other relevant books in plain sight.

Show visitors you keep current in your field. Current periodicals, which may be familiar to them, should be displayed in your office and/or in the waiting room. The good people you want to attract will be concerned that the company's leadership is on the cutting edge.

These ideas will help you show your concerns and interests to your current employees as well. Of course, if you read these publications and discuss the books or articles with your people, you will verify that you really care about what you are doing. You will also serve as an example for your people; there is a much greater chance people will read and learn if they know the boss does, and that the boss asks questions and raises issues from those publications.

Another comfort factor is your company's reputation for quality in its products and services. It has to be real, not just a sham or cover-up so things look good on the surface. To earn and maintain this reputation, it's imperative that you and other leaders in your company devote a lot of serious attention to quality. If you are sincere, and if you really focus on quality, you will earn respect and admiration for the way things are done in your organization.

That admiration and respect will motivate your good people, who are striving to deserve that reputation, to stay with you. Success begets success. If they're achieving, they will want to stay and achieve more as long as they are challenged and feel positive about the experience.

Focus on People Factors

Attitude is perhaps the single greatest determinant of decisions in our lives. We do things because we like something associated with those things. We avoid things about which we have a negative attitude. When we examine attitudes in the workplace, we soon focus on morale and team spirit.

Not everyone is going to be excited about work. Not everyone is going to throw total energy into being a team player. Each person comes from a different direction. Your challenge, perhaps obligation, is to pull them together so your people are all going the same direction.

So many books and magazine articles point to what has happened in Japan as being a good example for us to follow. Personally, I am a bit uncomfortable about that sort of reference. Many of the management techniques that have made Japanese industry strong originated in the United States. While the Japanese have applied those techniques diligently, Americans went off in search of new fads, new approaches. The advantage will belong to those who continually search for better ways. The foundation, however, will remain the basic, down-to-earth, caring involvement with the people who make progress and achievement possible.

For illustration, I will yield my resistance to "Japanese answers." Consider these guiding principles from Matsushita Electric (Panasonic), where morale remains very high:

- respect
- awards
- communication
- courtesy
- discussion
- negotiation
- consensus
- loyalty to employees
- socializing
- training
- few direct orders
- long-term thinking
- hope for the future

- innovative freedom
- job permanence
- stable conditions
- clearly assigned responsibilities
- special welcome to new people
- lots of smiles
- plenty of please and thank-you
- thoughtfulness and consideration
- receptiveness to criticism
- generous help with retirement
- dedication
- determination
- discipline
- industrious hard work

It isn't necessary to have pep rallies to get people turned on. People will turn themselves on . . . if they perceive a positive environment for the company and for themselves. People will get excited, and maintain a high level of enthusiasm, if they see results and feel the caring from senior management.

Your People Are Competing

As working people, we compete. Using all the resources at our disposal, we go after the best jobs, the highest income, the greatest status, and the strongest opportunity to make a valuable contribution to our employer and society. We strive to control our own destiny.

Look at your good people, those folks you want to keep on your team. How sensitive, how aware are you of their striving? Wise leaders will use all their communications skills to observe how people are competing, what is important to them. Ask questions. Listen. Listen some more.

If you want to keep your good people, give them as much of what they want as you can. Understand how they are, consciously or unconsciously, competing with each other for attention, favor, opportunity. Guide their competition to be positive for them and for your organization.

Encouraging people to put forth their best effort can easily produce winners. But, in competitive environments, you may also produce losers. If two people are competing for the same job, you may well want to keep them both. Consider what you can do for the person(s) who don't get the choice assignment or the promotion. If you aren't able to do something to make your selection a win-win situation, you risk losing those who don't "win" the one position open.

Give people alternatives of relatively similar significance. If someone doesn't get an expected or desired promotion, what else can you offer? A challenging special assignment? Promise of the next open promotion? Be careful not to make promises you can't keep. Don't manipulate the system beyond reasonable limits for personal reasons. Stay focused on the long-term. Know that different people want, or will be satisfied with, different kinds of rewards. Learn enough about each of your people that you can respond to individual needs.

Some people want higher positions just to have a more important position in the organizational hierarchy. They like to see their names in a box that's further up on the chart. Climbing that kind of a career ladder is paramount to some people. For others, the position they hold isn't that important. Don't make assumptions. What's good for Gail Goose isn't necessarily what Gil Gander wants.

Some people are driven to earn as much money as possible. Very little else even matters. They will be happy with a lesser position, very little recognition, low status, and so forth . . . if they have a strong income. There are a number of different ways to structure compensation packages to attract and hold good people. Warning: People who are driven by money as their primary motivator probably won't stay with you very long, and you can't afford to throw more money at them without seeing a strong return on your investment. The time will come, sooner than you'd like, when you'll have to refuse another increase and allow the employee to leave.

Status and prestige are very important to some of your good people. They don't need a higher position, necessarily, or obscene amounts of money. Perhaps they want the perceived high and influential status of a legislative lobbyist. Rubbing elbows with all those powerful politicians is reward enough. Others seek titles like "assistant to the president," regardless of the power or the income. Some folks are motivated merely by having a beautiful, embossed, multicolor business card. Feeling important, and/or being perceived by others as being important, is their driver.

For other workers, their status is more intrinsic. They feel more significant when they get things done. They thrive on the job, the task, and the results achieved. These folks compete more with themselves and the challenge or importance of the task. Their focus is often on improving their own performance rather than "beating" someone else.

Included in our country's diverse workforce are people who have an extraordinary level of social consciousness. They compete for opportunities to make significant contributions to society through their work. They are usually attracted, and bound to, organizations that are engaged in work for the public good. The range is wide today, including environmental protection agencies and companies, social service groups, health care, and the like. They are found in non-service settings as well, but prefer to work for companies that demonstrate their social conscience.

Many creative people compete for positions where they can design or produce something that will be a long-term benefit for society. Included in this category are people like architects, artists, teachers, landscapers, and many other career paths that provide goods or services for the common good and enjoyment of others.

Today's enlightened workers want to control their own destiny. It's not enough to work for a company forever just because a parent or some other relative spent a lifetime there.

Few people *want* to jump from job to job, but they feel it's necessary to grow their careers. Most people want to be independent and strong enough to make their own decisions regarding their employment, career path, and future.

We Compete to Keep People

Efforts to attract, inspire, and keep the best people we can find must be continuous. It's almost like creating a force field of protection around our people. They are "captive" as long as we continue our activity to maintain that force field. As soon as we relax our diligence, the competition can move right in to take advantage of all we have done to cultivate our fine employees.

You will find competition coming from four different sources. The first source I describe as being nonspecific. The second source is companies within your industry. Third is employers from other industries. The fourth is from within our own organization.

Our nonspecific competition is an internal attitude that can easily lead to proactive or reactive behavior. If our key employees are not satisfied, there will be a greater receptivity to alternative employment. Under these attitudinal circumstances, people are apt to be less productive—less motivated to work for the common good of the organization, much less themselves.

When there are no specific outside attractions, the competitor is really without form. The alienation feelings will often lead the employee to seek other opportunities, almost indiscriminately. The grass begins to look greener on the other side of the fence. You risk losing the employee because of what has happened, or hasn't happened, within your own environment. As the expression goes, you can be "your own worst enemy." You're actually pushing these people out, rather than having them attracted out by competitors.

The competition for good people you face in your own industry is dangerous. The companies that compete against you for sales and market share also want your people. You have trained them; they've proven their worth to an employer in your field. Even more valuable, perhaps, is their knowledge of your systems, customers, pricing, and a myriad of other facts that comprise corporate intelligence.

The risk here is that you could lose far more than a valued employee. And, what is worse, the employee could be "used" by the competitor, then discarded. With the pressure of competition today, some companies are offering hard-to-turn-down incentives to capture employees of other companies in their fields. They parasitically suck all the worthwhile knowledge they can from the unsuspecting employee, then terminate the employment. The poor drained employee is out on the street, while the parasite takes advantage of all the new knowledge and insight gained.

Many employers today feel it is heartily advised to build strong feelings of loyalty and competitiveness among their workforces. The fierce attachment to their company is directed against the competitors. This us-against-them power is aimed at encouraging innovation, efficiency, cunning, effectiveness, and profitability to make the host employer successful against the "hated" competitors. That same energy also stimulates resistance against even the hint of going over to the other side. Not wanting to be traitors, employees who leave the company also usually leave the industry.

Many companies deliberately recruit outside their industry. They seek recruits with applicable skills, talent, knowledge, background, or training. Bringing fresh perspectives from a different industry might enable a new employee to help keep the organization alert, innovative, responsive, and generally on the cutting edge. Hiring people with extensive experience in the same industry could spawn inbreeding and tunnel vision.

Some companies have grown so large that they have a number of separate divisions or subsidiaries. The people who operate the various entities may not know each other, particularly below the senior management levels. Even though they have the same core ownership, they function much like different companies in separate industries.

These divisions may try to recruit people away from each other. They can offer the attractiveness of being able to continue with the same health plan, the same retirement program, and other similar comfort factors. Sometimes the workers can even remain in the same city.

This interdivisional recruiting can be healthy for cross-training and cross-divisional cooperation. But, it can also cause serious conflicts. Any such recruiting and transferring of people, on a temporary or permanent basis, should be done above board with full knowledge and communication by the appropriate officials in each entity.

Appreciate the fact that we are operating in a multifaceted, multidimensional environment. While you should not spend your time looking over your shoulder for your competitors, know that they are there. Make your strategic decisions and implement those decisions as if the competition is right behind you. If you don't, they'll be passing you by before you know it.

4

What Good People Want

Understanding and appreciating what good people want from their managers and employing organizations is an important first step to meeting those expectations.

In the preceding chapters, we have touched on a number of the desires of good people. Some of these may have been new discoveries for you; most should be "old news." That employees want status, rewards, opportunities, recognition, and similar returns for their investment of time and energy should not be a surprise.

Astute managers already know what needs to be done. They know how to treat their people. Leaders of organizations know what their people want; most just don't concentrate seriously on meeting those needs. Now it's time to gain a better perspective of human needs and how they are met in the workplace.

Understanding Human Needs

Many have struggled to explain the range of human needs, but Abraham H. Maslow's hierarchy of needs is the most representative and the most helpful in gaining an understanding of what good people want.

Maslow placed all needs into rankings shown as levels. He explained that people will strive first to satisfy basic needs; then, once those needs are satisfied, they will focus on meeting higher-level needs. Each level of need must be satisfied, to a degree, before people will be motivated by the next-higher level of needs. There is no magic light that flashes when a level of need is met; that degree of satisfaction is different for each of us. As needs are satisfied at one level, the individual's focus shifts to the next higher level.

At the lowest level, basic needs such as adequate food, air, water, shelter, rest, and clothing (the fundamental things needed for physical survival) motivate behavior. In other

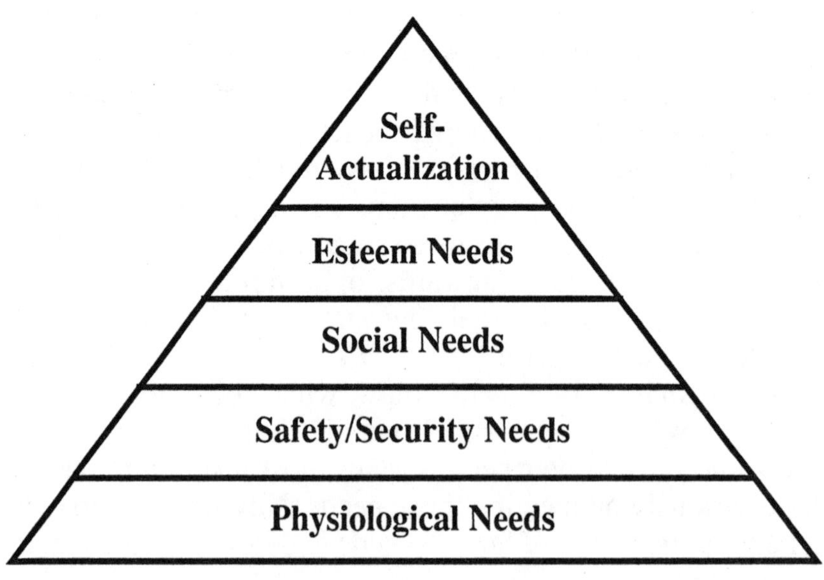

Maslow's Hierarchy of Needs

words, if people do not have sufficient food, water, clothing or shelter, their behavior is directed toward the acquisition of these survival needs. A person does not search for much else until these needs are met.

When sufficient physiological means for survival are present, their satisfaction no longer motivates behavior. Then safety and security needs become the motivators. Safety needs include knowing one's physical, emotional, and financial survival are not in jeopardy immediately or in the near future. At this stage, the person seeks avoidance of sources of anxiety or fear, along with the meeting of security needs of an organized, stable, predictable environment. Job security fulfills a safety/security need.

These two Maslow levels constitute a group of needs which predispose the individual to be self oriented. In other words, the person experiences life in general and all situations from a *self*-oriented perspective.

Continually looking out for self-survival, physical as well as emotional, is extremely stressful. Therefore, an organizational environment which either by design or accident induces fear of emotional safety is an environment which drains energy from employees. This energy could otherwise be applied to job productivity.

Such stressful environments do exist in American business today. Consider the feelings of employees of organizations in the midst of merger or downsizing. How about dictatorial, authoritarian environments designed to maintain control through intimidation? Such environments push employees directly into their most unproductive fear state, reducing their productivity, their satisfaction, and their desire to remain in that job.

Beyond Self to Others

Once the person's basic needs, as described by Maslow's first two levels, are satisfied, the employee's perspective broadens to include relationships with other people.

Now the concern is the fulfillment of social needs such as belongingness and love. Close relationships with friends, spouse and family, and fellow employees become important. These needs are met by giving and receiving love, both in the larger sense of friendship and the more intense sense of affection.

At this stage, people have a strong need to be accepted by others, to belong to a group. There is a desire for active participation: the individual contributes something valuable to the work group, and the group recognizes the contribution as worthwhile. Getting employees involved and building a sense of teamness helps fulfill this vital human need. This team feeling is fragile in today's organizations, where many people don't stay around long enough to feel part of a team. If this team concept of contribution and recognition, as a fundamental grounding, is begun early, the desire to have this need fulfilled will encourage people to stay.

Employees at this level of needs satisfaction require an entirely different organizational reward system, different work structure, different manager and supervisory and peer interactions than someone focused primarily on self. Since the respect and approval of others is important, the employee becomes positively motivated by the approval of management and the organization as a whole. This positive communication must be proactive; people will no longer assume everything is fine if they don't see the boss.

So, we understand that employees want to fulfill basic safety and survival needs through physical comforts, security, and financial reward. Once these needs are met, which happens fairly quickly in most employment relationships, the employee's concern is with the fulfillment of social and emotional needs.

Esteem Needs

Once the employee has satisfied social needs, esteem needs become important. Having a high self-regard and having respect for others are representative of this level.

At this stage, the employee is most concerned with self-concept. Self-estimations of strength, confidence, freedom, importance are supplemented by others' recognition of one's status, prestige, reputation, importance, competence, and value.

Respect from others becomes increasingly important. Employees are motivated by feelings of personal competence and self-confidence, which can be validated and enhanced by their supervisors. When you express your respect for an employee's ability, demonstrate your confidence in the employee, and show your appreciation and support, you help fulfill the esteem need.

When someone's self-esteem needs are met, it is easy and comfortable for that person to be able to build the esteem of others. Without that strong inner sense of personal worth, it is much more difficult—if not impossible—for one to be concerned with the esteem of others. This fact is why it is important for managers and supervisors, those in leadership position, to have high self-esteem. (See *Appendix C* for an in-depth discussion of self-esteem in the corporate setting.)

Self-Actualizing Employees

At the top of Maslow's hierarchy, behavior is motivated by self esteem and self-actualization needs, a perspective which re-introduces a strong self-influence. Behavior is motivated by a sense of making a significant contribution and attaining a high level of self-worth.

Self-actualization needs motivate individuals toward behavior which stretches them to achieve all they are capable of achieving. Creative expression and greater realization of personal potential become paramount. This motive is strong among Generation X employees, and will be felt throughout the workforce as more people adopt some of the values attributed to this generation born between 1965 and 1985.

It's important for us to recognize that employees at this level of motivation are again more self-oriented. However, a major difference is that the direction for the behavior comes from making a contribution, helping to achieve worthwhile objectives that validate a purpose for one's life.

Employees at this mature level of motivation require more opportunities for involvement and increasing organizational flexibility. The organizational structure, management style, work structure, and methods, must change responsively to create and maintain a motivational environment. People must feel encouraged to find ways to realize their work potential, comfortably within the "system." Sometimes the system must change.

An organization that is very authoritarian, that sends the do-as-you're-told message, is non-motivational for these employees. As a matter of fact, these employees may appear as nonconformists or renegades. Because these employees are motivated by self-esteem, they tend to think for themselves and see beyond the organization's parameters.

So why would your organization want such employees? Because they are internally motivated. They are the self-starters, the self-learners, the independent thinkers who are motivated to make a contribution to society and to your organization. Give them flexibility to be creative. Give them space to explore and time to think. Encourage their contributions, their thoughts, and their vision. You will not need to concern yourself with motivation. Traditional supervision will evolve to facilitation in support of these employees.

Any or all of these needs, from the basic physical needs to the highest level self-actualization, may be satisfied through interaction with others in the workplace. These needs are not mutually exclusive; the mix is different for different people.

So the message to organizational leaders desiring to keep

people and to keep them productive is to encourage employee development through these various motivational levels. The strategies outlined in this book are designed to help you do just that.

Specific Action Steps

The Maslow hierarchy and other theories have considerable value in helping us understand human wants and needs. The application of this knowledge is most critical for those charged with leading organizations and keeping good people.

Direct supervisors of good people—at all levels—are the vital link between the organization's philosophy and the way things are actually done. Supervisors must understand and appreciate what their people want from them before they can meet those needs. Equipped with this knowledge, these enlightened supervisors can modify their approach to respond to the wants and needs of each individual worker, rather than trying to satisfy everyone ("the masses") at the same time. Quite a bit of research has been done to look at practical applications of needs motivation theories.

In the late 1940s, a study was conducted to learn what motivates people in work organizations. Researchers were interested in how workers would respond, but also whether their supervisors' perceptions of the workers' wants were consistent.

People in a wide variety of work settings were surveyed, as were their direct supervisors. Their responses were compared with some surprising results. This research study has been repeated a number of times over the years with the same results.

The researchers gave respondents a list of motivational factors and asked to rank them in order of importance. The workers were asked to prioritize them from their perspective. The supervisors were asked to rank them in the order they believed the workers would prioritize them.

As you can see from the chart below, the results were dramatically different. Clearly, the supervisors responding to the survey did not have a realistic understanding of what really motivated their people!

Motivational Factor	Workers' Response	Supervisors' Response
good working conditions	9	4
feeling "in" on things	2	10
tactful disciplining	10	7
full appreciation for work done	1	8
management loyalty to workers	8	6
good wages	5	1
promotion and growth	7	3
help of personal problems	3	9
job security	4	2
interesting work	6	5

Note that the factors the workers ranked 1-2-3 were the same ones that the supervisors ranked 8-9-10!

Let's consider the strongest motivators:

1. Employees want to receive feedback on how they are doing. This desire means that supervisors—in fact, all managers—need to provide recognition of achievement or even just reports of progress toward agreed-upon goals. Without feedback and recognition, workers will have only a marginal commitment to the job. Alienation from supervisors and the organization increases. When commitment and recognition levels are low, workers will seek recognition elsewhere—perhaps from outside the organization. This lack of feedback communication could mean heavier labor-management polarization or workers leaving for other employment.

To overcome such situations, or perceptions, management may need to modify communications systems to provide stronger feedback in a continual and consistent manner. Supervisors can provide motivation by evaluating results of work personally with employees.

2. People want to feel involved in the job to the point of designing the job and establishing goals and objectives. Your employees are human beings, not just numbers or cogs in a machine. They have ideas about how things could and should be done and questions about why certain things are done or not done.

Employees are closest to the work for which they are responsible. They want to perform that work in the best way possible. They have the potential (Maslow's self-actualization level) and desire to use it. They *want* to be involved. Thus, supervisors can motivate workers by asking them to set their own work goals and to suggest better ways to do things. Today's workers want freedom and flexibility to determine the best way to achieve desired results.

3. People want help on personal problems. This desire for support doesn't mean that the supervisor must become a social worker. However, it does suggest that employees want the boss to care about them as individuals. Today's manager must invest a significant amount of time advising, counseling, coaching, guiding, training, and listening. Be sensitive and understanding. Help people over the rough spots and help them do their best.

Employees who are helped to perform will feel better about themselves, feel more secure, and receive positive feedback from others. It's easy to see how these feelings fit right into the Maslow hierarchy. The key is for supervisors to appreciate how their concrete actions on a day-to-day basis serve to meet those human needs.

When needs are met, when employees are getting what they want from their supervisors and their organization, they are more satisfied and more likely to remain in that motivational environment.

Current research confirms these same finding. Perry Pascarella in his book, *The New Achievers,* describes motivation of today's employees with the same facts. Pascarella insists that there is no lack of work ethic in America. Workers *do* want to make a lasting contribution, but they are prevented from doing so by American organizations and their managers. We get in our own way!

To keep good people, and to keep them productive, corporate leaders need to carefully examine the impact of their organizational structure, philosophy, policies, and procedures. These critical aspects significantly influence the corporate culture which governs both attitudes and actions. These essential concerns are deliberately covered in the *first* chapter of the strategy section of this book.

Other current literature supports the importance of being attentive to the needs of employees. John Naisbitt and Patricia Aburdeen, co-authors of *Reinventing the Corporation,* look with more depth at current trends and the current predicament. Drawing the same conclusions, they emphasize that the companies that provide for the wants of their employees will attract and keep good people: productive people committed to making lasting, valuable contributions. The authors describe these companies as the *Fortunate 500* with good reason.

Supervisors and managers are likely to be motivated by different priorities than front-line operations employees. The two groups have different perspectives and are driven by different needs. Operational workers are motivated differently than research and development employees. While the Maslow hierarchy is probably the best model to understand human wants and needs, we must be sensitive to differences among groups of employees and among individual members of the team.

To illustrate this point, compare the results shown in the chart on page 48 with the following presentation of results of another study. The chart below illustrates the weights given to the same categories by over 300 first-level and second-level supervisors in one organization over a three-year period. Note the similarities and differences, remembering that each factor is a potential motivator.

Motivational Factor	What First-Line Supervisors Say They Want	What Second-Line Supervisors Say They Want
good working conditions	6	6
feeling involvement in job	8	7
tactful disciplining	9	9
feedback on work well done	4	4
loyalty of supervisor	7	8
high wages (salary)	2	1
promotion and growth	3	3
help of personal problems	10	10
job security	5	5
interesting work	1	2

The marketplace is driving a renewed interest in productivity and quality. The economy is shifting away from an operations-intensive orientation in which quantitative concerns have a high value. In today's competitive environment, the new emphasis is on *quality*. Caring employees are the people who get the quality job done. The burden rests on the shoulders of the relatively few really good people on whom we can depend.

Now, more than ever, we need to reach those exceptional people, motivate them, and hold on to them. At the same time, we must build the same attitude and performance in our other employees with high potential. We can only do this if we know what they want from employers and managers, and if we manage in ways that will fulfill those wants.

This discussion could go on and on. But more examples would just take up space in this book and usurp your reading time. The essence of keeping good people is not in mere understanding, but in taking strategic action to make a positive difference.

Anecdotal Research Results

My conversations with people at all levels in organizations, in all walks of life, have generated an interesting list of what people want from their employers. Consider how you feel personally as you read this list, then explore how well these expectations and desires are met in your organization. Some will sound similar to earlier discussions in this chapter, so you'll sense some reinforcement.

- Appreciation
- Stable and secure work environment
- Accountability
- Greater responsibility
- Autonomy
- Involvement in decision making
- Empowerment
- Leaders who listen and *act* on suggestions
- Continual learning—formal and informal, including mentoring
- Freedom to experiment . . . and to fail without being punished
- Supportive, rather than restrictive, work environment
- Information—knowledge of what's happening with the company, the industry
- Rewards based on performance
- The opportunity to make a difference.

5

Why Good People Leave

Survey after survey has examined why people leave their jobs for supposedly greener pastures. A variety of reasons is given by workers in a various occupations, industries, and locales. The motivations for jumping for one job to another can be grouped into five categories. The conclusion is that there are five principal reasons that good people leave their jobs:

1. **It doesn't feel good around here.** This is a corporate culture issue in most cases. Workers are also concerned with the company's reputation; the physical conditions of comfort, convenience, and safety; and the clarity of mission.
2. **They wouldn't miss me if I were gone.** Even though leaders do value employees, they don't tell them often enough. If people don't feel important, they're not mo-

tivated to stay. No one wants to be a commodity, easily replaced by someone off the street. If they are regarded as expendable, they'll leave for a position where they're appreciated.

3. **I don't get what I need to get my job done.** Contrary to opinions heard all too often from management, people really *want* to do a good job. When they're frustrated by too many rules, red tape, incompetent supervisors or co-workers, inadequate tools and equipment, or insufficient information, people look for other places to work.
4. **There's no opportunity for advancement.** No, we're not talking about promotions, although many deserving people would like to move up. The issue here is learning. People want to learn, to sharpen their skills and pick up new ones. They want to improve their capacity to perform a wide variety of jobs. Call it career security. The desire is for training and development. If workers can't find the growth opportunities with one company, they'll seek another employer where they can learn.
5. **The compensation doesn't meet my needs.** Workers want fair compensation, but the first four reasons take priority. If they're not well-met, but money's high, you'll hear people say "you can't pay me enough to stay here." Even with the first four reasons in mind, there are a lot of employees who feel they can better themselves just by chasing more income.

Research shows that most people shift their loyalties to a new employer because of non-monetary factors. I emphasize this fact, because I have heard a great number of business owners, executives, managers, and supervisors express their belief that people "go where the money is." That argument simply isn't totally true anymore.

People are hungry for opportunities to grow in their jobs. They crave advancement, both in position and stature, and in responsibility and opportunity. If they can't find avenues for growth in one environment, they'll seek them in another. People want to make a difference, to be involved, and to be sincerely appreciated for their contributions.

Please Notice Me!

Human beings want attention and recognition. We get so little attention from others, we're really hungry for any kind of acknowledgment of our value (or even our existence).

Think about the reception you got when you went home last night. Remember how your spouse greeted you enthusiastically at the door? Remember how you were asked about how things went at work? And the genuine concern for the projects you're involved in? Did your solicitous spouse invite you to join in the preparation of your family meal—"Let's do it together"?

As you crossed the threshold, did your kids turn off the television with excited exclamations about your arrival? Did they come bounding over, eager to tell you about their adventures at school?

And did your dog leap off the hearth to share affection at your feet, tail wagging vigorously with expressive yelps punctuating the expressions of delight that you were home?

Maybe the dog sounds familiar, but the rest must have been at someone else's house? Welcome to the real world!

Few of us get the attention we'd like at home. So, we look elsewhere for satisfaction of the basic human need to be appreciated and cared about.

Wouldn't it be nice if we could experience that kind of attention at work? After all, we spend more of our waking hours at work than we do at home anyway. Research shows that people often leave an employer because they haven't received the recognition they want.

As an interesting side comment, a lot can be learned by

watching children. Ever notice how a child responds to positive attention? If children can't get positive attention from adults, parents and teachers, they deliberately misbehave to earn some kind of attention. Adults are just grown up kids.

Managers Set the Course

While peer "pressures" and norms guide the way many people behave and think in the work environment, let's recognize that managers have a significant influence on the attitudes of their employees. The way people are treated by their managers—several layers up, not just their immediate superiors—will determine their satisfaction, productivity, and longevity.

It's unrealistic to think that people will be happy with everything management decides or does. Camelot doesn't really exist. Reality is that some people will differ with management from time to time. This circumstance is expected by mature people in any organization. Often the key is not *what* is done, but *how* it is done . . . and explained.

People want to be treated with respect. They want to be seen as being important to the organization's success, and recognized for their parts in making positive things happen. When people issues are well addressed by management, employees will demonstrate their loyalty and dedication as team players under the most adverse circumstances. However, when people are not treated well, they won't "invest" themselves in the company even under the best of corporate circumstances.

Managers have to consciously and deliberately work with their people to get things done. The way they apply the principles presented in this book and other guides to leadership and management will determine their success in building stable, productive teams.

Enlightened employers who want to be successful will emphasize to their managers and supervisors the value of being people-oriented. Every indication points to the critical importance of building genuine, positive relationships with people—employees, customers, and suppliers.

Strategic Leadership

The "meat" of this book is an abundance of things that organizational leaders can do to keep good people as productive members of their team. Senior leaders set the pace, the culture, the example. Employee retention is a strategic objective. Therefore, these approaches are applied strategically, hence the description of these techniques as "strategies." This terminology is not to imply that only strategic-level leaders are involved with retention; all leaders, managers, supervisors, superintendents, foremen are involved. Whatever your title, if you lead, manage, or coordinate the work of others, you fit the role of "leader" in this context.

To do something strategically means to plan in advance, as opposed to responding to emergent conditions with a knee-jerk reaction. Certainly, there will be those times when a fast response is needed to keep a valued employee. However, the premise of this book is that those times will be infrequent—if the recommended strategies are applied.

Please note that strategies (plural) need to be applied. You can not simply apply one strategy or technique and assume that all your people will be loyal and productive forever! A variety of strategies and tactics have to be applied, with constant attention to how they are received by your people. Expect to do some fine tuning and solicit ongoing feedback, since each situation is different and each individual's needs will be different. Message: strive to retain each individual—independently, one-on-one. Needs and wants change over time, too, so it's important to stay in touch with each person. People typically don't leave or stay with an organization in groups; it's an individual decision.

Our emphasis is on having people be productive members of our team. We want them to achieve results, enabling the entire organization to achieve its objectives and maintain its existence with continual accomplishment of goals. We want these folks to be productive, dedicated, and loyal because they *want* to be, not because someone above them in the hierarchy says so. The motivation is internal, not external.

Before people can be productive, they have to know what is expected of them. Before they can be members of a team, there has to be a conscious team. And teams need leaders. Those team leaders do things, strategically and carefully, to build the team and empower members to "win" . . . individually and collectively.

Your task, as leader, is to apply the various strategies in this book in a deliberate fashion to meet those objectives. Some strategies will be applied uniformly, with all people treated the same way. Others will be applied on an individual level, meeting personal needs.

This differential treatment is quite legitimate, although many managers try to hide it behind insistence that everyone should be treated equally. As a good leader, you should not try to treat everyone equally; instead, focus on treating each person *fairly*. Today, more than ever, our workforce is composed of individuals. It is critical that their individual characteristics are taken into consideration.

The strategies presented on the following pages are interdependent. They can easily be applied on their own, without any consideration of any other strategy. They can be strengthened by combination with another strategy. You can mix and match as you wish. There is no predetermined formula. Some things you are probably already doing . . . or *think* you're doing. Challenge your assumptions; you may find that you aren't doing as well as you thought you were.

The collection of strategies in this book should not be considered to be complete. It represents the author's best efforts at time of publication and, to a degree, limitations of space. As you discover other strategies, by talking with fellow leaders, reading books or articles, or by trial and error, I'd be interested in learning about them. Ideas and techniques will be shared in *Workforce Stability Alert,* the newsletter of The Workforce Stability Institute. Some ideas may be posted on a couple of our web sites on the internet. See www.herman.net, www.employee.org, and www.leanandmeaningful.org.

Don't be limited by what you read in these pages. Stay alert for other ideas. Keep learning! Make notes in this books as you read and apply the recommended techniques so ***Keeping Good People*** may serve as a living reference for years to come.

6

Environmental Strategies

The primary strategies for keeping good people, and keeping them productive, deal with the working environment. "Environment" today means much more than it has in the past. We look at a much bigger picture than we ever have before. We're talking about corporate culture . . . and more.

The environmental strategies address three crucial aspects of the workplace:

1. the ethics and values foundation on which the organization is built
2. the policies that interpret those values and translate them into operative action
3. the physical environment that is a concrete manifestation of the organization's concern for the space that its people occupy.

While seemingly different, these strategies are all linked by the common thread of their impact on the human behavior that shapes what the organization is . . . and can become. Employees have become increasingly sensitive to environmental issues. They ask, "What does it feel like to work here?" If something doesn't "feel" right, in today's full-employment conditions they can easily leave.

As they choose where they're going to work, applicants ask a lot of questions about culture and environment. They want to talk with current employees to ask relevant questions. If they find a culture that doesn't feel comfortable to them, they may leave very shortly after they're hired. That's why a careful hiring process and strong new-hire orientation are so important.

Ethics and values establish an organization's character, its moral fiber. These strategies determine how decisions will be made, how people will be treated and how they will treat others, and how business will be conducted. Ethics and values create and confirm the organization's place in our Society. Employees watch closely to see how the company relates to customers, suppliers, employees, and other stakeholders.

The American public is focusing more intently on ethics issues. We see evidence of this attitude and concern in the way we respond when cheating is uncovered. Our response doesn't even require that we are the victim or even know the victim. If our sense of right and wrong, of fair play, is violated, we become angry.

Some of our most obvious examples, thanks to news coverage, are episodes involving inappropriate purchases by the federal government. Outrageous prices for things like hammers and toilet seats enrage the public, and rightly so. We expect a different kind of behavior from our public officials as well as those private sector vendors who deal with them. In the private sector, an often-deserved hue and cry has been raised about executive salaries that are dramatically far out of line with compensation of other employees. In a wide range of circumstances, people are asking, "is this fair?"

Policies are designed based on the organization's ethics and values. Our policies give us living guidelines regarding the way we function. Values and policies are so intertwined, it is hard to separate them in many cases. And it should be that way.

In a wide range of areas, we determine our policies to legitimize what we do. Those same policies also clearly delineate what we will not do. Following established policies, we move forward in our leadership well-grounded in the organization's values-based stance and direction. Clear polices help clear up dangerous and confusing ambiguities.

The physical place in which people work says a lot about the organization, its values, and its policies. The more comfortable the place is, as a work environment, the more productive will be those who work there. Satisfaction and contentment with surroundings greatly influence the way people work and their interest in remaining with the employer.

All these elements come together to establish and maintain the feeling your people have about their work environment.

Let's look at the ethics and values and policy strategies to keep good people:

Ethics, Values, and Policies

The successful companies of the future, let alone the present, will be based on solid ethical principles. Corporate values will be recognized as the vital lifeblood that pulls people together and keeps them together.

Dealing with these matters will be difficult for some companies and their management teams. Until recently such concerns have not been important enough, sensitive enough, to address directly. Now they are becoming decision points for current and prospective employees, for customers, and even for suppliers.

A company's reputation rests on more than just the quality

of its products, although that is one important value. Insiders and outsiders judge companies by their philosophy and level of customer service, their involvement in community activities, and their commitment to moral, environmental, and even political issues. Corporate management has dealt with these concerns in the past, but usually not to the extent of having defined official policies and positions.

Changing expectations of the employers' role and responsibility "forces" companies to examine carefully the way the organization functions. The companies are judged by where they operate their businesses, as seen by the reaction to companies with facilities in South Africa during the Apartheid struggles. They are even judged by the content of the television shows they sponsor and their response to learning about defects in their products.

Today's employees are becoming more concerned about moral and ethical issues in business. The corporation's values, as expressed in company statements, in annual reports, and in daily operative behavior, affect how people feel about remaining with an employer. Workers want to be comfortable with what their employer stands for. They seek compatibility of those corporate positions with their own personal viewpoints.

When good employees, aware of social issues, sense a strong divergence between their value positions and those of their employer, the likelihood of their divorcing themselves from the employer is greater than ever before in our history. Never before has such a high level of values consciousness been combined with a high level of alternative employment opportunities. The result is an understandably volatile situation.

With the seriousness of these concerns in mind, let's consider some values and ethics strategies for keeping good people.

Strategy 1.1

Clarify your mission.

Every organization has a mission—a reason for being, whether it's written or not. If the mission is clear, people can "buy into it" and support it. There's a cohesiveness that develops when everyone is on the same track. If the mission is fuzzy, then employees come to work uncertain about why they're there, what they're striving to accomplish, and why. If the "why" isn't clear and crisp, efforts (and attitudes and energies) won't be focused.

Four horses can be harnessed together to combine their strength to pull a wagon with a very heavy load. They can do amazing things as a team. But, if those horses are not in harness, not in sync, they may pull in opposite directions and rip the wagon apart! A clearly understood and expressed mission keeps the team pulling together.

We call the written expression of the organization's reason for existence a mission statement or statement of purpose. This definition serves as the foundation, the common thread, for everything the organization does. If you already have a mission statement, I'd encourage you to go through the design process again to affirm the legitimacy and currency of what you have and also to provide more opportunity for input from your people. The mission should be written and endorsed by as many people as possible, not just by some executives in corner offices. If the mission statement is written solely by company leaders, it's *their* mission statement. It may or may not be accepted and supported by all the other people in the organization.

Your statement should be succinct. It should fit comfortably on one page, typed double-spaced or typeset in at least 14 point type. Explain why you are in business. Validate the reason your company exists, and specify the kind(s) of business(es) you're in.

In developing your statement, I encourage you to make the process a team effort. Involve managers from various levels of the corporate hierarchy. Bring non-managerial employees into the picture. Solicit input from your board of directors. Invite your customers or clients to offer their description of who you are. Not only will you benefit from several perspectives, you will have the opportunity to cross-check the legitimacy of each element of your statement.

An important advantage of involving a number of key people is that *people support what they help to create*. Your mission statement is worthless if every member of your team doesn't support it. Discuss the concepts. Gain agreement on what you're really all about. Choose your words carefully and shape your sentences deliberately to say what you really want to say. Craft this important document to be permanent enough to serve you for a while.

Once you have an acceptable, legitimate mission statement, begin putting it to work. This document is a valuable tool for you to assure that everyone understands what your organization is all about . . . and why. The first step is to spread the word. Show all your employees what has been developed. Some companies share the draft statement with employees, offering opportunities for review and comment before the document is finalized.

When the Mission Statement is finished and approved by everyone who has to approve it, begin making it a part of your corporate culture. You accomplish this task by introducing it to all your employees with an explanation of what it means to the company and to each employee. Through group and one-on-one conversations, be sure that everyone understands the statement, its value, and what *they* can do to bring the words to life.

Next, introduce your new Mission Statement to your customers, suppliers, job applicants, and anyone else doing business with your organization. Here are some suggestions to consider:

- Post the Mission Statement on bulletin boards in your facility, where it will be seen by employees and visitors.
- Put framed copies of the Mission Statement in the offices of all executives, managers, and supervisors. The frames can be hung on the wall or placed on desks, credenzas, filing cabinets, or tables.
- Place framed copies on the walls in offices, employee lounges, near coffee machines or water coolers, and other places where employees will see it.
- Enclose copies in payroll envelopes so each employee receives a personal copy.
- Give copies to customers during sales calls. As appropriate, send copies to customers. Enclose a copy in each shipment of merchandise.
- Display a copy on the wall of the personnel office. Give a copy, or show one, to each applicant. Explain what the Mission Statement means, especially as it applies to the company's expectations of its employees and what the company sees as its obligations/responsibilities to its employees.
- Print the mission statement on the back of business cards. Produce similar-sized cards and laminate them for employees to carry with them. These cards can be attached to name tags for employees working in environments such as hospitals, labs, or airports.

To reinforce the concepts and importance of your company's mission statement, you might schedule periodic meetings of all employees, or groups of employees. During these sessions, discuss the meaning and relevance of the Mission Statement and how it is applied in the daily work of the organization. Emphasize each employee's responsibility to live the Mission Statement every day.

Discuss aspects of your mission and your vision for the future in regular staff meetings. Refer to it in disciplinary conversations, so that practically everything you do reflects your clear mission—your reason for being in business.

Make your mission statement real, legitimate, permanent, and influential on a daily basis.

Strategy 1.2

Create a Statement of Values.

The same process that was used to create your Mission Statement can be used to create a Statement of Values or a Statement of Guiding Principles. The results of this effort should be displayed prominently with the Mission Statement to emphasize how your organization is strongly values-based.

Talk with your people about what principles are important to them—personally, as well as in the work environment. Explore attitudes about honesty, integrity, ethics, orientation toward religious foundations, long-term relationships versus brief encounters, and being self-serving as opposed to other-serving, and fair treatment for all. Issues such as health and safety can be addressed, determining whether you will have a non-smoking environment, pre-employment and/or annual physical examinations, and enforcement of safety measures such as wearing earplugs and safety glasses. If it fits for your organization, include words about caring for each other, involving families, and/or being a part of your community.

Express the value you may place on your employees, your customers, your suppliers, and your stockholders. How do you treat them? Put these attitudes in writing to reinforce the beliefs that serve as the foundation for the way you do things, the way you run your business.

A caution: you may well get into spiritual issues in these discussions. Be very careful to word your values statements to be inclusive, rather than exclusive. Words describing particular religious beliefs may be uncomfortable to people you'll want to hire in the future. For instance, if you talk about believing in Jesus Christ, you might exclude Jews, Moslems, Hindus, Buddhists . . . folks who might be desirable applicants in the future. You might be happy to have some of those diverse employees, but they may feel less than comfortable about joining your company.

Be clear about what you stand for, what you believe. Emphasize ethics: no bribes, kickbacks, or other unethical practices will be tolerated. Describe how customers, suppliers, and employees should be treated.

If you post your Statement of Guiding Principles in your purchasing department and give copies to the salespeople calling on your company, you'll send a clear message about how your company does business. For most people who read the values document, your words will be a welcome breath of fresh air. For the others, it will be a subtle warning that no one should ask your people to do something they shouldn't.

The clearer you make your guiding principles, and the more those principles are consciously used in making decisions, the more they will become a part of your operating philosophy. Clarity supports independent thought and action—the empowerment and comfort that encourage people to stay with their employer.

Many employees will welcome the clear statement to guide and reinforce how they should conduct themselves as members of your organization. Sometimes people need something to point to, to refer to, in determining their behavior. Give them that support, that anchor, with a strong, easily-to-understand statement of guiding principles.

People in management positions benefit from corporate culture values clarification. When they understand the company's philosophical approach, it is easier for them to make decisions on their own. As a result, managers have more time to focus on the real business of the organization, reducing the time they have to spend trying to figure out how to make values-based decisions in your environment.

Strategy 1.3

Share a common vision.

Your organization's chances of success are much greater if you have a clearly defined vision that all your people can follow. Where are we going as a company? How do we view our future? How will we move from where we are today to where we'd like to be in the future?

What will your entity look like in the years ahead? Is your desire to grow? How large and how fast? Do you prefer to remain the same size, providing increasingly good products and services to a fixed geographic or demographic market? Will you diversify or limit the areas in which you are involved?

Attitudes and behavior can be quite different among employees of a company that is energetically laser-focused on gung-ho strong growth and one that prefers to maintain the status quo, deepening relationships with current customers. An organization that is seriously committed to research and development will think and behave differently than one that is more interested in gaining a greater return on investment from existing technology, products, or services.

Use a group participation process with your vision, but with top executive leadership. What directions should the company go . . . or not go? Solicit lots of input from all your employees, encouraging creative, out-of-the-box thinking. As people have an opportunity to become involved with the visioning process, they develop a sense of ownership of the company's future. Their emotional relationship with their vision will tend to hold them to the company . . . to help the vision become reality. Remember, as I emphasized earlier, "people support what they help to create."

Once your vision is crystallized, share it with every employee . . . and every new employee. Show them where you and your "partners" expect the company to move in the future. Today's employees are forward-thinking. They're looking toward the future and will feel more attached to an employer who is also looking seriously at its future.

Emphasize the excitement of the future, your vision, in your ongoing communications with your people. Your sharing and reinforcement will encourage your good people to stay to help you realize this vision, especially if they helped create it.

Strategy 1.4

Work together as a team.

The people who work for an employer are individuals. They apply their personal talents, knowledge, abilities, and energy to accomplish the work of the organization. People can contribute as individuals, or as members of a team.

The choice, to function independently or as part of a team, is made consciously. The more the employee interacts positively with other members of the team, the greater will be the bonds linking the employee with the organization. Those emotional bonds link people to your company in ways a mere paycheck simply can't.

When people work together in teams, they get more accomplished—both in qualitative and quantitative terms. While there are tasks that are best done on an individual basis, most work benefits from the involvement of more than one person's effort.

Whether people work alone or in teams is a consequence of the operating philosophy of the organization. This philosophy is established and maintained by senior management, but is also strongly influenced by middle managers and supervisors. By your actions, by the way you assign work and lead, you determine how much and how well people will work together.

To build an organizational climate that encourages people to work together, emphasize the value of working together as a team. Encourage cooperation, collaboration, networking, sharing, and camaraderie. Assign tasks or projects to groups, or suggest that individuals accepting assignments call upon others to assist them.

Teamwork involves a common striving for goals and objectives that are understood and agreed-to by all concerned. In your leadership role, strive to clarify those goals and objectives with your people. Initiate discussions that serve to build consensus in work groups and in the organization as a whole.

Effective teamwork involves members communicating with each other, assuring that everyone has access to needed information. Beyond access, teamwork implies a more active communications flow enabling all members to know what others are doing, why they are doing it, and what they will do in the future. It's a deliberate, assertive process.

You can make it easier for people to work in teams. Support the team concept by facilitating teamwork interaction. For example, provide work areas that are more conducive to team operation. Place people in reasonable proximity to each other and you make it easier for them to collaborate. This design includes giving people enough space to be together as they work on joint projects.

Don't expect people to work well as teams if their work areas consist of small one-person cubicles with no common areas. Cubicle forests are not usually the most conducive environment for collaborative creativity. As one client expressed it, productivity and loyal enthusiasm can be dangerously damaged by difficulties with "intercubicle communication."

Unless you take deliberate steps to build and maintain the necessary human relationships, don't expect close cooperation and collaboration among people at opposite ends of a plant or in separate buildings. Look for creative ways to keep people connected.

To enable your people to work better in teams, give them

ways to communicate with each other. A place to meet is a good first step, but team functioning is also enhanced by the use of communications technology such as good telephone systems, networked personal computers, and accessibility to e-mail and the internet. Facsimile machines, live video, conference call equipment, and other technologies still being developed, enhance the ability of people to interact in a quick, efficient manner.

Stay alert for any opportunity to reinforce the value and importance of people working together for the common good of the organization. Do whatever you can to support and strengthen people's capacities to function as a team.

Make a special effort to include part-time, flex-time, and telecommuting workers. When you're developing teams or building networks of communication, it's too easy to forget these important people. Use technology and good old human-to-human contact to keep everyone connected.

Strategy 1.5

See loyalty as a two-way relationship.

To keep your good people, you naturally want your employees to feel strong bonds of loyalty to the organization. If you treat your employees well, following the philosophy expressed through the strategies in this book, the feelings of loyalty will be there.

Loyalty is a two-way relationship. If you expect your people to be loyal to you, you have to be loyal to them. Being loyal to your employees means avoiding layoffs as much as possible. It means backing them up when they need help in dealing with a customer or supplier. Loyalty to employees includes understanding when someone makes an honest mistake, not terminating them or applying severe discipline when an employee's error or accident was unintentional.

Loyalty means giving your people appropriate support in their personal lives when they are in trouble. This kind of support is most often given through employee assistance programs offering confidential service from mental health counselors, alcoholism clinics, legal specialists, and similar professionals. A number of employers will grant pay advances or special leaves of absence to help their valued employees over the rough spots along the road of life.

Some companies show their loyalty by making company equipment or facilities available for employee use on personal time. As an example, many companies that have trucks will allow employees to use them on their own time to move furniture, dirt, or something else appropriate for the vehicle. Others will make shop tools available for employees to take home to work on personal projects. If your company values suggest supporting your people in such ways, be sure your corporate policy is clear to avoid misunderstandings. It's wise to be sure your insurance policies cover you and your people, too.

Do those extra things to demonstrate your loyalty to your people, and they will do extra things to show their loyalty to you. As a result of the perception of cold-heartedness associated with layoffs and downsizings in recent years, workers are understandably cynical and suspicious. Their feeling is that corporate loyalty is dead. They're not going to be loyal to an employer unless and until that employer demonstrates genuine loyalty to them.

Strategy 1.6

Be enthusiastic.

If you have reason to be enthusiastic about your people, your organization, your potential, and your success, show it! If pride and enthusiasm and team spirit are justified, support the expression of these feelings as a company. Make this kind of positive communication a shared value as part of your corporate culture.

When people operate as a team, and achieve success, they

should be able to celebrate their wins. If such celebrations are suppressed or prohibited, it dampens the motivation to work as hard for the victories. Think positive! Celebrate with parties—including food like pizza, cake and ice cream, cookies, hors d'oeuvres, or even complete meals. Pot luck meals can be fun, too—giving everyone a chance to share in the preparation of the celebration.

Enthusiasm can be experienced at the time of winning and also while the race is being run. You can even celebrate the race before it's run—remember pep rallies before high school football games? Build positive feelings among your people toward what you are doing. Emphasize how each person is contributing toward your organization's achievement. Stay excited!

Enthusiasm is contagious! If you consciously spread enthusiasm, it will be more difficult for negative feelings to infect your organization. Remember that negative feelings are contagious, too.

Strategy 1.7

Communicate positive feelings.

At first blush, this strategy may sound like it's a repetition of Strategy 1.6, Be Enthusiastic. We might view this strategy as a low-key version of hard-driving enthusiasm. Few people can be a walking pep rally every day—and if they did act that way, people would soon write them off as overbearing and their impact would diminish.

With this strategy, I'm encouraging you to always communicate positive feelings. Well, almost always. Most of the time, you can find a way to put a positive twist on negative circumstances, but there are those times when negative conditions really deserve some negative thinking.

I suggest that there are really only two types of feelings that people can have in the work environment (and I realize I'm generalizing here)—positive and negative. If people don't hear positive communication or sense a positive attitude, they assume the negative. There is no neutral.

Have you ever noticed that when a friend, colleague, or even a boss passes you in the hall or even in a shopping mall without saying hello, you wonder what's wrong? The other person may simply have been preoccupied or have not even seen you, but you assume the negative. It's a natural human tendency. Solution? Strengthen the flow of positive communications so others really "get" your positive attitude toward them.

Concentrate on greeting each one of your people at least once every day. Yes, that means you have to get out of your office and go visit them in their work areas. Trust me, the exercise will do you good. You'll clear your head, demonstrate an outreach kind of caring, and gain a better sense of working conditions in your company. Find positive things to talk about—the clothing people are wearing, the work they're doing, the appearance of their work areas, the weather, team success, or good news about matters of common interest.

You can even communicate positively when disciplining or coaching someone. Focus on what people are doing right and on the constructive aspects of how people can improve their performance, rather than merely pounding away on the negative. Yes, I know you don't just criticize people all the time . . . but could they get that feeling because you're not building in enough of the positive?

Build a solid, positive environment, the kind of environment that generates a positive undercurrent even without energetic enthusiasm. Find reasons to celebrate, to spread positive feelings. Occasions for celebration include birthdays, anniversaries of employment, the company's founding, completed projects, sales achievement, awards received (individual, team, company), or even the arrival of Spring.

Strategy 1.8

Stay focused on the customer.

Successful companies, today and into the future, will be those that are customer-driven. If you want to be competitive, on the leading edge of your industry, include deliberate high-level customer service as one of your company's principal values.

Building the most effective kind of attitude toward customer service will not come just from training people to smile and say, "Thank you for shopping at. . . . "Your attitude toward customers must be a deliberate strategy flowing from the very top of your organization. This attitude must be real, it must be genuine. If employees sense that it's phony, they may be uncomfortable enough to leave. Today's workers don't want to live a lie.

This concern is another one of those aspects, like most of the values we're discussing, where actions speak louder than words. All your people will be watching to see how senior management regards customer service. The employees on the front lines, interacting directly with your customers, will perform as they see their leaders performing.

If management treats employees well, there's a pretty good chance the employees will treat the customers well. If management treats employees badly, expect the same kind of treatment to be extended to customers. There's a moral here: Internal customer service influences external customer service.

Some companies have stopped spending thousands of dollars on customer satisfaction surveys. These companies discovered such a strong correlation with the results of employee satisfaction surveys, that they now concentrate on keeping employees happy (as internal customers) and find that their paying customers are treated very well.

To facilitate good customer service, give careful consideration to the design of your policies that affect the way your people can deal with customers. Begin with pricing, then look at the range of flexibility your salespeople have. Does your paperwork requirement support or frustrate the efforts of your people to serve your customers? How much do your policies enable or hamper your service staff and customer relations specialists as they seek to resolve the problems that always arise?

Some of the most successful companies in the customer service arena give their employees a considerable amount of authority to make things "right" for the customer. Some restaurants give not only managers, but servers, the authority to discount prices, give meals away, or give gift certificates when striving to satisfy a disgruntled customer. Clerks in retail stores have freedom to accept returned merchandise without receipts. Manufacturers' customer service representatives can replace parts or products at no charge to the customer to "make things right."

Giving front-line people such power strengthens their ability to respond to the customer's needs. Feeling the company's sincere desire to do business the "right" way inspires customers to return to continue doing business with such companies. This becomes a driving force and a source of pride for the employees who care about the company and the customer. The result is a win-win-win relationship. People who have the power to do what's right for the customer are more likely to stay with their employer; they feel that they can make a real difference. They have power, they really matter to the organization and to its customers.

Some employees will half-apologetically confess that they don't serve customers. Folks in positions in such as accounting, clerical, computer systems, or manufacturing often don't relate to the company's customers. Help them appreciate the impact they have on the company's success through serving their internal customers—employees in other departments of the company. Everyone in the organization serves the company's customer, directly or indirectly.

Internal customer service is a vitally important component of corporate success. Recognize good service internally, as well as externally. Bring departments together in meetings where they can explore how to better serve each other . . . and eventually do a better job for the company's ultimate customer.

Strategy 1.9

Offer stability, security, risk, as needed.

You can influence worker productivity and job satisfaction by the degree of stability and risk you offer. Although the terms sound opposite, both can be comfortably present in the same organizational environment.

The concept of risk usually goes hand-in-hand with change. Organizational change is a fact of life now. The three constants in our lives are death, taxes, and change. The problem with change, from the perspectives of many people, is the disruption of stability. When stability is shaken, fears of damage to security follow close behind.

Change is necessary in organizations. Without change, leading toward positive progress, organizations slide backward. The loss is either directly measurable or is relative to the competition. However you judge your position, it is clear that you must deliberately move forward to survive and thrive. Change is a necessity. While some people really like constant change, others feel really threatened by it, feeling a very uncomfortable lack of stability. Pay careful attention to your people; know who likes change and who doesn't, then feed their personal preferences.

When an organization offers a foundation of stability, change comes more easily. There is a strong platform to use as a jumping-off point. In a stable organization, the risks associated with change are more comfortable because of the sense of security felt by members of the organization. If you want to encourage positive change with minimal or at least calculated risk, take steps to maintain the stability of your organization to support the change.

These concepts are mutually supportive. Stability and security are enhanced by the organization taking the risks to make changes and trying new approaches to stay on the cutting edge. The more your people are "on the leading edge" in a positive way, the greater will be the excitement about making progress and staying "on top" of any situation. (See Strategy 2.31.)

Organizations that strive for too much stability tend to resist change, growth, and responsiveness. Those that aim for too much risk may endanger their own security by exposing vulnerability. Your greatest success will come from striking a reasonable balance between stability and risk to provide long-term security.

Involve your people in determining the right stability/change balance for your organization. Their participation in the decisions—philosophically and practically—will build their comfort and support of your approach. The resulting feeling of having helped to make the choices that will drive the organization's balance—and future—will build a commitment to stay around to assure the success they helped design.

Strategy 1.10

Prohibit discrimination of any kind.

Since the Civil Rights Act of 1964, we have become legally and morally sensitive to preventing discrimination. Beyond the legal implications, discrimination may inhibit your opportunities to gain the high potential of contributions and longevity of employment by those who may be targets for discrimination. If your good people believe they are being discriminated against, whether it is true or not, they will probably leave you for a more accepting environment.

Traditionally, we do not permit discrimination on the basis of race, creed, color, national origin, religion, sex, or age. These areas of difference are covered by federal law, so they are violated only at great risk.

There are other areas of difference that could serve as bases for discrimination, perhaps causing you to lose some of your best people. Even though, as human beings, people have prejudices, guard against discrimination in employment based on such factors as:

- level of education
- use of grammar in spoken or written communication
- home state (examples: people in Ohio often put down those from West Virginia. Indiana residents harbor similar feeling for folks from Kentucky. Texans may enjoy joking about people who live in Oklahoma.)
- style of dress or other appearance factors, including hairstyle, body weight or height, and skin blemishes
- regional accents
- neighborhood of residence
- type of vehicle owned
- marital or parental status
- sports activity
- political party identification
- use of tobacco products: cigarettes, cigars, pipes, chewing tobacco
- relationship preferences.

The list can go on and on. And, yes, managers and entire organizations still discriminate for or against employees or potential employees based on these criteria. Be wary that you aren't scaring away, or blatantly sending away, some of your best talent because of such short-sightedness.

When you discover discrimination, take immediate and definitive steps to negate the discrimination and clarify for all concerned that such discrimination will not be tolerated.

Strategy 1.11

Eschew profanity.

Now, there's an interesting word we don't see every day. Eschew. For years I saw that word in an expression, "eschew obfuscation," and wondered what it meant. Finally, when I grew mature enough to stop resisting my parents' insistence that I look things up in the dictionary, I discovered the meaning of the confusing words and phrase.

Eschew means to shun or avoid. Obfuscation is making things unclear or obscure. Thus, I discovered, that hard-to-comprehend phrase demonstrated very plainly to make things clear.

Eschew seems like a good word to attach to profanity in the workplace. Shun it. Avoid it. Profanity is totally inappropriate for people in management or other influential positions. Don't use it on a regular basis, as part of your normal vocabulary; and try to find alternative words when you are angry or frustrated. Yes, I know "fudge" doesn't seem to be as satisfying, but think of the people around you.

A lot of people, even in today's more liberal times, don't like cursing. Being around someone who curses is uncomfortable for them. They find it difficult to respect someone using profanity. It can be particularly distasteful if they don't use those kinds of words at all themselves. They may never say anything to you, but the feelings are there anyway.

Even those people who use profanity themselves, on a regular basis or on "special occasions," have less respect for others who use it. This attitude especially applies toward people in leadership positions. It lowers their opinion of you.

Appreciate that people follow your lead. If you curse, expect them to do the same. If cursing is accepted on an employee-to-employee basis, it won't be long before cursing will be easy to do in front of the customers . . . and then to the customers. On a recent trip, I stopped at a drug store for some cold medicine. Imagine my feelings when the pharmacist, helping me make my selection, used profanity in our conversation.

What do your personal and organizational values say about profanity? Can you legitimately establish a policy, and adhere to it yourself?

Strategy 1.12

Be fair and honest.

It almost seems insulting to include this concept as an environmental strategy for your consideration. But, it is something that must be addressed when constructing your overall statement of organizational values.

Do your people understand clearly the organization's position on fairness and honesty? You might be surprised. This situation is another one where what you do speaks louder than what you say.

If you're going to be fair and honest, those standards must be applied in *all* dealings with employees, customers, unions, suppliers, and the community. If you are not honest in your dealings with suppliers, don't expect your employees to believe you'll be honest with them.

If you expect your people to be fair and honest with others, including each other and you, set the example. Otherwise, you may end up like the drug-abusing father who couldn't understand why his kids "turned bad." Your people at work watch you just as much as your children do at home.

Strategy 1.13

Facilitate a family feeling.

Some business owners and managers shy away from the idea of having a family feeling among their employees. They believe that a business is just that, a business. A family is different.

A family feeling does not mean you're giving away the

store. It does mean that people can call each other by their first names or nicknames. More formal terms of address can be used when company's there, like a client, but the feeling of comfort with each other is present.

In a family, people care about each other. While they are bonded together, they are also free to be individuals. They hold a strong allegiance to each other, defending that togetherness against outsiders. They share responsibilities.

Family members also squabble from time to time. Differences are brought out relatively quickly, dealt with in direct and sometimes emotional ways, then put to rest. Parent-child relationships are productive.

There are many positive aspects to our sense of family in our cultures. Even the negative aspects have their positive attributes. If applied properly, the family feeling can be very healthy for any organization.

Strategy 1.14

Value professional standing.

Many professions, and some trades, have requirements for certain levels of education, experience, qualification, and continuing education. These elements of professional membership and designation are important to those in the professions. They should also be of value to the organizations employing those people.

If you want to attract and hold professionals, demonstrate that you value their status and respect their credentials. The respect and appreciation will be returned. Disdain the professional standing, and you will "force" some of your key people to seek positions where their professionalism is recognized and honored.

There are a number of ways that professional standings can be recognized. Let's consider some:

- Encourage framing and posting of certificates affirming

educational achievement and professional designation. Call attention to those credentials when taking visitors on tours of your facilities and when speaking to customers.

- If members of your team hold professional designations authorizing the use of identifying initials after their names, encourage the employee to use the designation in correspondence and when his/her name is shown on reports, proposals, and official documents.
- Support participation in professional organizations, including granting time and funds to attend appropriate meetings or conferences. Many companies pay the dues for their employees to facilitate their involvement in their profession.
- Recognize the status of your people in annual reports, newspaper, magazine, or newsletter articles, stockholder reports, and other publications. When professional accomplishments are made, publicize them proudly.
- Pay for subscriptions to professional journals so your people can keep current in their fields.
- Whenever appropriate, call upon your professionals for their expertise in solving problems or looking at alternatives.

Strategy 1.15

Promote integrity.

State and re-state your desire for honesty and honor in the behavior of all members of your organization. Emphasize the high value you place on righteousness, and refusal to compromise personal or corporate values.

Teach and discuss the meaning of integrity—the word and the concept. Even though most people have heard the word, not that many have actually talked about what the word means to them.

Abide by the code of ethics in your organization. Clarify your expectations that everyone will follow that same code, with termination being a probable consequence for violating that trust. (*See Strategy 1.2.*)

No more needs to be said. Either you have it or your don't.

Strategy 1.16

Encourage camaraderie.

Camaraderie refers to companionship. It's a fellowship, an enjoyment of being with each other, enjoying each other's company. The feeling is one of being pals, almost best of friends. It's a closeness that demonstrates that we enjoy being with each other.

In the business world, we can encourage people to build relationships with each other. Going out to lunch together, working on projects together, joining colleagues or coworkers in sports leagues, golf outings, family picnics, and carpooling all strengthen the bonds of camaraderie.

People who enjoy one another are usually more productive in the workplace. They have greater loyalty to each other and to the organization that makes it possible for them to be together, to work together for common good.

Explore opportunities for people to work together outside the normal working environment. When people work shoulder-to-shoulder on a community service project, they build bonds that can enhance their relationships. Great friendships, high degrees of comfort, can develop when your employees work with each other building a house for Habitat for Humanity, organizing and managing a walkathon, or collecting clothes and food for the needy. After checking for individual interest levels, put together a community service project for all your employees . . . and perhaps their families, too. Make a positive difference together.

Strategy 1.17

Promote a healthy working environment.

If you care about your people, you'll want them to have a healthy working environment. You can help create and promote it.

Make sure you have good engineering of heating, air conditioning, and ventilating systems. Maintain a healthy environment in which people can work. (*See Strategy 1.45 for additional information.*)

In areas that are not conducive to clean air, such as those in certain production facilities, provide breathing masks and "clean" rooms where workers can take a break. In "the old days," the emphasis was on getting the work out. Little, if any, care was given to the impact of the production environment on the health of the employees. Today, we still must have the same concerns for production, but certainly not at the expense of the workers.

An increasing number of employers have established smoke-free environments in the workplace. In some cases, an entire facility is declared smoke-free. This restriction may place a hardship on employees with a smoking habit. Employers are using the resources available from various health organizations to help people stop smoking. Some even offer cash bonuses for employees who quit smoking, payable after they have not smoked for some period of time.

For health, safety, and legal reasons, wise employers also ban alcohol and drugs from the workplace. If employees come to work under the influence of alcohol or drugs, they must be sent home. Coming to work under the influence of these substances is an offense punishable by discharge in many companies. Be firm about these policies for the protection of all your employees.

If your company has this value, enforce it among all your employees. Include executives who may now indulge in the so-called three-martini lunch. Include managers who may keep a bottle in their desk drawer for special occasions. Include salesmen who have cocktails when taking customers out to lunch. You may want to join those companies that simply don't reimburse liquor purchases on expense accounts.

To promote health, consider establishing a wellness program for your employees. Such educational and support programs can range from making health literature available to sponsoring educational seminars to launching a full-blown, organized exercise regimen.

Professional assistance is available to help you design and implement any kind of wellness program you want. Check with resources such as:

- the outreach people at your community's hospital
- registered dietitians who practice in your area
- training professionals who have wellness courses
- health clubs, exercise centers, and sports medicine clinics
- recreation departments operated by municipal governments
- local school systems.

If the kind of program you are seeking does not exist, your chances are pretty good that one or more of the listed resources will be glad to help you put something together. You don't have to be elaborate or spend a lot of money to promote good health among your employees and their families.

Strategy 1.18

Insist on workplace safety.

As the expression goes, "Safety is everybody's business." We practically take it for granted that employers want a safe environment, as do their employees. Taking safety for granted is foolish.

Safety needs to be demanded and emphasized from the top of the organization. Those senior executives responsible must also get out of their offices and go out to where people are working to assure safety measures are implemented. Enforcement by the federal Occupation Health and Safety Administration (OSHA) is not as strong as it used to be; enforcement is now up to the employer. And employers are legally and morally liable when accidents occur.

In the past few months, I have personally been in several manufacturing plants where senior management insists that safety is a paramount concern. In one company, when we toured the production area we counted almost two dozen obvious safety hazards. How many did we overlook because we are not trained safety engineers? In the other plant, we saw employees working without their required safety glasses and ear protectors. The message wasn't getting through, and certainly wasn't being enforced. How do you think employees felt about how much management cared about their safety?

It's not enough to say safety is important. The message must be conveyed clearly to front-line supervisors. Those supervisors, and their hourly subordinates, must have the authority, responsibility, and accountability to correct safety problems *before* someone gets hurt. It's perfectly legitimate to place the burden of accountability on front-line supervisors. Train and equip them to fulfill the safety aspects of their jobs.

Supervisors are traditionally caught in the middle, trying to satisfy all the demands made upon them by management, employees, and customers, without having to contend with additional duties or extra work dumped on them by outsiders. If you insist that a supervisor keep the work area clean and safe, you may get an angry question in response: which is more important— getting the work out on time or having a clean, safe work area? How you answer determines the value that will be placed on health and safety.

To emphasize safety, employers will erect signs showing how many days have passed since the last lost-time accident. The space where the number of days is shown is painted so chalk can be used to change the number of days each evening or morning. Other signs use cards with numbers and holes so they can be hung on hooks. One hopes that changing numbers will be infrequent.

Safety dinners are held throughout the country. Employees wear shirts proclaiming the company's safety record. Awards are given for safe operation. For more ideas and support materials for an ongoing safety campaign, contact the National Safety Council, 1121 Spring Lake Drive, Itasca, Illinois 60143. Their telephone number is 630-775-2231.

Strategy 1.19

Avoid stupid rules.

Every organization needs rules to guide its operation. The writing and enforcement of these rules is an obligation of management. Naturally, the company's leaders expect the rules to be followed. The rules have to make sense if they're going to work.

If you institute stupid rules that are not needed, that conflict with the corporate culture or with other rules, or that just don't make any sense, your people will develop a negative attitude toward all rules. The disdain for the silly rules easily carries over to apply to all rules.

Simple solution: make sure that any rules, regulations, policies, procedures, and operating methods are reasonable and appropriate. Rules should always support, not frustrate, the efforts of the organization and team members to get the job done.

Herman's Law of Rule Making says as organizations grow larger, there is a tendency to make more rules. Even if everything is running just fine, an increase in the number of employees or locations seems to generate a proportional increase in the number of rules. Rules are necessary for some situations. Concentrate on those and ignore the other issues. Assume that reasonable people can think for themselves and will make good decisions when provided with good information and training.

Guard against the propensity to create more and more rules in bureaucratic organizations. Cut through red tape; don't create more! Red tape is not biodegradable, so it is not healthy for the earth's environment . . . or your work environment, either! Eliminate superfluous rules whenever you can.

Strategy 1.20

Don't tolerate substandard performance; remove unsuitable people.

Sometimes we have a tendency not to terminate unsuitable employees as soon as we should. This hesitance is particularly true if we have developed close relationships with them, and/or if close bonds have been formed with other members of our team.

This toleration is a dangerous practice and should be avoided. When you determine that an employee is unsuitable to continue as a member of your team, take steps to terminate your employment relationship with that person right away. By allowing them to continue working, you're condoning a lower standard of performance or quality of team member.

In some cases, your efforts to correct the problem will have begun already through your progressive discipline process. In other cases, you will have to confront the situation differently. Beware of capriciously terminating any employee abruptly without just cause. Based on your personnel policy manual, which you should create if you don't have one, just cause might include use of drugs or alcohol on company premises, theft, life-threatening behavior, or insubordination.

In either case, you might want to counsel the employee regarding the employee's suitability for continued employment with your organization. Perhaps this person just doesn't fit in. You're probably better off if the employee decides to leave you and resigns.

If the employee does not take the initiative to resign, take the necessary steps to move toward termination. If you allow an unproductive, or counterproductive, employee to remain on your payroll, other employees can become "poisoned" by that person's behavior. It's something akin to the bad apple in the bushel.

Dedicated employees lose faith and respect for you if you do not take decisive action when one of your employees doesn't pull his or her own weight. The good employees become disillusioned, wondering why they're working so hard. Good people want to be surrounded by other good people and have low tolerance for substandard coworkers.

Strategy 1.21

Support telecommuting

More and more employers are allowing their people to do all or part of their work at home. With developing technology, such as modems, facsimile machines, audio conference call mechanisms, and videoconferencing, the possibilities are endless. Many jobs can be done from home or from a satellite work facility.

Many people can actually be more productive at home than at the office. With fewer interruptions, they can get a lot more done. They can still take care of children or other errands and get the company's work done by working when it's most productive for them. For some workers, this design means working early in the morning, during the evening, or even late at night. People are able to manage the schedule that's best for them, being measured by the results they achieve, rather than the time they're sitting at their desks.

The benefits to the employer can be significant. With fewer people coming to the congregate work site, the company doesn't have to spend as much money on real estate, utilities, maintenance, and other costs related to facilities operation. Since there are fewer people around to pull into useless meetings. less time is wasted in those meetings,

Telecommuting can be a challenge for supervisors not accustomed to managing people who are not in close physical proximity to them. Be sure to provide extra training and support for your supervisors of teleworkers to help them become effective leaders and not merely managers. And don't forget to provide extra training for the telecommuters themselves, to help them adjust to the new workstyle.

Strategy 1.22

Support family leave

An increasing number of women are earning college degrees and going to work in highly responsible positions. As their careers begin to develop, these valuable employees may choose to have one or more children. You can keep them on your team by giving them non-paid leave to give birth and care for the children for a reasonable period of time thereafter. When they are ready to return to work, welcome them back and enable them to continue along their established career path.

Be receptive to men wanting to take some time off during childbirth and infancy time. There is now more interest in this kind of family participation among men. Expand your thinking to permit this kind of time off when couples adopt an infant or toddler, too. The same kind of time and attention is needed at home, even when the child is adopted.

Strategy 1.23

Support military reservists

Some valuable employees with a high social consciousness may want to invest part of their lives in missionary work or community service. Others may be involved with the National Guard or military reserves. Support these people by giving them flexibility to pursue their own interests and they will demonstrate their loyalty to you by returning even stronger than when they departed.

Establish a company policy regarding the length of time you will hold jobs or opportunities open, how you will handle benefits and benefit eligibility (check with your carrier), and whether you will pay employees during their absence from work. Even if you give yourself some flexibility in your guidelines, set the policy and stick with it. Establishing a firm policy will help your employees understand your position and will eliminate confusion later.

These employees who dedicate themselves to helping others in time of need are worthy of your recognition. Consider an article in your company newsletter, a bulletin board showing their activities, or some other way to honor their contributions to your community. You might want to have your top executives host an annual luncheon or dinner to honor your employees who serve in the military reserves or in the National Guard. Those important organizations need employer support to encourage men and women to serve; they have retention challenges, too.

Strategy 1.24

Apply progressive discipline fairly.

There are two parts to this strategy. One is to apply progressive discipline. The other is to apply it fairly.

Progressive discipline means following a series of deliberate steps in disciplining an employee for infractions of company rules. By following these steps, you are fair to the employee, you avoid capricious actions, and your disciplinary process will stand up in court.

The steps of progressive discipline increase in seriousness and intensity as your proceed with the enforcement procedure:

1. The first step is informational. During this initial phase, make sure the employee fully understands what is expected in terms of behavior and performance. Applying this step will solve most problems that arise from unclear expectations.
2. If the problem persists, the second step is to initiate the formal discipline process with the verbal warning, or verbal reprimand. In this interview, the superior again informs the errant employee of the expectations and specifically how the expectations are not being met. Agreement is reached as to how the employee can correct the problem.

   The supervisor states that this interview is a verbal notification of dissatisfaction with the employee's performance. If the problem is not corrected, further discipline may result. (Use "may" instead of "will" to give yourself flexibility in the future. You might want to issue more than one verbal reprimand before moving to the next step.)
3. The third step is the written reprimand or warning. This notification is similar to the verbal reprimand, except that the communication is put in writing. The written memorandum includes a description of the behavior that is expected of the employee, then what the employee is perceived to be doing.

   Next, write down how and when you expect the employee to correct the behavior or overcome the problem. If supervisory support will be needed to get things back on track, indicate what kind of support will be given—by whom, when, and how.

Again, include the statement that if the problem is not corrected, further disciplinary action may be taken. The employee gets a copy of the memorandum, and a copy goes into the employee's personnel file.

4. If the problem still persists, your next step is a suspension. This action involves giving the employee time off without pay for anywhere from one to thirty days. Usually, one, two, or three days will convey the seriousness of your message. Again, state the expected behavior, the perceived behavior, what must be done to correct the problem, and the statement that additional disciplinary action may be taken if the problem is not corrected. Document that a written reprimand had been given, the date, and the employee's response at that time.

   Some companies are using a variation that involves a paid suspension. The employee is given time off with pay, but must return with a written plan for how the problem behavior will be corrected. Studies show that many employees treated this way either correct their behavior or resign.

5. The final step in the progressive discipline process is termination. If the other steps have not produced the desired results, it is usually necessary to discharge the employee. Again, this discharge should be done in writing, stipulating the dates of the verbal reprimand, written reprimand, and suspension.

   If the discharged employee appeals, the discipline was legitimate, and all the steps have been followed, the administrative or civil courts will probably support your position.

   If all the steps have been followed, and the discipline is legitimate, the administrative or civil courts will probably support your position if the discharged employee appeals. If you do not follow and document the steps, you are open for criticism and possible reversal of your discharge.

Strategy 1.25

Make work fun.

People should enjoy their jobs. If people don't enjoy what they are doing, they should resign their positions and go find some kind of work they can enjoy doing.

Happy employees are more productive employees. They are comfortable in their work environment, so they will want to remain there for a longer period of time.

Your challenge is to create and maintain an environment where people can enjoy their work, can enjoy being a part of your team. There are a number of ways to creat and maintain this kind of work environment, ranging from the way you decorate the work area to the prevailing attitudes toward enjoying work.

Bring out the positive aspects of your team's environment. Celebrate the victories. Celebrate birthdays. Do some silly things once in a while just to have some fun. Be careful not to ridicule anyone or cause any damage in the process.

Laugh!

Don't turn the place into a country club or a comedy fair, but have fun. Bring in a pizza once in a while for lunch. Buy ice cream bars for everyone on a warm day. Have costume contests around holidays. Invite employees to bring their favorite dishes for a pot-luck lunch. Decorate your work areas to recognize holidays, birthdays, or company anniversary. These things will carry over to support positive attitudes that will reinforce work being fun . . . an enjoyable experience, rather than an oppressive drudgery.

As the expression goes, "Take what you do seriously, but don't take yourself too seriously."

Strategy 1.26

Reduce meetings.

There are a lot of ways to communicate in the work environment. While it's important to keep in contact with what's happening, to share information, and to invite input into various kinds of decisions, sometimes we tend to overdo this communications thing. Too many managers have fallen into the habit of scheduling meetings for issues that really don't require meetings. This habit is a trap. We've talked with a lot of folks who leave companies—or think of leaving—because they have to be in so many meetings, they can't get their work done!

When meetings have to be held, keep them tight. Start meetings on time, even if all the participants haven't arrived yet. They'll get the message and be punctual the next time. Establish an ending time, and complete by that time. If you're dependable about your finishing time, people will trust you more and will support your moving through the agenda to stay on schedule.

Agendas: Prepare them—in writing—and distribute them to all participants before the meeting. Get the meeting plans and objectives into people's hands with sufficient lead time that they can adequately prepare.

If a meeting isn't necessary, use an alternative means of communication to convey your messages. With the advent of e-mail, quite a bit can be accomplished with higher levels of efficiency.

Strategy 1.27

Support privacy.

Appreciate the fact that people need some private time to get their work done. Just having time to think for a while can improve results dramatically. Establish in your culture the value of privacy and encourage people to respect co-workers' requests not to be disturbed for a while.

There are several ways to support privacy. One approach is to schedule certain times during the day when everyone has private time. No interruptions are permitted unless there's an emergency. You'd be amazed at how productivity, job satisfaction, and employment longevity will increase if you block off even an hour in the morning and an hour in the afternoon. An hour may not seem like much, but an uninterrupted hour is treasured in today's rush-rush business environments.

Another technique is to have signs for workers to post outside their work areas—on an office door or on a cubicle entrance—advising others that this person has asked for some quiet time. Include a place on the sign for the worker to indicate what time the privacy period will end and have some way people can leave notes requesting a call-back, visit, or specific answers or services. Make it easy for visitors to leave a message, allowing the visitor to communicate and also boosting the worker's efficiency in responding.

One cute idea we picked-up from a company in England is the "guard bear." Each employee brings in a stuffed animal of some sort. The teddy bear, or whatever animal it is, is placed by the door to your cubicle or office when you don't want to be disturbed. As the bear is on guard duty, he may take messages (slid onto a safety pin, perhaps). Employee creativity will produce a wide variety of protective animals, adding to the atmosphere of fun at work.

Strategy 1.28

Provide unusual benefits.

Look for unusual benefits that will be valued by your employees. You might even want to have a contest to see who comes up with the most creative benefit. [We would love to hear about your results—roger@herman.net.] Here's one to consider.

High school bands and similar groups are always looking for money to support their various projects. They hold bake sales, car washes, and similar fund-raising events. Call your high school band director and ask how much money they earn at a Saturday car wash. Invite the band members to come to your location to wash everyone's car while they work. You can even provide all the supplies for them and simply hire their energy and time. Bonus: this could be a really neat service for your customers, too. Free car wash when they buy something at your store. You help the community and your employees at the same time.

You can provide this benefit on some sort of regular schedule or spontaneously—surprises like this are fun! This kind of a benefit can also be a company-wide reward for some sort of achievement or celebration of a milestone.

Lean & Meaningful (Herman & Gioia, 1998, Oakhill Press) is filled with leading-edge ideas for your consideration. Experiences of over 200 companies—large and small—are cited.

Strategy 1.29

Celebrate achievements, birthdays, and other occasions.

Share the positive aspects of relationships among the people who are part of your organization's team. This celebration doesn't mean a continual party, but does suggest that once in a while some time out is appropriate. We've known for years that celebrating together strengthens bonds among people, as well as people and organizations.

When individuals, or teams of individuals, or the organization as a whole, has achieved something worthwhile, celebrate. Experience the moment together with soft drinks, a cake, cookies, or even a full meal. Watch out for alcohol consumption; it could turn a celebration into an event-not-to-be-remembered. Ban alcohol in celebrations on company time.

Birthdays, anniversaries of employment, retirements, transfers, goal achievements, and other noteworthy occasions merit at least a getting together as a team. Express congratulations, and perhaps say a few appropriate words of praise. There are many different ways to accomplish your purpose.

I know companies that have monthly get-togethers of all their employees. One or two people cover the phones while everyone else gathers to share cake and punch or coffee. One company combines celebration of the month's birthdays and employment anniversaries. The company president takes a few minutes to give a brief report to all assembled about company progress. Cost is low, lost production time is minimal, and the building of morale is noticeable.

Strategy 1.30

Conduct exit interviews.

Some of your employees will leave your organization just because it's time to move on. Most will leave because of something that happened, or didn't happen. Regardless of the reason, you should know why each of your employees leaves you.

To discover this information, conduct an exit interview with each person who leaves you. Find out what they liked, and what they didn't like, about working for your company. What would they have liked to see different? Why?

Ask about their plans for the future. Where are they going to work next? Why? What does the new employment offer them? How does it differ from what the employee is offered at your company? Would they have liked to remain with your organization; what would have motivated them to stay? What suggestions do they have for making improvements in your company? Would they be interested in returning some day?

Ask the employee what he learned working with you—about work, the job to be done, and about himself. Based on that learning, how will he structure his next job? Answers to those supportive and non-intrusive questions may give you some valuable insights into ways you might enhance the work experience for other members of your team.

Your entire focus during this open, non-threatening interview should be to determine what is happening in your organization that could have caused the employee to look for greener pastures. How can you do things better? Ferret out the problem areas so you can deal with them. Gain a deeper understanding of your organization's strengths so you can use that information in your recruiting.

You can actually conduct sessions similar to exit interviews with your current employees. Find out what they like about working for you. Why do they stay? What improvements would they like to see, and why?

Listen carefully to what people say. Take notes, during the interview or afterwards, to document what you learn. Meet with your colleagues to analyze what you have discovered, then assess the potential impact on other valued employees. Do you need to take any immediate steps to keep others from leaving?

Those managers who do not learn from departing employees why they are moving on, leave themselves wide open for a mass exodus. Stay in touch with the trends in your organization and in your industry.

Strategy 1.31

Establish clear policies.

The people who work with you need to understand very clearly what it is you want from them. They need to understand exactly what your company policies are, why those policies were established, and how tightly they will be enforced.

Company policies cover a wide range of topics, from security of company property to work release for jury duty. There are a number of books and guides available in your library, from local book stores, and from catalog services to help you construct a set of policies appropriate to your organization.

The key, from this book's perspective, is to establish clear policies to govern how things are done in your organization. If you are unable to be clear and definitive, it may be better not to have a policy in a particular area. Unclear policies often create more difficulties than the absence of any policy covering a topic.

To develop policies that best suit your needs, look at the kinds of questions a new employee may have. People who have been with your organization for quite a while will have a fairly consistent understanding of what should be done. They would usually decide each matter the same way. Those established practices can be put down on paper, in most cases, as accepted policies. You may find that a set of policies will be relatively easy to construct by following this process.

There will be other issues where the decision is not as clear-cut. In these situations, senior management must determine what the policy will be and put that statement on paper. Some of the long-term employees may be able to offer some valuable input, based on the way things have been done—or specifically not done—in the past.

Gradually, you can create your own unique set of policies for all to see, understand, and apply. When making them official, be sure to explain the reasons for the policy as well as what each policy is. Understanding the reasoning behind the policies will help employees decide what to do in cases where no written policy exists.

Strategy 1.32

Administer policies uniformly.

Once you have established the policies, exceptions to the rule should be rare. The policies should be applied uniformly to all employees and in all situations. If exceptions are justified, say with the way a particular long-term customer is treated, all concerned should be told about that exception.

If there are too many exceptions, your policy is written too tightly. Some fine-tuning might be necessary.

If you are administering personnel policies, they should apply the same way to all members of your team. If you are administering customer service policies, all customers should be treated the same way according to those standards. The same criteria apply to interactions with suppliers and anyone else who deals with the organization.

The standardization provides some of the stability that is so essential to solid, long-term operation of any organization.

Strategy 1.33

Provide advancement opportunities; promote from within.

When your organization has a policy of promoting from within, your good people will set their sights more deliberately on opportunities for professional growth in your employ. If there are few potential openings and you seem to hire more people from outside for middle- and senior-management positions, your people will "see the handwriting on the wall," whether it is really there or not.

Good people will look for growth opportunities, for paths to greater career enhancement. If they perceive that those avenues are not open to them within your organization, they will quite naturally look elsewhere.

To hold good people, demonstrate that they have at least an equal chance in the competition against outsiders for high positions. When comparing outside applicants to internal applicants, give credit to the value of the years of service by your employee. Not only does that individual know something more about the job, but has a deeper understanding of the organization, the personalities in various key positions, and what will be expected of the successful candidate in the new position.

Whenever an outsider is chosen over a home-grown candidate, ask yourself very seriously why you did not choose your current employee. You owe that examination to yourself and to your employee, and you should share the results of your evaluation with your employee. Why was your team member not prepared for the opportunity? Will that same circumstance still exist when the next opening occurs? What are you doing to prepare your people to move up in your organization?

If you haven't already done so, it might be wise to invest some time and thought to developing a succession plan. How will people move up in the organization if (name the position) is vacated through promotion, retirement, death, or resignation? (*See the chapter on growth strategies for ideas on preparing people to move up the ladder.*)

A word of caution and concern is in order here. While it is important to promote from within to build stability, longevity, and a strong sense of opportunity, remain open to considering candidates from outside. If all your people in management are from "the ranks," you may limit the infusion of new ideas and perspectives from those with leadership or specialized experience in other organizations. Strive for a balance that demonstrates how you value your people, but select the best candidate for each position.

Strategy 1.34

Give permission to fail or succeed.

It's easy to give your people permission to succeed. Everyone wants to do well and wants others to do well. Our problem comes with the flip side of this coin.

Some of the things people try, particularly if they are innovative and relatively prone to risk-taking, won't work. They may not work as well as expected, or they may just plain flop. Bomb. Fail. Crash and burn.

Don't punish your valued employees for trying. Failures

help breed successes. Accept the loss and keep moving. Encourage them to try something else . . . quickly. Don't let the hurt fester very long before getting them involved in other projects. The failing employees will feel bad enough already. You don't have to do or say anything to be sure the employees know their efforts were a failure. The shame, frustration, and embarrassment are already having a negative impact. Rescue your Don Quixotes quickly, dust off the knights and shine up their armor. Emphasize the positive aspects of the unsuccessful efforts and move the valued employees ahead in a positive, we-learned-something manner. What can we learn from the next endeavor?

While you don't want to encourage failure, you do want to encourage experimentation, innovation, and the drive to make positive changes. Let people know that you accept the fact that some projects won't do everything we'd like them to. But, that failure brings us that much closer to a success.

Give people credit and support for just trying. Most employees are afraid even to try. Cheer on your risk-takers! They're the ones who can help you make a difference!

If you criticize or punish those responsible for failure, expect two consequences: first, they'll be reluctant to try something else new while working for you. Second, they'll begin searching for another company that will accept their failures and encourage them to keep trying.

Strategy 1.35

Management Commitment: People are our most important resource.

Every organization uses a number of resources to accomplish its mission. Capital, space, time, equipment, materials, people, and other resources are allocated according to their availability and need. While all the resources are important, the most valuable are the human resources, your people. At the same time, those resources can be your most volatile.

Personnel costs are most often the largest portion of the organization's budget. Good people are the most difficult resources to acquire, develop, utilize, maintain, and retain. You can sometimes "make do" with less quality or quantity in another resource, but you'll always need to earn the greatest possible return on our investment in human resources.

Let your people know that they are your greatest asset. Tell them how important they are to the organization's success, and that you appreciate what they do to help you achieve success.

People are also your most responsive resource. Through their efforts, people can overcome the weaknesses in other resources. The other resources can't do that to compensate for a weak human resource.

If your building were to catch fire, your first concern would be the safety of the people. Equipment, raw materials, even records, would be secondary. People are, without question, your most important resource.

While it would seem to go without saying, it is worthwhile for management to verify through written expression that people are important. Give the support to people, and the rest of the puzzle somehow comes together.

Strategy 1.36

Maintain comfortable atmospheric conditions.

People like to be physically comfortable when they work. A significant part of this comfort results from control of the temperature, humidity, ventilation, light, color, smell, noise level, and cleanliness.

Sometimes one or more of these factors may be outside your ability to control. A stamping plant, for example, will have noise; that just goes with the territory. In consideration of this situation, the management of that plant could provide a quiet room where employees could take breaks in a pleasant area with less noise.

The more you can do to provide a good working atmosphere for your people, the more they will appreciate it. This correlation is especially true if you do some innovative things that are ahead of, or different from, what your competitors are doing.

Your employees probably have some ideas on things that could be done, and will enjoy being part of generating, influencing, and implementing "cutting edge" ideas. Solicit their contributions regarding the shaping of their environment.

Strategy 1.37

Invite employees to bring their pets to work.

Yes, I know this one sounds a little far out, but more and more employers are doing it. Obviously, the pets have to be tame and well-behaved. Make arrangements for appropriate confinement—in the work area or in some area set aside for pets. You may need to hire an employee or an outside contractor to care for pets during the day, if you'll have a number of them together in one place.

Strategy 1.38

Respond to complaints with solutions.

When things don't go just right, people usually respond emotionally. Their first step is to gripe. People gripe about everything from the frustration of rush hour traffic to irritation with recalcitrant photocopy machines.

Most of the time, griping is just a way of letting off a little steam. When gnawing problems are not solved, the gripes can escalate into complaints. If complaints are not dealt with properly, they can become grievances and seriously affect performance of the people and the organization.

The answer is to be sensitive to the gripes, and highly attentive to complaints. When one of your people complains about something, respond quickly with interest and concern.

Let them know you care about the problem and finding a solution.

Ask for their ideas on how the problem can be solved. Listen to that input, then determine what temporary or permanent solution you can apply. Take action to follow through to assure that the solution is implemented to defuse the complaint and solve the problem.

A very effective leadership technique is to insist that anyone presenting a problem also present at least one possible solution. This approach reduces problem-solving time, gathers solution ideas from the people who are closest to the problem and can see answers most clearly, and places a greater sense of "ownership" of the solution on those who must implement it.

Unsolved problems that generate complaints become proportionately more serious as time passes. If you don't respond to complaints with viable solutions, people begin to think you don't care. If not managed properly, these attitudes can grow to create a rift between you and your people.

Those who don't want to be part of an organization where there is dissension will be receptive to alternative employment opportunities. Perhaps it's hard for you to envision an unanswered complaint ballooning into a full-blown conflict between leaders and team members, but it happens. It happens more often than you would imagine.

Listen for complaints. Listen to what people have to say. Respond with action, not patronizing lip service or promises. Do something.

Strategy 1.39

Use your business plan.

"Plan your work, then work your plan."

That familiar saying rings true again and again. It applies to your efforts to keep your good people.

Employees like to know their management team has some

sort of plan that is used to move the organization forward. More and more, people are interested in the content of the plan, as well as its existence. They want to see that company leadership has its act together, and they want to know that they have a part in achieving the targeted success.

An increasing number of companies have established plans that chart the course for all functions of the organization. The role of work teams can be seen as the plan unfolds. People will respond to the expectations of the plan...if and when they become aware of those expectations.

If you have a viable business plan, you can use it as a motivator, as a set of objectives or targets, as a way to get people more involved with the achievement of desired results.

Explain your organization's plan to your people. Help them understand what you are trying to do (the big picture) and how they can help make the plan a reality (their picture). As people appreciate the importance of their contributions, the plan can become a driving force in total team accomplishment.

Each work team strives to get its part done and done well. As this happens, teams can feed off each other and collaborate for bigger results than any one team can reach on its own. The plan helps bring all these aspects together, so the pieces of the puzzle fit.

As the understanding of the plan grows, and people see that it works over a long enough period of time, you can involve people from all over the organization to help design future plans. This planning becomes powerful, as people will support what they help to create.

Your plan becomes like a song sheet for a choir. It's a lot easier to make beautiful music when everyone knows his/her part as well as an understanding of the whole piece.

Strategy 1.40

Within safety constraints, permit refreshments at work stations.

When people are working, they often like to sip coffee, have a soft drink, or enjoy a glass of water. Some folks like to munch on a candy bar or a carrot stick. This snacking might help keep people alert, make them feel refreshed, or satisfy nutritional cravings.

As long as such refreshments, or their consumption, do not endanger safety, quality, or work flow, it's usually a good idea to give people the freedom to snack.

Why mention something like this, you might wonder. Some companies do not even permit employees to drink a cup of coffee at their work stations, whether in a manufacturing, office, or service environment. People must leave their work to sip some coffee, tea, or some other refreshment. They may not want to leave their work; all they want is a cup of coffee or a soft drink. Getting a snack becomes a serious inconvenience.

If company policy forces people to stop their productive work for some refreshment, think of the message that workers could receive: "Being human and enjoying some refreshment is separate from working. Therefore, being human and enjoying what I do is different than work. The concept of enjoyment should not be connected with work." Consequently, work is not enjoyable. Does that sound far-fetched, or very real?

It is usually more productive to engender feelings that personal goals mesh with organizational goals. A worthwhile positive goal, from both personal and organizational perspectives, is to get work done. Employees should believe,

"Meeting my personal needs, like having some refreshment and going to the bathroom, are part of my work experience, not separate from it. My personal energy is well-invested in accomplishing the work I am expected to do. Everything I do supports my meeting or exceeding productivity and job satisfaction expectations."

Give people the freedom to manage their work time, their break time, and the accomplishment of their assigned tasks.

Strategy 1.41

Offer freedom of choice: break times, dress, vacations, and more.

It's important to have rules to set limits in various areas of how people operate in the work environment. But, if you make the requirements too tight, too stringent, those people who feel they are mature enough to manage their own lives will object.

More controls are needed in some work areas, such as those with constantly moving assembly lines or highly standardized work procedures. The people who work in those kinds of jobs understand that need and will accept the limitations that go along with that sort of work.

The key is not to make the rules any stricter than they absolutely must be. Give people as much flexibility as you can.

Strategy 1.42

Choose employees carefully the first time.

A wise corporate policy to establish and follow is to strive to select the right people to be your new employees . . . the first time.

Surprisingly, a number of employers hire people they think (or hope) will make it. During the probationary period, it becomes obvious that the new hire won't make it. So, that person is let go, and someone else is hired to "try out." Other employees see this continual flow of new hires and begin to wonder about management wisdom, company stability, and future integrity of the workforce. I've heard hourly workers at some companies suggest that the traditional swinging door designated as the "employees' entrance" be changed to a revolving door.

Take time to consider a number of applicants, conduct sufficient interviews, check references, and look carefully at each potential hire. Use aptitude tests, behavioral profiles, skills test and work try-outs to screen out those who have little chance of success in the job. Achieving workforce stability requires more than merely trying to hold on to "warm bodies." You have to hire the right people to begin with. Striving to retain people who are not appropriate for the company could actually be quite damaging.

Be wary of hiring people with no potential for advancement in the organization. If you bring in a disproportionate number of such employees, you limit your capacity to manage the succession stream. Be very conscious of the place and the potential of each of the people you invite to join your team. This conscientious screening will increase the success rate in hiring: more new hires will stay with the company over the long run.

Avoid what human resource professionals call the "mirror test." The joke is that you hold a mirror below the nostrils of your applicants. If it fogs up, hire them!

Careful selection will produce a better return on investment in training, reduce turnover, minimize extra overhead costs in processing people who don't last, and will enable the company to hire the people who will stay with the company over the long haul. You owe it to your current employees to select new members of your team cautiously. Both the present and future effectiveness of your organization are at stake.

Strategy 1.43

Provide a safe, secure environment.

While they will endure unfavorable working environments, good people prefer surroundings that support their productivity. The less they have to worry about, in terms of their physical environment, the more they can devote their attention and energy to meaningful work.

Your location will influence the safety and security of your facilities. Some locations require more safeguards (and more expense) to secure. Consider socioeconomic and other conditions relating to your work site(s), present and future. Remember that the degree of safety is gauged by statistical reality coupled with employees' perceptions.

Begin your analysis of facility security with the neighborhood in which your company is located. Is this location a place people like to be? Are there things that your company, as a corporate citizen, can do to clean up the neighborhood and make it more attractive? Next consider the property around your building. Is there a safe parking area for employee use? Are fences, security personnel, video surveillance, lighting systems, or other measures employed to minimize risk to your people?

Next, consider access to your building itself. Are entries as secure as they need to be? Many companies use door controls with security systems, mechanical, electric, or electronic to monitor and control who enters. Some organizations use security guards, armed when necessary, to assure protection of people, equipment, materials, inventory, information, and documents.

Some companies provide internal security within the physical structure of a building. An example is restricted access to certain work or storage areas. Even locked file cabinets are part of an internal security system.

Provide special secured areas as needed to protect company and personal property. As an example, a female employee may need to leave her purse somewhere while she moves around your facilities getting her job done. The employer should provide locking desks, lockers, or other places where personal belongings may be stored. Criminal activity makes most employees very uneasy about their safety, their security, and even their lives. Most people don't like to be out of control in such a way . . . and they'll change jobs to escape that feeling.

Consider your security status when people are working and when they are not working. Can an employee leave papers or project materials out overnight without worrying about their security?

I'm not suggesting that you create an armed fortress, but do consider both your actual conditions and the feelings your people have about their own security while working for you.

Strategy 1.44

Use color constructively in decoration.

Psychologists, artists, and decorating professionals will tell you unequivocally that colors have a measurable impact on productivity, comfort, attitude, and job satisfaction. In designing or redecorating work areas, consult a decorator specializing in work environments and/or do some research on your own.

Colors can affect perception of spaciousness or of temperature. For instance, in areas where workers are exposed to relatively high temperatures, cool colors such as light green or aqua will offset the discomfort psychologically.

Soft greens, golds, and blues are said to support worker concentration where you want to minimize distractions and help people see detail better. Reds, oranges, earth tones, and all the rest of the colors in the spectrum have their place in various kinds of work environments.

Bright or contrasting color is more impelling than neutral hues. It can help bring order out of chaos in the eye's perception of the surroundings. Used strategically, color can help workers distinguish important from unimportant elements. An example is the yellow paint used to call attention to safety hazards or zones in industrial plants.

Color should support the task, not distract from it. While the judicious use of color may inspire workers, too much color or the wrong colors may distract people from their tasks. Color should fit the environment, not stand out uncomfortably. You can improve visibility, help people stay organized, and contribute to mental attitudes by choosing the right colors for the work environment.

Strategy 1.45

Consider the physical environment.

There are a number of physical comforts, or lack of discomforts, that are important to people in their workplace. Employers who ignore such concerns are doomed to lose their best employees to other organizations sensitive to such needs.

The physical concerns don't focus entirely on the work area. They even extend to the appearance and location of the place of employment. Keep in mind the feelings of the valued team member, in terms of self-worth and comparison to others. Comparison is a natural tendency. Can your people be proud and hold their head high among their peers—inside and outside their organization?

Is your facility worth putting on a picture postcard to send to prospective employees? If not, what can you do to change the appearance so your physical structure better represents the culture of your company?

Strategy 1.46

Locate your company in a suitable environment.

To the extent possible, locate your company in an environment suitable to the kind of work you do. Consider your employees in making the decision. Invite their input.

While central cities are quite appropriate for many companies, more and more employers are seeking locations in suburbs and smaller outlying towns. If most of your work is done by computers and high technology communications systems, do you really need to be in the high-rent district downtown? Messenger services deliver just as well, or better, to locations outside the downtown area.

People who have to fight their way through rush-hour traffic jams on highways and sidewalks are under quite a bit of negative stress *before they even reach your work site.* The commute has eaten away personal time, and during the day they may (un)consciously worry about the risk and hassle of the trip home. This stress cuts into their productivity. And few people are excited about paying huge amounts of money to park in downtown parking garages, cutting into their take-home pay.

Official work hours in downtown areas of major cities are often 9:00 a.m. to 5:00 p.m. Some employees arrive closer to 8:15 because of rush hour congestion, then have to leave by 4:45 or even 4:15 in order to catch a train to get home by a reasonable hour to meet family obligations. Or, they may feel "forced" to work later to avoid the commuting hassle. Think of the loss of working time on an annualized basis. It can amount to about three and a half weeks a year.

We know people who work in major cities, facing a two-hour commute in the morning and again in the afternoon. Some of these folks try to manage their schedules to work four long days to save the hassle of the commute on the fifth working day of the week. Seek creative ways to overcome the negative aspects—if there are any—of working where you're located.

So, if you don't need to be downtown, consider locating at least some of your people in more accessible, less stressful locations. Can some of your people work from home, from remote work sites (satellite work centers), or from client or customer locations?

Having said that, here's the counterpoint: Not everyone wants to move out of the city. I'd recommend, if you're contemplating a location change, that you ask your people for their input.

Recently, a company in a major midwest city began planning a major move to a suburban location. The company's employees heard about the plans and indicated their desire to remain in a downtown locations. Result: the company expanded its facilities in the central city area and everyone is happy.

If a possible expansion or relocation is in your future, consider employee preferences along with availability of essential services, transportation patterns, supplier proximity, costs, available sites, tax incentives, and other factors.

Strategy 1.47

Create desirable work areas.

Everyone would like a corner office. Or so the prevailing popular myths perpetuated by the media would have us believe. Actually, while some really do want a corner office with all the trappings, most people just want a suitable work area conducive to their task accomplishment. However, they often also want that work area to reflect their value to the organization.

Use creative office-scaping to design some different and varied work environments. Use plants (real or "plantus plasticus") to engender a more natural feeling. Use color and a variety of decorative materials to create an environment that is inviting, unique, and practical. The unusual workspace can become part of the attractiveness of remaining with your organization, instead of going to work for some company whose work may look sterile and plain (read: unexciting, boring) by comparison.

Strategy 1.48

Encourage people to personalize their work areas.

Give people control over the decoration of their work areas. Allow them some privacy and an opportunity for self-expression. Some employers worry about what sorts of limits they should place on how someone decorates his or her work area. Usually, the fears are unfounded. People will respect office decorum. If their work areas are more comfortable for them, they will be more productive and satisfied with their working environments. This feeling encourages them to remain with your organization, where they have some personal freedom.

Outside the office area, this same kind of philosophy can apply to production facilities. For safety reasons, there must be more concern for limitations. But, many work areas would allow for display of family photos and perhaps some flowers. There is value in the unusual. Don't allow yourself to be limited by tradition or "this has never been done before." Be bold!

Some manufacturing companies encourage their production employees to paint their machines or work areas in a favorite color. True, it may give the plant the appearance of a circus . . . but, aren't circuses fun? Work should be a fun place to be. If people can enjoy their work environments, they will enjoy their work . . . and be more productive and loyal. Part of the work is linked with part of the physical aspect of the company.

The same effect can be gained by encouraging tasteful decoration of lockers. The ideas for self-expression are limited only by your imagination, within the bounds of what can be done in your kind of work areas. Not everyone will take advantage of the opportunity to personalize his/her workspace, but each will appreciate having the right to do so.

Strategy 1.49

Eliminate reserved personal parking.

Current thinking suggests that reserved parking spaces are passé. They promote status levels that are based on position, rather than on respect for a person's leadership role or accomplishment. If you emphasize teamwork in your organization, reserved parking areas suggest that some team members are better than others. Beware of status separations that may inhibit teamness.

The attitude that some people are better than, or deserve more than, others fosters a sense of alienation. Alone, that irritant may not cause someone to leave your team, but combined with other factors, it could become the proverbial straw that breaks the camel's back.

Strategy 1.50

Provide for appropriate childcare services.

Provide childcare facilities and services for your people. You can provide these services on-premises, in a company-operated facility nearby, or under contractual arrangements with outside providers.

With the increase in the number of working women and the increase in single-parent families, there is a significant concern today for the children of working parents. The concern is not limited to the women in our workforce. Men assume more and more responsibilities for childcare, particularly when the mother is working a different shift or the father has custody of the children.

Employees have a wide range of needs in the childcare area. With small children, the need is for competent, caring people to provide for the kids while the parent(s) work. This goes beyond babysitting today, addressing quality and service issues such as planned learning/growth activities for preschoolers. Some childcare facilities even provide computer literacy training for pre-schoolers. The desire for a healthy environment has taken on a more holistic interpretation.

School-age children may go home to an empty house, where as latch-key kids they have to fend for themselves. They may go to a neighbor's home, or to a relative or childcare provider in the neighborhood. Making these arrangements can be a major challenge for working parents, especially if a key player (including the child) is ill. Expect last-minute problems to occur, causing parents to miss work.

Seek ways to provide for the children of your employees. If your employees live and work in the same community, there will be one set of needs and solutions. If there is a distance factor, another set of needs and possible solutions comes into play.

If you don't want to get into the childcare business, with its attendant challenges and liabilities, you might consider some sort of cooperative alternative. Nearby employers sharing your circumstances might welcome an opportunity to coordinate efforts and resources in some sort of consortium. You might jointly contract with an existing or specially created childcare provider to serve your employees.

In many organizations, providing referral services, special pricing arrangements with approved providers, and/or childcare subsidies may be the best answer. Similar concerns may apply to other challenges faced by today's workers: eldercare and pet care.

Again, before proceeding, talk with your employees who are concerned about childcare and similar issues. Solicit their ideas, discover what approaches would best respond to their needs. Seek creative solutions. You may be amazed at the wisdom, resourcefulness, caring, and appreciation you'll see from those working parents.

7

Relationship Strategies

In this chapter, we will consider strategies that revolve around the way we treat the people on our teams . . . and the ways they treat each other. Positive relationships are essential for retention and productivity. It is your responsibility to be attentive to people's personal needs—both individually and collectively.

Relationships are most often based on emotional bonds, as opposed to logical foundations. Work relationships are no different. An employee's association with an employer is an emotionally based relationship, much like a marriage. The ups and downs will be there, just like in a marriage, but the emotional bonds strengthen and maintain the connection.

As people relate with each other in the work environment and through various work experiences, emotional bonds form. The stronger the bonds, the more difficult they are to break. If an employee feels that bond—with co-workers, supervisors, the company as a whole . . . or even with customers, the tendency will be for the employee to remain with the organization. If the emotional bonds are not built, there is little holding the employee from moving on to another opportunity.

Strategy 2.1

Know why your people are working for you.

Why are your employees working for you? Why are they working in your industry? Why are they working for your company? Why are they working in your community? With today's full-employment economy, your employees could get jobs elsewhere without much difficulty. There are plenty of opportunities out there.

So, why are they working for you? Chances are, it's not because you're on the bus route! Even in those situations where public transportation is necessary for people to get to work, your workers pass plenty of "now hiring" signs on their way to your place of business.

Talk with your people about why they work for you. Include the question in hiring interviews, then address it again during the orientation process. Open the issue again during performance evaluation interviews, in counseling sessions, and in informal discussions. As long as the employees are part of your team, solicit input about their thinking. Why are they working for you? What are they looking for in their employment with you? What are their career objectives? What do they like about working in your industry? Why do they prefer your company over others that do the same or similar work?

Keep asking these questions. The answers you get will give you greater insights into why they chose to work for your company . . . and why they choose to stay. Their answers will probably reveal some of the things that motivate them to work for one company rather than another. Pay close attention! They're giving you clues about how to hold on to them.

Strategy 2.2

Understand Behavioral Styles.

Understand the behavioral style of each of your team members. The best way to gain this knowledge is through the use of a self-assessment instrument that enables you, and your team member, to understand each other's styles. While there are a number of such learning tools on the market today, we have found the Performax Personal Profile (Carlson Learning Company) to be the most effective.

A person's behavioral styles, learned throughout life or learned specifically on the job, are strong determinants to how that person will function, respond to various motivators, and fit in with the rest of your team.

Some people will be in conflict with each other, quite expectedly, as a consequence of their behavioral styles. Others will be highly compatible and will work extremely well together. Obviously, this kind of information is important to understand and appreciate when you are building a team.

See Appendix A for further information about the four basic behavioral styles and how you can learn more about them.

Strategy 2.3

Understand values and ethical standards.

Be sensitive to people's values and ethical standards. Each of your people grew up learning a certain set of values. If those values are in serious conflict with the values of others in your organization, the person who is different will probably leave to seek a more congruent working environment.

While some discussion may be in order regarding a person's values, you should not attempt to change the person's perspectives. Your role should be to facilitate an understanding of the values, by both the individual and other team members . . . including yourself.

Discuss also how the team member's values compare to the values of the organization. When faced with irreconcilable differences, it's usually best to part company. Regardless of how talented that person might be, the continuing conflict could be very disruptive to the entire group.

Carlson Learning Company, the same people who distribute the Personal Profile described in Strategy 2.2 and in Appendix A, also offer a values profile. These learning tools can open discussion and stimulate greater understandings, more acceptance, and closer relationships.

Strategy 2.4

Resolve conflicts.

Conflicts will always be present. If they are not dealt with promptly and constructively, they can easily cost you dearly in time, productivity, future cooperation, or valued employees. They must not be ignored.

If an unresolved conflict goes deep enough, it can destroy an entire company, particularly as other employees take sides and turn a relatively minor disagreement into an uncontrolled brouhaha. Be alert to potential difficulties among your people. Act promptly in response to developing conflicts before the problems become serious.

Conflicts may deal with work issues, with personality clashes, or outside influences. Conflict is not, in itself, bad. It can be a positive interaction. The key is how the conflict is handled, both by the participants and by you as their leader. Don't hide the conflict, or your involvement in getting it resolved. Get it out in the open so everyone concerned knows that you are aware of the problem and you are responding to it.

Your role in conflict resolution should be to reduce the

emotional involvement that usually accompanies conflict. Help those involved concentrate on the issues that are causing the conflict. Sometimes there are real problems that must be addressed; sometimes the differences are petty or even just imagined by one or more of the parties. Focus attention on the root causes of the disagreements with a solution-oriented exploration of the issues.

When conflicts arise, recognize that you have an intervention role to play. Conflicts rarely go away by themselves. Some companies have a conflict resolution system established where solving such problems becomes a high priority on the agenda of a senior manager. You can even formalize it to the point of holding a hearing to let everyone "ventilate."

While these approaches may be appropriate in some cases, most companies have found that informal resolution at the lowest possible level in the organization is best. Teams are like families. They work beautifully together, but from time to time have little problems that have to be worked out. Consider your team to be like your family and help the antagonists resolve their difficulty.

If the conflict gets blown out of proportion, one of your valued people may feel the need to leave to save face. Solve problems quickly to avoid the need for such drastic response.

Strategy 2.5

Hold meetings of your team members.

Hold regular team meetings to provide opportunities for open communication. These gatherings seem to be most often held on a weekly basis, in companies where they are used. Some organizations get people together on a daily basis, several times a week, bi-weekly, or monthly. Do what seems best for you and your people. These gatherings are commonly called "staff meetings."

A recommended approach is to hold semi-structured meetings. Have a basic agenda—matters that are usually discussed at each meeting. These topics could include information about new products, new customers, new employees, current employees, or other changes in the routine flow of activities.

It's helpful for people to share, briefly, what they are working on. This exercise lets everyone have a sense of the bigger picture and provides an opportunity for specific input from one person to another. The sharing also provides a platform for people to report their accomplishments. Recognize those achievements publicly in the meeting. The conversations can also give people and opportunity to ask for help when they need it. Facilitate that mutual support. When this involves extensive one-to-one communication, the leader should suggest that the participants meet afterwards to discuss details. Respect the time of all involved.

After the semi-formal portion of the meeting, open the session to the sharing of ideas, problems, gripes, or anything else that anyone has to say. In our work with scores of companies, we are amazed at the lack of opportunities for people to just share with each other. Today's employees, caught up in a fast-moving work environment, need to just talk, to just "be" with each other once in a while.

This togetherness takes a little time, but as long as it is work-focused, it can be highly productive. The investment of a relatively brief amount of company time can reap tremendous rewards in terms of people feeling more a part of the team. Remember that emotional bonding.

Your people are smart. They are close to the action of what your company is trying to do. Many of them have ideas about how things could be done better, but never share them. Why? "No one ever asked." "I didn't think anyone was really interested." "I did say something, but no one listened."

When ideas come up, make some notes and follow through. Let the entire group know about your follow-through, not just the individual who made a suggestion. This open communication will support the individual who spoke up, and send a clear message to everyone else that you want to hear their ideas and that you will respond. Even if something suggested can't be done, at least explain why—in a positive way—so your people will feel encouraged to offer more ideas.

Strategy 2.6

Call spontaneous meetings.

When something comes up that everyone should know about, bring your people together to share the news or the concern. Some things should not be put off until the next regular meeting. The spontaneity alone can be positive in many organizations, especially when the normal course of business is to follow an established routine.

Spontaneous meetings can share good news, problems that need solution now, or news that could be easily misinterpreted through the grapevine. Bringing everyone concerned together for a short meeting also sends a message that you want them to be involved in the important day-to-day happenings of the company.

People want to feel a part of things. The more you help them feel they have a strong awareness, an opportunity for input, and some control over their destiny, the less likely they are to look for opportunities outside your company. When other employers make positions available, your people will be less receptive to those overtures, if they genuinely feel a part of what's happening within their current employment.

Incidentally, not all meetings have to be held in the same place. Different messages are conveyed when you hold meetings in a conference room, the Chief Executive's office, the lunchroom, or the employees' work areas. Consider the best place to hold meetings, relative to the message you want to convey.

Don't limit your meeting sites to company property. Some companies have been highly effective holding meetings off company premises. An all-employee gathering at a local motel meeting room, a restaurant meeting room, in a nearby park, or the meeting room of a nearby church can be very effective. Consider serving light refreshments; it builds comfort and gives people something to do while waiting for the meeting to start. It also shows consideration and a certain amount of generosity and commitment on the part of company management.

Strategy 2.7

Hold individual meetings.

Stay in close touch with each of your people on an individual basis. Don't confine your communication to the group meetings. Talk with your people frequently to learn of their progress, their difficulties, their frustrations. You may discover that an employee is challenged by an obstacle that seems insurmountable, but that you can handle with a phone call. Stay in close touch, so you'll know where the problems are. Prevention or solution when the problem is small keeps things running smoothly. The smoother the operation, the more people will be comfortable staying with you.

Meet with people in your office, in their work area, in a neutral place like a cafeteria, or even outside of the building. Again, your choice of venue says a lot. Going for a walk together—outside the building, away from telephones and other distractions—can provide a relationship environment that will encourage more open communication and a less stressful treatment of the issues.

Strategy 2.8

Facilitate open communication.

Help people understand the best ways to share various kinds of information . . . or to seek answers to work-related or personal questions they may have. Each company's culture suggests appropriate ways to communicate; become familiar with patterns in your organization, then institute changes as necessary.

Saying you have an open-door policy doesn't reduce the level of intimidation of your office. Telling people they can take their problems to "Personnel" won't work if their supervisor won't let them leave their work stations. And too often workers go to "Personnel" instead of resolving their issues with their supervisors or the people directly responsible. Be wary that Personnel, your human resource professionals, are inundated with problems that shouldn't concern them. Avoid using Human Resources as a crutch or as an excuse not to solve your own problems. Simply directing people to communicate more won't make it happen; show them how, make sure the communication channels are open, and provide mediation alternatives if people have difficulty resolving their differences.

Talking with business owners and managers, the problem I hear expressed more than any other is the lack of effective communication between employees, between departments, and between company locations. The complexity of this issue could form the basis for an entire book in and of itself.

Interpersonal communications in the corporate environment are complicated, yet simple. Sometimes we erect or support barriers to communication, often without realizing that we are blocking opportunities or motivations for people to share with each other. Many of those [perceived] blockages are addressed in other chapters; the organizational influences on communications are intricate and related. Much of your problem will be resolved as you focus on the concerns described throughout this book.

Facilitate open communication—first by practicing the technique yourself. In personal contacts, memos, meetings, newsletters, letters, and other means of sharing information and feelings, be open, honest, and thorough. If you are closed, protective, or cagey, expect your people to behave the same way. The negative energy will cause paranoia, resulting in diminishing results, employee unrest, and increased turnover. Set the example for open communication, then encourage others to follow your lead. It will take some time to transform your organization to one of greater internal communication, but you will see the progress and eventually reap rich results.

Reward success in communications whenever you find it. Remember that people will emulate what they perceive to be appropriate, favor-winning behavior. Recognize with your praise any project or task done well because of strong, productive communication. Call attention to those situations where communication is particularly effective. Reinforce doing it the right way.

To inspire communication, call meetings of key players and ask questions about what's happening. Have participants explain to each other what they are doing. Look for ways people can work together; encourage them to talk openly about those opportunities in group meetings where others will observe the cooperation improving.

Ask interrogative questions (using words like who, when, where, why, and how), then ask the people responding to talk directly to others in the group who could benefit from the answer. After a while, you will be able to pull yourself out of the center of conversation, leaving the other participants to communicate directly with each other. You may need to plant seeds with one or two participants to get the process started, but others will join in when you get out of the way.

Many people will let their superiors, or other people they perceive to be leaders, act as "switchboards" to share information. They will tell you something to be conveyed to another. They will ask you to find out about something that someone else has knowledge of. The more you allow yourself to be a switchboard, instead of having those people communicate directly with each other, the more they will rely on you and not interact productively with each other. Unless you need this control over communications for some reason, let go. If you still need information, ask for it.

Strategy 2.9

Stick up for your people.

You certainly expect loyalty from your people. They expect the same from you. Show people you support them, that you'll back them up. They need to know that you'll be there for them.

In the natural course of work, people have disagreements or difficulties of one kind or another with members of other work groups, other managers, or even other companies. When these situations arise, be there for your people. Empower your people to defend their position or to pursue a sought-after solution knowing that you support their efforts.

To be most effective in supporting your people, you need to know what they are doing. "Blind loyalty" is foolish; high awareness is wise. Encourage people to keep you informed about their work and any difficulties they anticipate. Work with them to assure the appropriateness of what they are doing, strengthening their position and efforts. Be able to defend them in a disagreement because you know what is happening.

Obviously, it is much easier to support someone when that person's position is right. When someone is wrong, or if their position is not the best solution or approach, you must be diplomatic and tactful in the way you intervene.

Advice given to parents is to tell erring children that you love them, but you're not pleased with the specific behaviors you see. The same approach can be applied with an employee who does something inappropriate or who takes an untenable position.

If, as a corporate manager, you can not support your employee's position, be sure you at least support the employee. "Love" the employee, but not necessarily the employee's behavior or position. People know when they are wrong, but still expect you to be there for them. This posture does not mean you'll support people when they're wrong—in their perspectives, but you *can* support them because they're members of your team.

Take time to learn more about what your employees are doing and help them understand what is right and what is wrong. Or better phrased, explain what is easy for you to support; explain what would make you uncomfortable, perhaps unable to give them the full back-up they would want.

Be realistic. Remember that while you represent the employee, you also represent the company. You have to balance your loyalty on a fulcrum of reasonableness. For example, an employee may want and deserve a salary increase. You'd like to see the employee receive greater compensation for work done, but you are also sensitive to the structure of the wage and salary program and budgetary constraints. You may be wise to document your support and your faith in your employee, but not recommend the increase. In this case, you might lead the search for alternative solutions.

There may be times when you assume some big risks taking an employee's side. Do it when necessary for the good of all concerned. When you take a risk position, or when you find you can not provide full support for someone, explain your position so you are not viewed as unconcerned and unsupportive.

Remember that people don't expect to get everything they ask for. But when they don't get something they request or anticipate, they should be given a full explanation of why you are responding differently than they desire.

Strategy 2.10

Give recognition strategically and deliberately.

When people do a good job, they deserve recognition for their accomplishment. One popular management philosophy encourages leaders to "catch people doing something right" and praise them.

The idea here is to be deliberate and intentional in your recognition of the work done by others. Don't wait until a job is completed, or until the annual performance review. Praise and appreciation should be shared regularly, and spontaneously, whenever opportunities arise.

Sometimes recognition is given quietly on a personal basis. Even just eye contact and a smile, or a pat on the back or a thumbs-up gesture are all that's needed. A few words of thanks or a short note are sincerely appreciated by good people who are diligently working to get things done. A little bit can go a long way.

In other situations, the recognition becomes much more significant if you shout from the rooftops, proclaiming your employee's achievement. While that metaphor may be a little dramatic, you get the idea. There are times when the praise will be much more appreciated if shared with others. Public recognition can have a very positive impact—on those being saluted, on others who care about them, and on those who could earn the same treatment.

There are numerous alternative means to communicate your messages of satisfaction, appreciation, or pride. These range from the one-on-one expressions to press releases sent to trade or professional publications. In between, you can use letters of commendation (copies to personnel files and perhaps to the employee's home), articles in company newsletters or magazines, plaques and certificates, special parking places for employees of the month, cash awards, dinner for two (and/or with the boss) or a nice evening out, time off, special assignments, flowers, or even a candy bar. The list can go on and on. Be creative! Something unique that speaks to the employee's particular interest will make the reward that much more meaningful—and appreciated.

The way your express your appreciation is really a strategic decision. What are you trying to accomplish with the recognition? If your objective is to quietly build an employee's confidence, a personal communication is probably your best approach. If your objective is to strengthen the employee's reputation and stature in the work group, a more public announcement might be appropriate. If your objective is to inspire others or to show off the talent or accomplishment in your industry, a different tactic may be applied.

With an understanding of why you are giving recognition, you can determine the techniques to use. If you have several different objectives, you may well employ more than one technique to communicate your message(s) to the target audiences. Know what you want to accomplish, design the strategy to achieve your goals, then implement it deliberately.

Giving awards for length of service is appropriate to reward longevity and dedication. However, if people are rewarded only for years of employment, the emphasis is on survival in the system instead of ongoing achievement. Pay attention to the "messages" that people receive as a result of your rewards. Remember that rewards reinforce behavior. What behavior do you want to inspire?

Strategy 2.11

Recognize the "new woman."

A new style of female employee is becoming more visible in the work environment. No longer are women limited to clerical, production, or similar routine tasks. Many women are moving competently and confidently into important management and leadership positions. This new generation of women in the workforce is different from its predecessors. This difference opens powerful opportunities and, at the same time, puts many men (and some women) in an awkward position. Traditionalists often aren't sure just how to deal with these "new women."

Unlike the previous generation, today's working women

tend to be fiercely independent, risk-taking, pioneering, and tough. These are not traits normally associated with the romantic or social side of women. They demand and deserve equal opportunities for participation, professional growth, advancement, and opportunities to play a significant role when merited and appropriate.

Company owners and managers would be well-advised to open their organizations to this new breed of working woman. You will find that these employees are often assertive, and even aggressive when they feel the situation warrants such a response. They stand up for what they believe and can make a tremendous contribution.

These valuable employees are typically well-educated and, on the average, even score higher in IQ tests than their male counterparts. They are characterized as being competitive, smart, politically aware and active on social issues. While they may not instantly understand your "old boy" network, they understand power and politics. They can play the games as well as, or perhaps better than their male peers.

A shortage of eligible men—accompanied by a drive to succeed on their own merits—has caused many women to be strongly career-oriented and independent. Your valuable female team members will probably resent suggestions that their place is in the home. The more traditional roles of wife and mother have become secondary for many; in many circles, those roles are not seen as crowning achievements. Single parenting is on the increase, as are changes in the male's role in the family.

Career women want to retain their identity as women, but at the same time compete equally with men in the working world. This combination of drives creates internal conflicts between "traditional femininity" and the demand for respect as equals. Be sensitive to the personal career concerns that your high-performing female employees may have. They are on the cutting edge of a changing corporate culture and their position is not always a comfortable one. Help them identify and resolve personal or work group issues, but don't try to "take care of everything" for them.

Some men are confused about interacting with these women on a professional level. The new cultures and interpersonal ethics at work, have little resemblance to chivalry and other old-fashioned values of courtesy and consideration that most men were raised with. No longer is it "ladies first." Women want respect, but in different ways.

Managers, both male and female, should spend time with all their employees to learn about their feelings regarding woman's role in the workplace. While I don't want to make too big an issue of this trend, it is important. It's one of the changes in our society that can cause sufficient discomfort to motivate good employees, both male and female, to leave insensitive or difficult situations to go to an environment perceived as having less stress.

Our research suggests women want both the rewards and burdens of equality in pay, status, opportunity, professional growth, respect, and influence. Women ask men to forget sexual distinctions. Common courtesies, such as opening doors for others, should extend to colleagues of both sexes. Don't shy away from being critical with women if criticism is called for. Tell it the way it is; don't "be nice" to a woman when you would not behave the same way with a male employee in the same position.

Given our changing demographics, the open nature of our educational system, and the increasing need for good people to work with us, we can expect more and more highly talented women to move into vital positions in organizations. To attract and hold the best people—regardless of their sex, take whatever steps are necessary to create and maintain a receptive and supportive work environment.

Strategy 2.12

Recognize other "special employees."

Your workforce probably has, or will have before long, employees from a variety of other special backgrounds. How well do you relate with employees such as immigrants, young people, older workers, mothers returning to work, military retirees, people coming off welfare, and others who may not "fit the mold" of your so-called typical employee?

There's a lot of potential for significant contributions from these people, as well as from "nontraditional" employees with longer hair, unusual clothes, or different vocabulary.

Be careful not to let someone's uniqueness get in your way of appreciating their value to you and your organization. Sometimes the people who are "different" can be your greatest asset. In some fields, like the media, research, and other creative endeavors, a personal expression of freedom of thought and behavior is prized.

Re-read Strategy 2.11 with these people in mind. You will discover that much of that section applies to other people as well as your rising female stars. In the years ahead, you will experience increasingly greater diversity in your workforce. In fact, diversity, with its variety of perspectives, can sometimes be the key to organizational growth.

Today's changing workforce also includes a growing proportion of workers with physical disabilities. More slow learners are being trained to function quite well in industrial environments. Emotionally challenged workers need opportunities and support. Wise employers give all these employees a chance and usually find that they've discovered a whole new field of dependable, productive—and loyal—performers.

Celebrate diversity.

Strategy 2.13

Show respect for others.

Each of the people working for you is an individual. Every one of those people has unique qualities, background, expertise, capabilities, potential, and feelings. Each person's values, ethics, behavioral style, talents, and achievements become an important and integral part of the fabric of your team, your organizational strength.

Respect and appreciate what power and potential these people bring to you. Empower them to use their strengths in the most productive and satisfying ways possible. Appreciate that, along with their strengths, they also may have areas of deficiency. As much as possible, design their jobs so they can contribute on the basis of their strengths, without letting their deficiencies get in their way.

Respect the privacy desired by most people in the workplace. Allow them a place where they can find some solitude or at least call their own. People like to have special places where they can put things they own or use. Enable each of them to have a personal "space."

High achievers need freedom to work independently. Respect the fact that many of your people might need to prove something on their own before introducing it to the rest of their work group. Give them the space, the time, and the resources to do what they believe is important.

Naturally, your high achievers should have a clear accountability to perform for the good of the group. If it is appropriate, articulate your expectations and your support. High performers need to understand what others want, what they have to offer, and what support they need to get their jobs done.

Some highly valued people are not as polished or sensitive in their interpersonal skills as they are in their own particular talent. They may be hard drivers, reclusive, relatively independent, or uncooperative. You may need to invest some time and energy in helping their coworkers appreciate what these folks have to offer. Build those bridges of understanding from both directions and you will increase the return from all concerned.

Building relationships in the workplace is a vital responsibility of leaders. You will naturally be concerned with professional relationships more than social, but you should play a stimulating, connecting role in helping people appreciate each other on all levels.

Strategy 2.14

Give people freedom and flexibility.

The adults who work for you want to be treated like adults. They want freedom to make some decisions on their own, to be in reasonable control of their own lives. They enjoy freedoms outside the work environment and don't want to be constrained when they come to work.

Find ways to give your people freedoms and choices. Some alternatives are very simple; others are more complicated in their implementation. Let's look at some possibilities.

Other than in the uniformed careers, people should be entitled to choose the clothes they wear to work. Before you say, "of course," please know that there are employers who still require their male employees to wear white shirts, "corporate" ties, and jackets in office environments. The men are not allowed to wear any colors or designs in their shirts. Some companies require women to wear skirts; slacks or pant-suits are not permitted. Such restrictions may stifle creativity and productivity. Within the limits of workplace decorum, give your employees as much flexibility as you can. People understand limitations based on safety or propriety, but restrictions based on seemingly arbitrary rules are not so easy to fathom.

More than we've seen in the past couple of generations, today's workers are sensitive to their relationships outside work. With both parents working in an increasing number of families, employees work consciously at maintaining healthy family life. They like to have pictures of their families at their workplace to serve as happy reminders and as a way of showing their pride in their spouses, children, and grandchildren. Plus, it makes them feel more comfortable to be surrounded by pictures of people they love.

It's important to give people the freedom to display pictures of family and similar personal items. Office workers can put pictures on their desks or walls. Factory employees can attach pictures to their lockers or put them near their work stations.

The creativity continues for all kinds of employees . . . if you give them the opportunity. It's hard to believe, but there are still employers today who refuse to allow their valued people the freedom to display family photos on their desk.

How much freedom can you give employees to set their own working hours? While some jobs simply don't have the flexibility to allow modification of the work schedule, many do lend themselves to flex-time, job-sharing, or other approaches to adjustment of start and finish times. There are a number of reasons employees want more control over their schedules (*see Strategy 3.40, Provide flexibility in working hours*). Strive to accommodate them.

Looking at the work itself, some of your people may be able to modify the way a job is done. They may have suggestions about procedures that, while not consistent with existing company policy, might make a lot of sense. Be alert to opportunities, and flexible enough to be responsive to ideas your people have. Ask for input . . . and listen to what your employees contribute when they believe they really have the power to make positive changes.

When people fully understand the results they are expected to accomplish, you can give them freedom to determine for themselves how they will achieve those results. Workers can often vary the order in which they do things, vary the sequence of jobs they perform, or pace themselves differently to work more comfortably or efficiently while still achieving the desired results.

Can your people schedule their vacations to fit the needs and desires of their families? Can they work *directly* with their counterparts in other departments to solve problems or get things done? Can they take breaks on their schedule, rather than only at times specified by the company?

Given sufficient information, most people can make the right decisions among the available choices. The more power people have to distinguish for themselves among those choices, the more responsible and happy they will be . . . and the more they will want to stay with your company.

Strategy 2.15

Trust your people.

If you can't trust someone who is a member of your team, that person should not be working with you.

The first question to ask is, very simply, why don't you trust your employee? Has something been done by that employee that causes you not to trust? Is it something you are directly familiar with, or is your evidence hearsay? If your knowledge is not direct and personal, you owe it to yourself and to your employee to verify the facts.

If the employee did, in fact, do something to affect your level of trust, was that action a one-time occurrence or is it a continual problem? If it was a one-time thing, are you holding an unfair and unwarranted grudge? Harboring such feelings could inhibit your effectiveness as an inspiring leader and could be severely limiting for your employee's career.

If the problem shaking your trust was continual, has the problem stopped? If it has stopped, can you put the matter behind you? How can the employee regain your trust and restore the relationship? If the behavior causing the mistrust has not stopped, then you need to confront the employee, express your concerns and your feelings, and bring the matter to some sort of closure. That resolution will either be termination of employment, transfer to someone else's area, or clearing up the misunderstanding and re-establishing the trusting relationship.

When you do trust your people, do they know it?

There are two ways to verify your trust so your people will produce more comfortably and confidently for you. One method is to express your trust matter-of-factly in words that are easy for you to say. There's no need to get flowery about it. Just tell the trusted employee how you feel. Yes, this will be difficult for some people . . . especially those who have trouble or discomfort sharing their feelings. Try simply saying, "I trust you." Express yourself; the feeling of satisfaction and the enhanced relationship you will experience afterwards will be worth it.

The other way to demonstrate your trust in an employee is to give the employee a position or task where your trust is an obvious prerequisite. Those who receive important assignments given only to trustworthy team members feel pretty good about the "givens" that are usually left unsaid.

When you share privileged information with someone else, that also demonstrates your trust. Depending on the nature of the information, and your reason for sharing, you may also send the employee clear signals that you value that individual's opinions and/or judgment. The phrase, "this is confidential," also conveys your high level of trust.

Yes, it is good to trust your people. It is even better to trust them and have them know that they are trusted.

Strategy 2.16

Show genuine, sincere appreciation.

Using "genuine" and "sincere" together almost sounds like a redundancy, but it isn't. The appreciation you show to your people must be genuine; it must be real. And it must be sincerely shown; people see right through insincerity.

Give appreciation when it is deserved. Find legitimate reasons to compliment or thank people. Most of the time, actions, performance, or results worthy of appreciation will be obvious. In other cases, you may have to look a while to find something worthy of note.

There are things deserving of attention and praise that are not easy to see. Many of your employees will simply do what has to be done without bringing their achievements to your attention. Some may even be modest and make a conscious effort not to bring things to your attention. They don't want to be a nuisance or cause a stir. Some of your most conscientious employees will not want to call attention to themselves. They are proud of their work, but are not comfortable bragging about it. Often these low-profile workers are your most valuable assets.

Reward "final" achievements, like completion of a project or special assignment, but also give praise while good things are in progress. Don't just wait until something has been done to tell your people you approve of their work.

Look for the positive aspects of your organization and the good results being achieved by your people. Find out who is responsible for those positives and show your appreciation. It may be that one particular person is worthy of praise, but often you will find *more* than one member of your team who should be recognized.

If you don't see outstanding achievements shouting for recognition, keep looking. You may find some routine accomplishments that deserve your attention. Some managers and advisors warn us not to recognize or reward people for doing routine things like coming to work on time or picking up after themselves.

I feel differently about this issue. Many employees do those "part of the job" things every day without anyone ever thanking them. Yes, those things are *expected,* and that's why people get paychecks. However, if we don't thank our employees for the routine tasks once in a while, they will probably feel taken for granted. People who feel taken for granted do not feel valued as individuals. They expect that they will not be missed if they leave and become highly receptive to other job offers.

Even without significant achievements on any sort of frequent basis, each of our people deserves praise just for being a valued member of our team. Not every day, but every once in a while, it makes sense to thank people for coming to work. Let them know, plainly and directly, that you're glad they're there and that they're members of your team.

An example of routine work worthy of praise might be helpful to clarify and emphasize this issue. Your bookkeeper, accountant, or controller keeps your financial house in order. Part of the job. Suppose that routine work were not done as well as it is, one hopes, done. You could be in a real mess! Those people are doing a fine job for you, even though their accomplishments don't usually leap forward for attention. That kind of valuable routine work is deserving of a word of thanks once in a while.

An opportunity awaits you here. Think of all the unsung heroes in your organization. Start making a list of all the fine folks who may not be in the kind of position that normally gets a lot of attention or commendation. Consider all those special people who, by getting their jobs done well each day, keep your entire system running smoothly. Here are some categories of employees that may be deserving of your recognition for their dependability, reliability, and support: receptionist, custodian, clerk-typist, mail room employee, gardener, security guard, busboy, driver.

Sincerity is critically important. If you are the least bit insincere in your appreciation, it will be apparent to your people. Therefore, a word of caution: if you don't really mean it, don't say it.

Your expressions of appreciation will be much more meaningful if they come from you personally. A letter of commendation, for instance, is much more significant when it is hand-delivered instead of sent through the mail. It takes on even more importance when you convey your appreciation directly to the deserving employee(s) in the presence of peers.

Contrary to some popular opinions in working America, appreciation does *not* have to be in the form of more money in the pay envelope. Sure, everyone wants more money. None of us ever has enough. We can always find things to do with more. Few people will decline a pay increase or cash bonus. While some will surely say they'd rather have money, there are other ways to show appreciation.

Why not just use money? First, it creates an expectation that good work—or even routine work—will be rewarded with more money. A what-have-you-done-for-me-lately attitude will generate ill feelings if people do not receive continual increases in income. Second, by rewarding average or good or exceptional behavior with money, you can easily establish a precedent . . . and a basis of measurement.

You can get caught in the trap of not knowing how much money to award for each kind of achievement. You can be sure your employees will be monitoring the amounts and placing artificial values on various kinds of rewarded behavior. Be careful. Be clear that each achievement is judged independently, with the reward appropriate for the individual as well as the performance. Avoid precedents.

An exception (isn't there always an exception?) is the program used by a number of companies to encourage and reward suggestions that save money. When employees make suggestions for changes in procedures, suppliers, materials, or other factors that result in a savings, employers pass on a percentage of the documented savings to the person making the suggestion. If you implement such a system, establish specific guidelines regarding calculation of the savings, the amount to be shared with the employee, and the duration of the determination period.

Some other ways to recognize performance or achievement are, in no particular order:

- a word of thanks
- a personal recognition and praise in front of peers
- a quiet, one-on-one word of thanks
- a letter of commendation, with copy to personnel file and perhaps copies sent to the employee's family and posted on a bulletin board or even announced through an employee or community newspaper
- a certificate (framed) or plaque
- a special parking place (employee of the month)
- dinner for employee and spouse with boss and spouse
- tickets to theater, concert, ball game, or other event
- a special assignment of importance
- a day off with pay
- a pin, certification patch, ball cap, tee shirt, or other item of clothing or attachment to clothing
- a job title change, promotion, or new position
- a priority position in choosing vacation days or working hours or other workplace variables
- a pizza party, lunch on the company, or dessert treat
- a limousine ride to work, and back home again on the day of recognition
- a small gift suitable for display in the office or home.

And the list goes on. Be creative. Seek unique ways to show your appreciation to the people who make your team success possible.

Depending on your company's culture, you might be quiet and conservative or wildly flamboyant. Ask your team members for their ideas; you'll probably get some wonderful ideas and maybe even some crazy, off-the-wall suggestions that just might be appropriate in some cases. Be receptive! Be responsive.

Remember, your praise is not for your benefit. It's for the benefit of the recipient(s). If they deserve recognition for something, they should get what they deserve. They will half-expect it from you. They'll be overjoyed (at least inside) when you reward them. Don't worry about those people who seem grumpy or unappreciative; remember, some folks just don't know quite how to receive your plaudits. Inside, they probably feel warm and happy that you noticed and you care.

One final word of caution. Don't overdo appreciation. Make it legitimate. Reward and recognize when it is appropriate. If you do it too often, the act loses importance and value. Make it special.

Strategy 2.17

Listen.

Probably the most important communications skill is listening. We learn the most through listening, and other people appreciate us when we really listen to what they have to say.

Interestingly, listening is the one communication skill we don't teach in our formal education system. We teach speaking, writing, and reading, but we don't teach people how to listen effectively. We learn how to listen by ourselves, with varying degrees of success.

Some of our listening strength is a part of our behavioral style (*see Appendix A*). People with some styles of behavior naturally listen better than people with other styles. Most of us have to work consciously at being good listeners. It doesn't come naturally.

We learn listening skills as adults through trial and error, or simply by trying harder. Participation in listening workshops, given by professional trainers, has helped countless executives, managers, supervisors, salespeople, and others enhance their ability to listen better.

There are a number of listening techniques we teach in workshops. Here are a few ideas for your consideration:

- Block out as many distractions as you can. Closing an office door may remove most of the noise distraction.

Having someone take your phone calls can allow you to concentrate without interruptions. Focusing consciously on the person to whom you are listening will help; depending on the nature of the communication, you might need to use intense concentration to hear what is being said.

- Face the person to whom you are listening. This body positioning accomplishes a couple of things for you. First, it communicates plainly that you are giving the talker your full attention. This body language builds confidence and comfort for the other person. Second, it enables you to use your senses of both hearing and sight to listen.
- Use your eyes, your ears, and your "sixth sense" as you listen. Pay attention to the words that are spoken, the tone and volume of the person's voice, and the intensity of the communication. Listen for both content and feelings. Go beyond the words to grasp the meaning and intent of the speaker. Sometimes the emotion shown is much more meaningful than the words used to convey a message.
- When appropriate, take notes on what the other person is saying. This technique accomplishes several things for you. It shows the other person you are serious and caring enough to write down their message; the writing also suggests you will probably take some action as a result of the communication. It helps you organize what is being said, making more sense of the message as you write it. (Some of us are more visual learners than auditory.) A third benefit of writing key points is having a set of notes to use in responding to the other person in a more prepared fashion after your time together.
- Control your own emotions and tendency to respond before the speaker is finished talking to you. Isn't it annoying to have someone start responding to what you're saying before you're finished? The practice is not only rude, but your thinking about what you will say will

cause you to listen less effectively to what is being said to you.

Remember, your objective in listening is to gain a clear understanding of what the other person is sharing with you. Listen on both a logical/rational and emotional level. Sometimes words alone do not fully express what is being communicated. Your purpose as a listener is not to defend, argue, direct, inquire, or give people the answers they seek. Your whole purpose is to grasp what is being conveyed. Then, equipped with strong comprehension, you can respond in a way that will best achieve the goals of your conversation.

You can't talk and listen at the same time. We have two ears and one mouth for a reason, it is said. We should listen twice as much as we talk. To learn, close your mouth and open your ears. Keep the other person talking long enough to gain the knowledge and understanding you need to respond legitimately. If you don't understand, say so, then ask for clarification so you can "get it."

Practice a technique known as "active listening" whenever emotions are high, the issue discussed is sensitive, or you are unfamiliar with what is being told to you. Active listening is a cooperative two-way communications process. It assures both participants that the messages are getting through in a clear, concise, understandable form.

As the term is usually used, active listening employs feedback as a mechanism to assure accurate communications. As an active listener, paraphrase what you hear and feed that back to the speaker. It's a deliberate, almost formal, kind of interchange.

Listeners begin their response to speakers with phrases like, "if I understand you correctly, you said . . . ," "so, what you're saying is . . . ," "then the essence of your message is . . . ," and "to be sure I understand what you mean. . . ." These phrases are followed by a synopsis or summary, in the listener's words, of what the listener heard.

The speaker, responding to the listener's reaction, then confirms that the communication has been received as intended. If the listener didn't quite get the message, the speaker indicates that there is a problem and endeavors to restate the communication so the listener can better grasp the meaning.

Active listening can be initiated by the speaker as well. After saying something, the speaker can ask the listener for a response to make sure complete communication occurred. The speaker would say something like, "I'd like to be sure I've explained myself clearly. Would you please share with me what you heard me say?" You'll be more effective with an almost apologetic request, as opposed to a demand.

This process works best when exercised in a conscious, cooperative way. Confrontation and defensiveness will reduce the effectiveness of the technique considerably.

In the phrases shown above, please notice the use of "I" words in assigning responsibility. The initiator of the active listening process assumes the burden for assuring the accuracy and completeness of the communication.

For best results in applying these, and other listening techniques, remember that listening is serious business. It takes careful concentration, a real desire to hear the other person, and honestly understand what is being said.

Strategy 2.18

Let people be who they are.

Your team of competent people is comprised of a wide variety of interesting folks. Chances are they come from diverse backgrounds, have disparate kinds and levels of formal education, have unique combinations of talent and ability, and are driven by different motivators.

One of the reasons your team functions well is the individualistic nature of your team members and the special way they complement each other. If your team membership is too homogeneous, you'll have much less opportunity for healthy conflict and creativity.

With homogeneity, the clones will become so like one another that the group's uniqueness will evaporate. Life will become bland due to the overwhelming sameness. Atrophy will set in, kicking the group back to mediocrity and apathy.

Diversity is healthy. Encourage your people to be who they are, not to try to be like someone else within the organization. Sure, you might like to operate like the leader, but when you play that role you lose some of the value you have in being just like you.

Accept and treasure each of your people for their uniqueness. Each will bring something different to the party. Your opportunity as team leader, is to mold the diversity into something each of the members can identify with. At the same time, it is important that members not lose the special individualities they have to offer.

Strategy 2.19

Find opportunities to talk with your people.

Interestingly, one of the reasons people leave companies is because of the perceived lack of a satisfactory relationship with the boss. While I'm not suggesting that you should establish a close social relationship with your people (or that you shouldn't), it is important to develop and maintain some sort of one-to-one rapport with them.

Today's workers want to know their leaders really care. They want to see and talk with their leaders, have some sort of personal contact. It is the fulfillment of this need that makes the Hewlett-Packard Management-By-Walking-Around (MBWA) technique so effective.

You don't have to invite each of your people into your office for an in-depth conversation on the meaning of life as we know it. But you do have to get out of your office and talk with the members of your team. You have to see and be seen throughout your organization. I can't emphasize this technique enough. In company after company, workers tell us that they "rarely see the boss." If they have no relationship with you, then you have not used your position or your charisma to build longevity and loyalty.

Your closest relationships will be with your direct reports. These people, of course, need more of your time and input. They can give you suggestions regarding other people in your company that will be most receptive to your communications overtures. You can—and should—serve as a communications tool to represent your company's leadership.

On a regular basis (not a schedule, please), get out of your office and wander around your facility. If you are responsible for more than one physical location, deliberately plan visits just to be there. Your presence shows you care, that you really do exist, that you are human, and you do look like your pictures. Plain and simple: get out of your office and go spend time with your people.

As you wander, stop and talk with your employees. Ask how they're doing, or what they're doing. Give production workers, for instance, an opportunity to brag to the Big Boss about how they do their job. Share some things with them about your pride in what they are doing, your appreciation.

You don't have to be the president of a huge conglomerate to be perceived as being in an ivory tower. The same feeling of distance can occur in a one-location operation if the leader is not relatively closely and personally involved with what is happening. This MBWA doesn't mean you have to make decisions at the operation level of your company, just see and be seen. Demonstrate that you know what's going on, that you're really interested, that you care.

If your organization is small enough, you probably should be right out in the middle of things on a constant basis. You have to be the judge of what frequency is most appropriate. Remember, the closer you are to the action, the more chance you have of positively influencing results.

If your schedule is too demanding during the normal working day, arrange to greet people as they come to work or go home. Attend company informal functions, such as bowling league nights or celebrations. Company picnics are, of course, a must. When families are there, invest your time with them, too; get to know them and let them get to know you. Employees with families loyal to the employer are less likely to leave that employer. Family influence keeps them where the spouse and kids are included and appreciated.

Merely wandering around and observing is not sufficient. You have to talk with people. Long conversations are not necessary, just enough communication to allow you to demonstrate that you don't think you're better than they are.

Warning: As people become more comfortable with you talking to them, they'll start talking with you. They will ask questions and make suggestions that will keep you on your toes. Be sure to respond with the same speed and attention you would give a customer or other important person.

The people who work with you are the most important people you know in your business life. You can't achieve your desired results without them.

Strategy 2.20

Balance praise and criticism.

As you give feedback to your people, be careful to maintain a balance of praise and criticism. If they think they hear more of one or the other, employees can form impressions that can be counterproductive to what you are trying to achieve.

Praise is good. People like to hear they are doing a good job. They like to know they are appreciated. However, if you give too much praise, it begins to sound empty and loses its impact.

Even with a top-notch employee, it's important to mix some constructive criticism with the praise. If you can't find something with room for improvement, worthy of meaningful critique—that can be done in a positive way, ask the employee. A question addressing how the employee thinks his/her work can be improved will help balance the praise load. Interact with your high-achieving employees in such a way as to let them know you want them to keep growing . . . and that you are there to help them become even better than they are.

Too much negative criticism can be even more damaging. Some people get so much bad news about their performance, they begin to have negative thoughts about themselves—especially as they relate to their lives working for you.

For people who are vulnerable or sensitive, even a little criticism without a counterbalancing dose of praise will make them feel put down. Some folks very easily feel put down so badly, they have to look up to see their shoes! This non-constructive criticism does not build positive feelings!

If people feel good about themselves, then experience a lot of negative criticism at work, they quickly associate negative feelings with that work environment. In such cases, those people will take the first reasonable alternative employment opportunity that comes along. They want to get away from the negative "vibes" to go to an environment that gives them positive feelings more congruent with who they feel they are.

It is not necessary to keep a log of the number of negatives versus the number of positives shared with each employee. Just be alert and sensitive not to go overboard in either direction.

Strategy 2.21

Build everyone's self-esteem.

People will naturally perform better when they feel good about themselves. When those good feelings are associated with their relationships with their employers, stronger bonds are felt between employees and employers.

Self-esteem should not be confused with self-image. The concept of self-image refers more to looking good to others, an outward appearance. Self-esteem is an inner feeling of personal worth. Self-image without self-esteem is a role, a façade. Self-esteem is the foundation.

To help your people build their self-esteem (and each individual has to do this internally—we can not do it for them), there are several things you can do. In no particular order, they are:

- create opportunities for personal growth and confidence-building
- reinforce people for who they are
- accept people for themselves
- value everyone's worth highly
- encourage people to talk about what they're good at . . . and what they have to offer.

Today's forward-looking thinkers foresee a vital role for self-esteem in organizational identity, strength, and success. This attention to personal self-perception takes on increasing importance as we become more oriented to a workforce of individuals.

For a further understanding of this concept and critical importance in organizations, see Appendix C for an exclusive interview with the late Bill McGrane, Director of The Self Esteem Institute.

Strategy 2.22

Don't gossip.

Gossip and rumors can easily have a negative effect on an organization. The result can be feelings of discomfort, suspicion, and even paranoia among members of the organization.

It's hard to be productive and feel positive about your position when you are constantly worried about what others are saying about you. The need to protect yourself from what you perceive to be personal attacks gets in the way of both production of good work and personal satisfaction on the job. When you have to watch your back, it's difficult to look forward at the same time.

You won't be able to stop all the gossip and rumor-spreading in your organization. Some people engage in this kind of activity almost as a hobby, or a diversion from what they are supposed to be doing. What you can do is set an example by not engaging in gossip or rumor-spreading yourself.

When you have something to say to or about someone, do it directly. Don't complain to others about your attitudes: that activity won't solve your problems. Confront issues with others on a one-to-one basis. Even though there is a natural tendency to talk about others, guard what you say yourself. Be particularly careful not to spread negative news that may affect someone's capacity to continue to serve your company comfortably.

When you hear others gossiping, intervene as appropriate and discourage the practice. You don't have to get formal about this process. Just quietly suggest to those gossiping that such behavior is not desirable in your organization.

Some high performers rise above the gossip and don't let it bother them at all. Some are highly sensitive to their interpersonal relationships and won't stay in an environment where they think others talk about them in inappropriate ways. Even those who ignore gossip can be affected by it, as coworkers form opinions that affect their working conditions and relationships.

As you create and maintain an open working environment, the closeness and positive feelings among your team members will naturally limit potentially damaging gossip. This issue is not something that requires official action, as much as a sensitivity to the informal interactions among people.

Strategy 2.23

Look for positives, not negatives.

It's easy to see the negative aspects of practically any situation. Finding things to criticize does not seem to be a problem for most people. Spotting the *positive* things is sometimes more challenging, and perhaps not as much fun.

To overcome natural tendencies, we must focus on the good things in our lives . . . and in the lives of our people. Frankly, it is not as simple as it seems. It is something we have to do with a high level of consciousness and intention.

When all you seem to see is the negatives, the shortcomings, your people will categorize you as being more critical than supportive. Before long, they will avoid coming to you or inviting your input. No one likes to hear negatives all the time. As they endeavor to protect themselves from your criticism (nit-picking?), your key people will withdraw and avoid doing anything that might be attacked.

Not saying anything, or doing anything, when positives are there (or thought to be there) to be noticed, can be just as bad—or even worse—than saying negative expressions. In my speeches and seminars, I emphasize that it's essential to communicate the positive aggressively. If people don't hear the positive, they assume the negative. There is no neutral. People feel either the positive or the negative.

So, the message is: find positive aspects to talk about in everything you see. Even when you know the negatives are there, and even if you have to say something about the negatives, be sure to emphasize the positives. Let people save face and feel a sense of pride about those things that are good.

A word of warning: beware of "yes, buts" in your speaking. It can be self-defeating to say something like, "you did a find job with this, but . . ." The "but" neutralizes the positive comment, and may even overpower it. In this kind of a situation, many people go around nervously waiting for the other shoe to drop. Use the word "and" instead of "but."

Employees can quickly tire of not hearing the positive things they want to hear. Hearing the negatives only wears people down—something they don't want to happen. No one likes living under a dark cloud for very long.

In your communication with others, be realistic. And

wherever possible, brighten up your life and your environment with a positive approach. When people hear you make positive statements, they begin to view you as being positive. People want to follow positive leaders. Workers want to associate with positive companies led by positive people.

Strategy 2.24

Express confidence in your people.

Confident employees are more productive employees. They feel better about themselves, about what they are doing and about their place and value in their working environment. As a result, they have a greater tendency to remain in an employment situation where they feel confident.

Employees get their feelings of confidence from two different sources: external and internal. You, as the leader of your people and a principal influencer of their environment, can have a significant positive impact on both of these important sources.

One external source of confidence is your personal relationship with your team member. You send clear messages, consciously and unconsciously, that express your feelings. When you have confidence in someone, it's wise to express that confidence. Telling people you have faith in them, that you believe in them, that you trust them, that you respect them, or simply that you have confidence in them, will have a great impact. Employees want to know how their superiors regard them, since that affects their present and future career positioning. It also affects how they feel about themselves.

Other external sources of confidence are fellow employees, management people beyond their own supervisor, customers, suppliers, and peers employed by other companies in the industry.

You can build your employees' confidence by passing along the thank-you notes and expressions of confidence you receive from customers and suppliers. As appropriate, you might even solicit letters from satisfied customers so you have something more to share with your people.

Most managers could all do a lot more to share feelings of confidence and appreciation within their organizations. Their achievements are often possible only because of the support they receive from others in the company. They take that support for granted, don't they? It's easy to just keep moving, rarely taking time to express confidence in those people who make success possible. When was the last time you sat around the table in a staff meeting and shared your mutual confidence with your peers?

Hearing how your fellow managers, at your level and perhaps a level above and/or below, feel about you could really boost your morale and self-esteem! Hearing others express how much they respect your knowledge, experience, talent, ability to get things done, insight, and leadership would sure make you feel good! Your people get the same "high" hearing that sort of affirmation.

When people appreciate each other, they feel closer to one another, more like a team. The more cohesive that team, because of shared attitudes, respect, and experiences, the less likely it is that people will want to leave the team. Moral: if you want to hold your people and help them feel part of a team, encourage them to share their positive perceptions of each other . . . and of the team itself with the combined strength of the members.

How can this sharing be done in a non-threatening, comfortable way? There are several methods.

The first one is to express your own feelings, setting an example for others to follow. Remember the potential impact of a role model. People are watching you all the time, whether you are conscious of their observation or not. Be open, honest, and consistent in your communication.

A second way is to gather together from time to time those people who are connected by their work. It could be a project team, a group of peers from cooperating departments, or managers of facilities in several locations. Create the mix of people in whatever common threads seem appropriate. When people are together, get them talking about possible solutions to a shared problem or a problem they can all relate to.

After they have worked on the problem for a while and have become comfortable interacting with each other, change the subject. Focus their attention on themselves and have participants share what they see as the positive contributions made by each other. Have them explain why they feel fellow group members can help the group solve the current problem and other problems that challenge the organization.

A third method of sharing confidence and appreciation is to have people write little notes describing their respect and confidence in others. You can do this in a group setting by putting pages of a flip chart on the wall or on tables. Put each person's name at the top of a page and let participants wander around the room writing their comments under each person's name.

Outside the group setting, you can have people write their comments on 3" X 5" cards, putting the name of the described person at the top of the card. You can collect all the cards and distribute them to the described individuals, or you can post them all on a wall or on a bulletin board. This process does not have to be a scheduled exercise; create a special place in your facility to post cards or notes . . . an "I like you because" board. You could also create a "you're valuable because" board.

Customers and suppliers may express their confidence or appreciation for your people. Whenever this happens, be sure the positive messages are posted, circulated, or announced so everyone knows that so-and-so earned some valuable recognition from the outside organization. Notes or letters could be posted on the "I like you because" board for all to see. Be sure a copy goes into the employee's personnel file.

Internal sources of confidence for your people are personal competence and experience. See the chapter on growth strategies for ideas on how to foster growth to build competence among your people. The more people learn, the more they know, the more confident they become about their work.

The same applies to experience. The more experiences a person has, work-related and not, the more confident that person will be. Work experiences, life experiences, and just general exposure to what's going on in the real world, can build confidence. Sending production people, supervisors and hourly workers, to a trade show or a customer visit, can expand horizons and provide new perspectives. That helps build confidence.

Strategy 2.25

Enable people to be together.

Strengthening relationships through social contacts as well as business contacts will also build confidence and cooperation. Arranging for people to meet, with or without an agenda, to work on a project together or just talk, can have a positive impact.

There are a number of things you can do, as a leader, to facilitate people getting together, feeling more comfortable together, and functioning better together as a team. Interestingly, managers complain about people not working together, not communicating, but don't act positively to build that togetherness.

You won't usually have to "force" people to come together. Most will welcome your initiation of opportunities for greater communication and interaction. Let's consider some approaches you might take to build relationships.

People eating a meal together can strengthen bonds of friendship and cooperation. Eating together is one of the oldest methods to break down barriers of distrust, ignorance, and fear. Our history books and legends are full of stories of enemies or strangers breaking bread together to resolve their differences or better understand each other.

You can arrange meals on a personal or small group basis. Inviting one or two people to join you for breakfast, lunch, or dinner can set the stage for resolving an interdepartmental conflict, investigating or introducing new policies, building relationships, or just sharing valuable information about the industry or the company. A small group is more intimate and gives you more of a chance to interact personally with each person. It also enables you to give more attention to fostering stronger bonds between those present.

One approach is to schedule Breakfast with the Boss on some sort of regular basis. The frequency really depends on company-specific factors, so we won't recommend any sort of schedule here. You can invite guests to just drop in, or you can pre-arrange who will participate. A random selection process works in a lot of organizations using this meal with the boss process. The selection process may not be purely random, as schedulers strive to achieve a diversity of departmental and level representation.

Lunch with the boss has also increased in popularity, with all sorts of venues being used. Be creative. A number of years ago when I was doing some consulting for a truck manufacturer, the plant manager used to take employees for lunch—in one of the company's newly built trucks. This approach sent some very positive messages and gave the selected employees a first-hand look at a finished product they helped produce.

Dinner is considered to be a more formal meal. Even the thought of having dinner with the boss can be intimidating. Be especially sensitive to this wariness. Dinner interactions may be something you want to avoid, or they may provide opportunities for get-togethers with executives or higher level managers who are accustomed to dinner environments.

Part of the discomfort with dinner venues comes from the after-work circumstance. In many organizations, people would go home, change, then go to dinner. That's where the problem may come from. Consider after hours hors d'oeuvres gatherings—informal, without liquor. Even though some people like alcoholic beverages and may expect them in that kind of setting, the possibility of something unpleasant happening is too great to risk.

In companies where people work multiple shifts, the second shift lunch period might be convenient for the top executive from time to time. Take care in building closer relationships between top executives and others in the company, to include *all* workers—whenever and wherever they work.

In our society, people place different values on sharing breakfast, as opposed to lunch, as opposed to dinner. Lunch is most convenient. Dinner is sort of special, because it is usually after working hours and more formal. Breakfast is a little inconvenient; it may require an adjustment in schedules.

Breakfast is favored by many leaders because it occurs at the start of the day, is less formal, and can be concluded more quickly than a lingering dinner. Alcoholic beverages are not a part of breakfast meals, where they may well be a part of lunches or dinners. It is wise to avoid consumption of alcohol in these kind of sessions, so everyone can operate with a clear head.

Meals can be formal or informal. They can take place in restaurants, in company facilities, or at meeting sites such as hotels, conference centers, or resorts. Many companies design management and sales meetings deliberately to encourage more open communication among participants. It makes it easier for people to share their experiences, ideas, problems, and solutions.

The larger the group you are bringing together, the more you may want to consider using a more formal agenda. As the number of participants increases, the gathering becomes more of a meeting than a social occasion. To overcome this tendency, design your seating to make communication easier. Having six or eight people at a round table, for instance, will open more communication than having those people sitting across from each other or as part of a larger group at long banquet tables.

I've seen some companies host quarterly or bi-monthly breakfasts for all their employees. Lots of round or four-person square tables are set up so people are eating in ad-hoc small groups. People from all levels and departments of the company enjoy eating and talking together.

A series of meal-based meetings can encourage partnering between persons A and B, then A and C, then B and C, then A, B, and C. It may take some time, but gradually you can enhance the way people work with each other.

In some gatherings, you may want to ask participants to talk together about particular company problems or concerns. This suggestion deliberately creates an environment where people with varying backgrounds have been brought together as a company team to accomplish something. This approach can be very powerful, especially if you have already had some meal gatherings where you *didn't* ask for help. Now you come to them, as a team unto themselves, and ask for their input.

You'll enjoy benefits to all these approaches, depending on what you are trying to accomplish. Consider what you are trying to do, then design the best strategy to meet your goals.

Other ways to bring people together include sports activities. These can range from bowling leagues, to softball teams, to company-sponsored participation in charity walkathons. Both organized programs and informal activities can be effective meeting and communications opportunities.

Another way to bring people together is to recruit volunteers from your company to support civic activities such as United Fund, Junior Achievement, Boy Scouts or Girl Scouts, or industry education programs. The additional benefit of doing something, as a company, to support your community will also be worthwhile.

Company picnics are traditional in many organizations, with varying degrees of success. The picnics are more successful if they involve people from all levels of the organization. (I am amazed when I learn about managers and senior executives not attending company picnics.) When leaders don't attend company functions, participants get a negative message, regardless of whether that message was intended. When management people go to company picnics, they should make a point of circulating among *all* the people present to become better known and show that they are human.

Some companies enhance their picnics by holding the events in special settings like amusement parks. If you already are using special settings, consider providing company tee shirts or ball caps to all your people . . . and their families, too. You can imprint them with your company name or logo, and even the date and location of your picnic. Imagine the impact on your people, and others, as you all move around through the entertainment facility in your identical shirts. They'll see so many people in identifying clothing, that it will seem that you dominate the park. The fellowship, the kinship, will be palpable.

There are many more ideas you can use to bring people together. Depending on your company and your people, you can arrange theater parties, progressive dinners, brown-bag lunches, continuing education lectures or seminars, and other activities. The objective is to bring people together to enable them to build relationships that will facilitate them working together in their official company roles.

Strategy 2.26

Care about people as individuals.

Each of the people working with you is an individual. Each of those individuals is unique and special. While they think of themselves as part of the organization, their first self-descriptors will focus on themselves as individuals.

As human beings, each of us wants our own identity. We want to be special, different from everyone else. We want to be recognized for who we are, personally, not just as part of some larger group. Most of us don't like anonymity. We don't want to just blend in.

Get to know your people, so you can relate to them on a personal, one-to-one basis. Learn something about their backgrounds, their interests, their families, their ambitions. Understand what makes them unique and special.

Use that knowledge of your people to interact with them as individual human beings. Talk with them about their families, their personal interests.

Value each person for who and what he or she is. Recognize what each person can become. Appreciate the contribution each person makes to the organization and to fellow team members. When people accomplish things in your company, reward them as individuals. Extend that individual attention even when you are recognizing group performance. The two levels of attention are not incompatible. You can encourage team performance and salute personal achievement at the same time.

Provide opportunities for people to assert their individuality. These expressions may include freedom in decoration of work areas, business cards for people who don't normally carry them, and name signs hanging over machines in a production area.

While working with your people as a group, never forget that each of those people is an individual. They see themselves as part of the team, as part of your organization. But, even more importantly, they see themselves as individuals and should be respected and treated that way.

Strategy 2.27

Be accessible.

An oft-heard complaint is that managers are not accessible to their subordinates. Part of the problem is real and part of it is perception. And, in people's thinking, perception is reality, so the inaccessibility problem is widespread.

A primary concern is the manager's attitude, and how that attitude is expressed to others. Do your people believe that you hide from them, that you deliberately try to be hard to find? How much is true, and how much is perception?

If your people don't see you on some kind of a regular basis, they may assume that you are avoiding them. It's a legitimate perception; there are managers who want to have little to do with their people and practically hide from them. The attitude and expectation can easily affect people's thinking, even if it is not the actual situation at their company. Just *hearing* that some managers behave that way creates certain expectations, attitudes, and behaviors.

An open-door policy is fine, *if* people feel comfortable coming to your office. Employees in many organizations are intimidated by the boss's office. This intimidation might be the case in your company if offices are not easy to get to, if secretaries screen employee visitors and act as a barrier, or if people are not familiar and comfortable with the managers' offices. Getting into the boss's office should not be difficult.

Have employees in your company been in the management offices? Surprisingly, in many companies the offices are off-limits to non-office personnel. This separation was the case in an organization where I took over as Chief Executive Officer. I let it be known that employees were welcome in my office. For a solid week, people came to see me, just to have the experience of actually going into the CEO's office. They really didn't have anything to see me about; they just wanted to see what the office looked like, and to test whether they could actually get in.

To build the comfort level of people coming to your office, invite your employees to visit your office on a routine basis. Hold meetings and discussions in your office with the involvement of people from all levels of your organization. The more comfortable it becomes, the less people will be intimidated when you call them in for an uncomfortable serious conversation.

Even taking these steps might not be effective enough for you. In your organization it might be more appropriate to take your "open door" to your people. Go to where your people are working and communicate with them on the job. Meet them on their turf. Break through formality so your team members feel more comfortable talking with you. Listen carefully to what they have to say. Follow through promptly with whatever actions may be necessary to respond to expressed concerns. Make promises, as appropriate, then be sure to keep them.

Depending on your environment, there may be other things you can do. One approach might be to spend an entire lunch hour just sitting in the company cafeteria. Invite people to join you and talk informally. If you provide these informal get-togethers on some sort of periodic basis, your people will look for you and take the initiative to join you if they have something to say.

Some executives schedule regular meetings with their staff just to listen to what they have to say. Dedicated employees want staff meetings where they can voice their concerns and where they can get some sort of response. These meetings don't have to be formal, but they must provide opportunities to talk and listen.

Think creatively to find other ways you can be more accessible to your people. Opportunities will vary from company to company. Seek those solutions which are best for your circumstances.

Strategy 2.28

Have a sense of humor.

"Take your work seriously, but don't take yourself too seriously."

This old adage is meaningful for us in today's working environment. You have to take what you do seriously. With the "lean machine" staffing philosophy in most companies, everyone has a significant amount of important work to do . . . and seemingly never enough time to do it all. The pressure can build up some serious stress.

However, you can have fun while you work. Happy, relaxed employees are more productive. They work well in an environment with less stress and enhanced camaraderie. Most people are basically happy and positive, enjoying life. The same feelings should be experienced at work.

Unfortunately, many employers do not condone their people enjoying their time at work. The emphasis is placed so heavily on production that employees are made to feel more like robots, unemotionally plodding through their workdays. The understandable expectation is that work will not be an enjoyable experience, and therefore many people do not look forward to going to their places of employment.

Enlightened companies can break through this barrier of negativity by lightening up a bit. Young people today encourage us to "chill out." As employers and managers show their sense of humor and encourage enjoyment of working together to accomplish results, employees will develop better attitudes toward their jobs. As a consequence, absenteeism will drop and productivity and job satisfaction will rise.

When people enjoy their jobs and the positive companionship of the people they work with, they will be more likely to remain with the employer who fosters those special benefits.

How can you make the work experience more enjoyable, more lighthearted? The opportunities are limitless. First, enjoy doing your own work and being with the people on your team. If you don't enjoy what you're doing, your people will sense your feeling. Your attitudes will affect their attitudes more quickly and more deeply than you might suspect.

If you hear a good funny story, share it with your people. Find the right time and place for this sharing. While some people might benefit from having their work interrupted for a laugh break, others might prefer to share the laugh during a break or at lunch. Others pass along the jokes that seem to find their way to us through e-mail. Be careful to tell "clean" jokes. While they may laugh out of courtesy, many people are embarrassed and uncomfortable hearing "dirty" jokes.

Celebrate birthdays, promotions, and other special events with short parties. Lunch together with fellow workers, a piece of cake, sharing the moment builds teamness and positive feelings about work. Inexpensive funny gifts can add a lot toward the enjoyment. The celebrations do not have to be long at all; just a short period of fun together can go a long way.

Balloons are a popular way of recognizing a celebrant. The old-fashioned rubber latex balloons or the foil balloons can be attached to someone's desk or work station in areas where safety is not a factor. The recipient can take the balloons home to share with the family if desired. Fresh flowers can serve the same purpose, as can silk flowers or planters.

Be mindful of your power—use it wisely to get things done, but don't let it get in your way as you build relationships with your people. You have a lot of power just from being a boss; we call that "position power." Reduce the social distance that power can produce by relaxing the way you interact with your people. When you visit them in their work area, and they're sitting down, you sit, too. If you remain standing, you're intimidating—even without meaning to be. Have people call you by your first name. Relax. Lighten up.

Strategy 2.29

Set an example.

The people who work for you look to you as a role model. If you're a leader, by position or relationships, others see you as something special. They will watch your actions and reactions and will follow your lead. They're observing you closely, more than you think they are.

People watch the way you walk, talk, and treat others. They note the clothes you wear and how you wear them. They see the car you drive, observing cleanliness, maintenance, and driving habits. Your actions, and reactions, are seen, along with the way you treat your peers, customers, superiors, and subordinates.

If you are enthusiastic, your people will be enthusiastic. If you are angry, your people will be angry. If you wear nice clothes to work and have a smile for everyone, others will follow your lead. More than you realize, you set the tone for your organization.

To enable people to excel, to be highly productive, and to feel good about themselves and their employer, you need to exemplify those behaviors and attitudes. Alert, loyal team members mirror their leaders. Even those who march to the beat of their own drum are influenced by the way you perform. Without realizing it, many of these people will emulate those they respect and admire.

Assuming people want to achieve, we can appreciate why dedicated workers prefer high performance, results-oriented managers and supervisors. Unwittingly, we follow the example of those above us—in position, achievement, seniority, age, and other categories. You set the pace for your team.

Live each day as if you were influencing the lives of all the people with whom you come in contact. You probably are having a significant impact without being conscious of the messages you send every day.

Strategy 2.30

Show leadership at the top of your organization.

A great many people want to be led, or at least guided, by the leader of their organization. While people look to a variety of intermediate leaders to set an example, they look to the *senior* leader(s) to provide leadership and direction.

The top people play a vital role of forward-looking leadership in our companies, governments, educational institutions, non-profit organizations and other groups. Senior leaders set the direction and pace for the entire team. It is not a role that can be delegated or abdicated; the responsibility "goes with the territory" of chief leader.

Intentionally or unintentionally, when you're at the top, you are watched by everyone below you. When you're at the head of the line, everyone is following your lead. It's an unavoidable obligation. People depend on their leaders to show the way. You're in a fishbowl.

If there isn't someone to show the way, people feel as though they are adrift at sea in a rudderless ship. They're at the mercy of the currents of life, with no control over their own destiny. No one wants to be in the kind of position, so those who perceive their circumstances to be like that rudderless ship will abandon ship.

Executives who want their good people to stay with them have to demonstrate, continually, that they have a firm hand on the wheel . . . and the throttle. If people don't see that control and focus, their confidence in their leadership begins to erode. If not stemmed by middle managers and front-line supervisors, the erosion will affect good people at all levels of the organization with potentially damaging consequences.

Senior leaders must assure that they exert deliberate, visible guidance and inspiration for their followers. Just as important, executives must communicate the exercise of their leadership to all the people in their organization. The guiding presence has to be felt by everyone in a positive way.

Strategy 2.31

Reduce stress. Keep anxiety to stay sharp.

Psychologists tell us there are two kinds of stress, negative stress and eustress ("good stress"). Everyone is under stress, since there is some level of tension in everything we do, in every aspect of our lives. The only human body without stress is a corpse.

Eustress is the stress we experience through the positive events in our lives, such as marriage, job promotion, wearing a new outfit, taking a vacation, or winning the lottery.

Negative stress, called "distress," is what is usually meant when the word "stress" is used. This feeling affects us when we believe that things are not going well. Causal experiences include divorce, death of a loved one, family problems, trouble at work, an accident, or a flat tire when we're late for an appointment.

To maximize productivity and to keep good people sharp, there should be a positive stress in the organizational environment. This feeling creates a sort of positive "edge" in the environment. Where eustress is seen working *for* company achievement, there may be a sense of competition with another company or with previous accomplishments. There may be a desire to lead in a chosen field of endeavor. Tight schedules, close tolerances, and high levels of customer service can be sources of pride and excitement for employees when approached in a positive manner.

Good people usually work well under some sort of eustress. If the feeling does not already exist in the company, these people may create it for themselves. There are folks who "work best under pressure" and those who are out to prove something. They build a positive anxiety that empowers them to produce more.

Many good employees, found in sales, research and development, and aggressive management positions want to be on the cutting edge. They want to be where the action is, making those important footprints in the sands of time. They want to do something significant for themselves, for their employer, for their profession, for their industry, for society. If you can create and maintain the kind of environment that will encourage and support their endeavors, you can attract and keep these valuable employees.

Those who concern themselves with accuracy, quality, correctness, and detail are also valuable members of your team. They don't necessarily want to be the movers and shakers in their field, but they are usually proud to be supportive of organizations that are striving to make a difference. Their roles are to be sure that the company's important work is being done properly. A different kind of environment may be needed to hold these people.

The environments desired by the movers and shakers and by the controllers are not incompatible. You may have to act as an interpreter once in a while to help different kinds of people understand each other. The sense of positive anxiety, the desire to do the right things, the right way, can be a powerful motivational force.

Strategy 2.32

Don't question or second-guess your people all the time.

Good people enjoy a feeling of independence in their work. They want to be entrusted with an assignment or a role and left alone to get the job done. These folks want others to rely on their expertise, their experience, and their personal motivation for accomplishment.

When you give them an assignment or a role to play, good people will usually move forward deliberately to achieve the expected objectives. They want to be left alone along the way. When a superior, or even a peer, continually questions what they are doing, they may feel an erosion of trust from others. This relationship is, at the least, counterproductive. At the most, it can be irritating enough to drive a good employee away.

If you are the kind of boss who wants to know what's going on, what progress is being made, ask your good people to keep you informed. Explain that you may ask some questions to increase your awareness of their work. Make this request in a positive way, rather than in a way that suggests you don't trust them to work alone (without your advice/control).

Good people feel they are competent in their work. They can get the job done if just left alone. If you are looking over their shoulders too much, they may be "turned off" by the over-supervision and tend to seek employment opportunities elsewhere. If they discover you are second-guessing them by following up on their work, doing the same things, or checking too much (in their opinion), they may feel a lack of trust or lack of autonomy. This situation creates a discomfort that leads to a search for greener pastures.

If you don't trust your people, you may have problems deeper than we can address in this book. If you do trust your people, but just want to know what's going on, share your interest with them. Unless they are hiding something, most good people will be happy to share their efforts with you.

Strategy 2.33

Be firm and fair.

Good people want to be treated fairly, and they want to know that others are also treated fairly. At the same time, they expect those charged with leadership to be firm in enforcing company policies and organizational standards.

Fairness means open, honest dealings with each other. It means equitable treatment of all members of a group, whether it is a group of employees, customers, or suppliers. This equitable treatment doesn't mean that everyone has to be treated the same; it means that everyone has an equal opportunity for accomplishment and that standards are applied in an objective, even-handed manner.

Firmness is equally important. If circumstances call for definitive action to be taken with an employee, customer, or supplier, the action must be taken. Good people do not expect their leaders to be wishy-washy. They want to know where people stand; they must be able to depend on that standing to be firm and reasonably unwavering.

This firmness doesn't mean that there may not be exceptions to the rules. However, exceptions should not become the norm. Good people desire the organization's managers to have strength, internal fortitude to see that things are done, the plans made are followed through. When there are tough decisions to be made, good people expect them to be made—even if those decisions may be unpopular. Good managers are expected to "bite the bullet" when necessary.

To be firm and fair, there will be times when your difficult decisions will produce uncomfortable consequences . . . at least in the short run. Good people will understand and appreciate those situations. They may not fully support your position, but they will lose confidence in you if you don't do what you must do.

The same conditions apply with the "good" decisions. When there are exciting opportunities open to the company, good people will expect you to accept the challenge and the risk. After fairly evaluating the consequences, make a firm decision and stick with it.

Good people appreciate leaders who will "face the music" in any kind of situation. Their environment becomes one of clarity and almost predictability. The alternative, capricious and arbitrary reactions to changing conditions, unsettles many good people. An anchor of stability provides a calming effect that enables good people to create and produce without an undue amount of distraction or worry.

Strategy 2.34

Celebrate longevity.

Honor your employees who are most senior in terms of time worked for the company. By giving positive recognition to them, you send a message to others that longevity is something to be valued.

The traditional approach is to hold a dinner or similar

event each year recognizing those people who have been with the company 5, 10, 15, 20, 25 years. The senior executive typically presents them with a service pin or some other momento acknowledging their years of service. Often these awards have jewels set in them, signifying the progressive achievement.

People with those long lengths of service are still around, and some workers will prefer just to stay at one company. Continue to recognize them. However, with the increasing tendency to leave after a much shorter tenure, begin recognizing length of service much earlier than the five year mark. In your annual recognition event, pay attention to those with one year of service, two, three, and so forth. Have them stand up, perhaps tell a story of something memorable that happened during their history with the company.

A client was having difficulty with people leaving within the first two years of employment. Their studies showed that if people stayed for six months, they'd probably stay for two years. If they stayed for two years, they had a greater tendency to stay for five years. We recommended recognition at the six month point with a "graduation" from trainee to regular employee. Several things were done to note the change in status: a different name tag, notice in the company newsletter, a small party with a modest cake, and a letter of congratulations from the employee's supervisor. At the 12-month point, the employee was again recognized—small party including presentation of a service pin, and a letter from the manager at the next highest level (the letter was presented in person, with a copy sent home to the family.) At 18 months the employee received business cards and a phone call from the next highest management level. At two years, flowers, a small decorative gift for the home, and both letter and phone call from a company vice president were added to mark the occasion.

Increase the employee's status in the organization with progressively greater experience on the job. Find some way to mark the employee's work station with the recognition. Think in terms of something unobtrusive that would note the tenure: a paperweight with the number of years show, the employee's photo included in a special wall display of photos, something different on the employee's name tag or company identification card, or a modest sign outside the employee's office or cubicle. Use your imagination to create the right recognition for your environment.

Strategy 2.35

Go to a play.

How many of your employees have ever attended a community theater production? This kind of cultural exposure is usually healthy, wholesome, and enjoyable. When you attend an amateur production in your community, you're expressing an important kind of support for what is happening locally. If you have employees involved, directly or indirectly, with the production, you can send a strong and well-received message of support by your attendance.

Tickets to productions community theater groups or high school or college students are usually very inexpensive. This happy circumstance makes those tickets an affordable gift to give to all your employees or even to a select group being recognized for their particular contribution. This kind of a prize can work beautifully to honor a department of the month. Most theater groups would be delighted to sell you a block of tickets for a show at a reduced price. They're filling seats, generating some revenue, and enjoying a higher community audience involvement.

There are multiple benefits to this idea. Your employees will enjoy the evening in a non-intimidating environment and gain a cultural experience. You will have shared something with them in a positive, human way—be sure they see you there; join them, don't just send them. And, as a good corporate citizen, you are supporting your community.

Strategy 2.36

Value all your people.

Each and every member of your team plays an important part in the success of your organization. Each has a different role and makes a different kind of contribution, but each also does something to help the overall team achieve its objectives.

Value *all* of your people. The custodian and the brand-new employee are valuable human beings, valuable team members. In that regard, they have the same kind of value as the president of the company or a long-term employee.

Show your people how much you value them by the way you treat them, the way you care for them. You are probably respected for your position and for your knowledge about the company, the industry, the market. Remember the old adage, attributed to the Greek philosopher, Anonymous:

> "People don't care how much you know until they know how much you care."

Demonstrate your caring for your people. Let them see how much you value them as members of your team. Tell them what is going on. Ask for their advice. Express your appreciation for their efforts in helping the team get its job done. Genuinely care.

Strategy 2.37

Strengthen your employee orientation program.

Invest time and other resources in conducting a thorough orientation program. Our research has shown that, in general, the more time an employer invests in the employee orientation process, the longer participating employees will stay with the company. Each company has to determine for itself what should be covered in orientation and how long the educational process should take.

In designing your employee orientation program, keep in

mind that new employees will very quickly hit "information overload" if you throw too much at them too quickly. You may want to stage several orientation sessions over the first few days or weeks. Assume that some of the initial information will be forgotten in the excitement and stress of assimilating into the new job; repeat the teaching of key points at a later date. Repetition is a valuable learning method.

In your orientation, include the following kinds of information:

- history of the company
- leaders of the company
- mission statement
- statement of guiding principles
- success stories
- career path opportunities
- corporate organization
- company's position in marketplace
- importance of each individual
- employee's job and its relationship to the rest of the organization
- benefit programs and their value (cost to company)
- company policies—especially attendance, pay days, holidays
- customer service procedures
- on-the-job training, who to go to for help

Resell the company and the employment opportunity through the orientation program. Assume the risk of "buyer's remorse," especially if the new employee had other opportunities to consider. Now is the time to reinforce that the worker made the right decision in choosing to join your team.

Strategy 2.38

Re-orient experienced employees.

Understandably, most companies concentrate their orientation efforts on new hires. What about the people who have been around for a while? Are they current on what the company's doing, what happens in each department, the importance of the Statement of Guiding Principles? Include people who have been with you a year or more in orientation programs. Establish a schedule so your existing employees experience the orientation process every year or two.

Avoid the Oh-darn-I-have-to-go-to-that-orientation-thing-again attitude by getting the employee involved. Ask existing employees to share their perception of the company with new hires. Have them introduce their department as you explain the responsibilities of each of the departments. Ask for their critique of the process after they've experienced an orientation session. Invite current employees to sponsor newcomers, to show them the way around.

As they feel more a part of the important work of properly introducing new people to their company, experienced employees will gain a sense of ownership in shepherding their charges. They'll assume some accountability for the assimilation of the new employees into the company's culture . . . and reinforce the positive feelings for themselves at the same time.

8

Support Strategies

Much of the attention of your people is focused on task responsibilities . . . getting their jobs done. The strategies in this chapter address task-oriented concerns, supporting employees so they can get their work done more efficiently, more effectively, and more enjoyably. If people feel positively about the way they perform their work, they will be more comfortable remaining with their employers.

There are a number of different kinds of support that leaders can give people. Much of the support starts with attitude. If managers assume that people are trying to avoid work, just trying to get by with mediocrity, the attitude expressed to workers will be much different than if the assumption is that people really want to excel in all aspects of their work. Today's workers really want to see and feel the positive attitude: expect that people *want* to do a good job, then support them in ways that help them do just that. Moral support makes a big difference.

Support can include providing the tools and equipment needed to perform. A clear understanding of what is to be accomplished is a valuable part of support. The way managers work with people, the way departments interact with each other, the application of rules and regulations, and the sharing of knowledge of the jobs to be done all make a difference. When people feel that support, they build a sense of confidence—a sense of accomplishment—that inspires them to stay.

Strategy 3.1

Give people real work to do.

People really don't like "busy work" very much. They much prefer to be engaged in some sort of *productive* work that makes a contribution to the overall success of the company. They want their work to be meaningful.

Each of your people wants to feel valuable to the organization. That value is derived from what the employee does to help the organization achieve its goals. The more you can link each task to productive, mission-oriented results, the more valuable the employee will feel. Help people see how their work contributes to the company's success.

To overcome the depreciating impact of routine work, you can attack the problem from two perspectives. First, strive to schedule work so your people can maximize their productive activity on the job. Second, recognize the value of what may be perceived as "busy work," giving it a level of importance higher than just stalling or killing time.

No one likes to "hurry up and wait" in their work. In your scheduling, avoid pushing people to the point that they have a period of downtime while they are waiting for others to catch up to them. Try to balance the work among people and among departments so people can pace themselves better.

To overcome this problem, plan the so-called busy work tasks ahead of time. Don't just look around at the last minute for something to keep someone occupied. Have a deliberate system of specific tasks to be done in time available. Make these responsibilities part of the employee's job, individually or as part of a team assignment.

One kind of task that is considered busy work by many employees is cleaning up and straightening merchandise, tools, or inventory. Unless that work is the employees' primary responsibility, your team members may feel that such tasks are inappropriate extra busy work that you are dumping on them just to keep them working.

In actuality, most employees are usually so busy fulfilling the primary functions of their jobs, they have little time left to straighten up or clean up. That kind of work is put off or ignored until it becomes a relatively serious, noticeable problem. It becomes a nuisance, rather than an integral part of the job.

Make these tasks part of the jobs; with a lower priority perhaps, but still part of the job. Whenever the employees have time available, attention and effort should automatically be directed to the secondary tasks. Make this clear to the employees, placing a value on the non-primary tasks that also have to be accomplished.

For example, clerks in retail stores have a primary responsibility to serve the customers. However, when there are no customers to be served at a given moment, the clerks should automatically straighten stock on shelves, replace purchased merchandise, and perform similar tasks to present the right kind of buying environment for the next customer.

"Condition" your people to look for things to do when they have some time available. Give them ideas, perhaps a list of what they might do. As you build the team feeling in your organization, people will be more and more willing to pitch in. In many cases, they can help fellow employees catch up on work overloads. Encourage this kind of collaborative effort; praise it whenever you see it.

A side comment: when work is caught up, there are times when it is wise just to let people take a break and relax for a few minutes. It is not necessary for people to "push" every minute of the work day. In fact, balancing breaks with work, especially when the balance is maturely employee-controlled, gives the mind and body a break and enables people to become even more productive overall.

Strategy 3.2

Provide challenges.

People like to be mentally and/or physically challenged at work. They like to "stretch" beyond their norms. There's a certain excitement about doing something that hasn't been done before, expanding existing limits, or improving efficiency.

Interestingly, many workers would create their own on-the-job challenges and would really stretch themselves . . . if they knew it was permissible or desired. Some employees can't visualize and pursue challenges on their own because they are not able to grasp the "big picture" of the company's mission and the value of their role.

You, as the leader, may have to create and design the challenges that will stimulate your people to stretch for higher achievement. In some cases, this stretch will be a cooperative adventure with your team members; in other cases you will have to show them the path and encourage them to walk that path.

Without putting them down by making them feel they are not doing their jobs, show your people that there is more they can do. In your communication with them, describe the acceptance and meeting of new challenges in positive terms.

Don't make challenges too big. Experience has shown that the most progress is made in small steps. Seek little improvements that eventually add up to great strides. People are naturally overwhelmed by goals that are too big to understand and achieve. Help people make incremental improvements, getting a little better each day. It's better to have small successes than big failures.

Strategy 3.3

Prevent frustration.

One of the reasons that people leave one employer to go to another is to escape an intolerable level of frustration.

High performers don't mind obstacles and challenges; in fact, they often welcome them. The problem arises when they can't overcome those obstacles and challenges because of frustrations they encounter in the workplace. Frustrations may be caused by any number of circumstances—real and imagined barriers to high performance.

Raise your sensitivity to be highly alert for feelings of frustration. When you sense those feelings of frustration, even at the not-a-problem beginning stages, take deliberate steps to eliminate the causes. Let your people know that you want to remove unnecessary frustrations from their lives. Show them that you are acting aggressively to make work go more smoothly. Ask for help in your efforts so a sort of partnership develops. Workers will want to stay with you to join in your crusade.

Strategy 3.4

Encourage cooperation.

One frustration that becomes so irritating that it chases away good people is a lack of cooperation from fellow workers—especially management. People want and need support to get their jobs done. When they don't get it, and don't understand why, the frustration level can build.

The solution obviously is to assure that the needed support is provided. If, for some reason, you can't provide all the support the worker desires, explain why that type or level of support is not available. Work together to explore better ways to get the job done.

To be sure that you are aware of employees' expectations and their level of fulfillment, ask questions. No, I don't suggest you ask your people how frustrated they are! Instead, ask what else *you* can do to support them so they can get their jobs done. What else do they need? How can you help? The answers you seek may not be immediately forthcoming. Workers may be taken aback by such questions; no one has ever asked before. Keep asking, gently. Responses will come eventually.

Strategy 3.5

Provide lots of information.

Another source of frustration is ignorance—a lack of the information needed to get the job done.

The old idea of "mushroom management" won't work today. Where did that expression come from? Mushrooms are grown in the dark, with lots of "fertilizer" being piled on them. That process may work for mushrooms, but it sure doesn't work with people. They don't like to be kept in the dark, or having a lot of "fertilizer" dumped on them by management.

People want and need information to make decisions and get things done. Establish a clear company policy to make every effort to provide the information people need.

Unless you deliberately open the flow and exchange of information, people will tend not to share what they know with others. This tendency is not a malicious withholding of knowledge as much as it is a lack of emphasis on sharing. It's a problem of omission, rather than control or protectionism. It's just not done unless there is some impetus, some inspiration, for assertively sharing knowledge with others.

To facilitate the open exchange of information, establish a means of making knowledge available. Reports, summaries of activities, notices on bulletin boards, staff meetings, and teamwork can all help get the word out. The opportunity to access information through local area networking of personal computers helps a number of companies.

Sometimes information is not communicated from one person to another, from one department to another, because people are not sure what questions to ask to gain the knowledge needed. This obstacle can be overcome, to a degree, by helping everyone see the "big picture." Once people start relating the parts together, the questions to enhance understanding come easier.

Communications deficiencies are one of the biggest problems that organizations face today. The best way to overcome the problem, even though it's time-consuming, is to schedule meetings where key players can explain to each other what they are doing. The real understanding will come during the question and answer period.

Emphasize to everyone the importance of investing the time and energy to be sure people know what each other is doing.

People may need information from somewhere else in your organization, from outside your organization, or from some sort of creative process. Stay alert to possible ignorance irritants and work with your people to overcome them as well as you can. Again, when it is difficult to solve the problems for some reason, keep your people advised.

There are all kinds of information to share. You can even go so far as to practice "Open-Book" management, a process in which full financial information is shared with all employees, accompanied by classes that help everyone understand the meaning of all those numbers.

You don't have to go so far as full disclosure if you don't want to. One intermediate measure is to share sales figures. If you show what's happening in each product line, that information would help production workers understand why they're producing certain amounts of each product. If there are problems with customer satisfaction relating to product quality, sharing the actual letters from the field could have an educational and inspirational impact on those people who have the power to fix the problems.

Provide information about decisions that are being made, showing all affected workers what facts influenced the company's choices. Where appropriate, present the information and ask affected workers for their ideas, for their input. The decisions may be the same, but workers will support them more because they had a part in making those decisions. Since they're closer to the problem, when presented with critical information, workers may suggest a solution that management had not even thought of.

Clue: explain the "why" of running your business. Explain the causes of opportunities and problems as they present themselves to you. Help people see the bigger picture and they'll feel more involved, more a part of what's happening. This feeling of being "in" on things will stimulate greater loyalty, participation, and productivity.

Strategy 3.6

Reduce uncertainty.

Uncertainty is irritating. It's unsettling. It's demotivating. When people are not sure what is going to happen, they are cautious, concerned, and feel as though they are not on firm footing. If other employment opportunities are offered, people experiencing uncertainty are vulnerable to being attracted away.

The very nature of doing business in today's world is, in itself, uncertain. People in leadership positions are more accustomed to dealing with uncertainty as a "given" than are the people working as part of their teams. Leaders take uncertainty for granted, often assuming that their people regard the frustrating condition the same way. Uncertainty is viewed differently at different levels in the organization, partly because of the information available and partly because of the attitude training received as a result of working at a particular level.

It's wise to help others put uncertainty in perspective. It's easier to understand and accept the situation as a part of corporate life when you see the big picture. Whenever possible, reduce uncertainty by giving people clear answers about matters that concern them. Provide sufficient information and insight to reduce the negative aspects of the uncertainty; make the uncertainty almost fun.

Whenever you make changes in your organizational structure, modify your product/service offering, alter your marketing direction, or initiate other changes, expect your people to feel insecure and unsure until you tell them what is happening and how it affects them and their work. People will be concerned for their jobs, for the nature of the work they will be expected to perform, and for the security and future of their employer.

As a metaphor, consider how boats are tossed about by choppy seas. If you're in a small boat, like a rowboat, you're in for a wild and dangerous ride. If you're in a medium-sized yacht, you'll still feel the tossing and the rolling, but the ride will be a little more stable. However, if you're in a big cruise ship, those same waves may have very little affect on you. Same waves, different stability.

Strategy 3.7

Sympathize with the irritations of life.

Your employees are vulnerable to other frustrations of life in general. Challenges such as having to fight traffic to get to work, dealing with a recalcitrant phone system, wrestling with computer problems, or trying to get things done with equipment that won't function properly can be very irritating.

Be sensitive and responsive to these issues. We all face these irritations, or others that are more related to our life styles, habits, and circumstances. Accept that we all have these challenges. Roll with the punches, go with the flow. This too shall pass. Life goes on. Offer a willing and sympathetic ear to your co-workers facing challenges. Help where you can, but appreciate that sometimes just listening and caring is all your people really need from you.

Strategy 3.8

Remove barriers to task accomplishment.

One of the ways you can keep your good people happy and productive is to remove the barriers that inhibit them from completing their tasks. Remember that most people honestly and sincerely want to accomplish things at work. When they are not able to achieve that completion, they feel they are lacking something in their work lives.

Removing barriers may involve a number of different kinds of interventions. With so many variables in the work that people do, we can not possibly list every barrier and intervention. We can, however, address some of the most common.

One barrier that irritates good people is supervisors who don't seem to care. People want support and dedication from their supervisors. Studies have shown that many hourly workers perceive their supervisors as being more concerned for themselves than for their people or for the job that has to be done.

Another barrier cited is managerial indecisiveness. It seems that many companies are plagued by supervisors and middle managers who can not, or will not, make day-to-day decisions. Is their problem a lack of information, lack of knowledge about how to make decisions, or the fear of being second-guessed by their superiors? If this indecisiveness is a problem in your organization, evaluate your situation, determine the cause(s), and take action to assure that managers actually manage.

Hourly workers, and other types of employees in American companies, complain that their superiors don't listen to them. The people on the front line see ways that things can be done better, but no one will listen when they try to bring about needed changes. Eventually, these "blocked" employees feel that company leadership really doesn't care. And, if management doesn't care, why should anyone else?

The "system" is often perceived as a blockage. If the official way that things are supposed to be done is time-consuming and laborious, the system may be part of the problem, not part of the solution. Many operating systems need to be overhauled, streamlined to bring them into congruence with the demands of today's environment.

Tradition can get in your way. "We've always done it this way" is a common lament. The old ways may have worked fine in days gone by, but they may not fit for today. The hierarchies and "old boy" networks of the past are viewed as counterproductive and even counterculture today. It's time to challenge everything we do and how we do it, say today's enlightened workers. Without inhibition or restriction, look for better ways.

These barriers are only some of the obstacles that productive employees feel they must struggle to overcome. Learn what your people are doing . . . and are not doing. Listen carefully to what they say, staying ever-alert for the identification of perceived barriers. Then work quickly and diligently to remove those barriers so that your people can be, and feel, successful.

Strategy 3.9

Adjust jobs to fit strengths, abilities, and talents.

Few people like to fit into boxes created by others. They want to have some control over their environment, over the way they do things, and over our destiny. Many jobs can be modified to respond to the individuals filling the positions. Employers would be wise to be flexible, allowing employees to make the adjustments that will enable them to make a greater and longer contribution.

Each person has a unique set of knowledge, skills, abilities, attitudes, and talents. Each of your good people brings a special combination to you. To best utilize these resources, allow each employee to modify the way the job is done to suit his/her preferences.

As you design or re-design a job, consider the person now performing the tasks. How can you take advantage of that person's strengths? Are there other jobs that can/should be restructured in your organization? Are the various functions of your company distributed in the most effective way?

You might be able to increase productivity and employee satisfaction significantly by allocating tasks differently among the members of your team. The happier people are with the way work assignments are arranged, especially theirs, the more likely they will be to remain in those employment situations.

Strategy 3.10

Empower people to work as a team.

While many good employees can—and do—work just fine independently, the work to be done today often is best accomplished by two or more people working together as a team. Even work that can be done by one person can be done with more enjoyment, faster, more efficiently, or more effectively when done in partnership with someone else.

Human beings naturally enjoy work and social relationships with others. The joint efforts can be quite productive, while building important bonds among fellow employees.

As previously discussed, your work environment, physically, functionally, and psychologically should be conducive to people working together. If it is not, you might want to make some adjustments to facilitate a team working pattern.

Some businesses have very small offices or cubicles for key employees. The space is so small and cramped, there is no room for an extra chair for a second employee to sit down and discuss a project with the occupant.

If people want to talk with each other about a shared interest regarding their work, where can they do it? Are conference rooms available? Are those rooms booked so heavily with formal meetings that a couple of people can't sit down and discuss a timely issue? How about conversation areas with couches, chairs, and maybe even large pillows for people to sit on as they discuss issues, projects, desired results?

By not providing floor space, furniture, and supportive arrangements (such as privacy, flip charts, tables to spread papers), you may be sending clear messages to your people that you don't want them to collaborate. If they become less productive because they aren't communicating with each other, take a critical look at what you are doing to encourage or discourage people working together.

Do your managers know how to supervise teams of people? While many supervisors can often do fairly well in coordinating and supporting groups of workers or building productive one-on-one relationships, they often fall short in the vital skills of team-building.

Let your people know you like them to work together. Tell them you are anxious for them to strengthen creative problem solving by working more with their colleagues. Support the two-heads-are-better-than-one approach, providing semi-structured opportunities for people to interact, share, and cooperate to get even better results.

Strategy 3.11

"Mickey Mouse" should be fun, not fundamental.

Good people become quickly frustrated by "Mickey Mouse" rules, regulations, and procedures. People don't want to put up with nonsensical rules and regulations.

Take a good look at your policies and procedures. Look for anything that might call for extra paperwork, unnecessary steps, superfluous approvals, or similar nuisances.

Slash red tape. Eliminate burdensome bureaucracy. Cut the harnesses. Get the clutter out of the way. Remove anything that may be an obstacle to the effective and efficient operation of your business. Stop the silly stuff that makes life a challenge.

Check out your approval system. How many levels of approval does it take to get an OK to move ahead with a project—even a minor one? I once consulted with an organization that was overpoweringly bureaucratic and fearful of a control freak at the helm. As many as fourteen levels of approval were required for decisions that could have been empowered to front line supervisors.

Do whatever you need to do to make it easy for your people to get things done. Your streamlining efforts will probably make it easier for your customers to do business with you, too.

Strategy 3.12

Keep the promises you make.

This advice seems basic, doesn't it? It's one of those "of course" things in life.

In my consulting work, I've found that countless employees don't feel they can trust their employers to follow through on the promises they make. This lack of trust is, quite naturally, unsettling for good employees who are trying to help their employers succeed.

Be alert to the effect your seemingly minor actions have on the rest of your organization. When you make a promise, even an announcement of the way things will be done differently, people expect to be able to rely on that statement as true.

If and when you have to change course from what your people are expecting, explain the change to them. If you don't properly convey the reasons for the change, they may perceive you as going back on your word. If you leave them in the dark too often, you could lose credibility with your people.

Loss of credibility usually leads to loss of loyalty, which usually leads to the loss of your good people.

Strategy 3.13

Provide the resources to get the job done.

To support your people in the accomplishment of their work, provide all the resources they need to get their jobs done. They may want more people, more or different equipment, more space, more time, or bigger budgets. If they don't get the resources they want, they will feel a lack of support from management and wonder whether management really cares and wants them to perform well.

Resources are scarce today, as they always have been in prudent organizations. While we have to make do with what we have, people feel better about it if there is a clear understanding of the situation.

Furnish your people with all the resources you *can* provide to support their efforts. Then, take the time to explain why they can not have more resources. If it is possible for them to trade one kind of resource for another, perhaps with another department, help them understand their capacity to manage their limited pool of resources.

When people understand what they have to work with, and why, they become more focused on achieving the best utilization of those resources instead of complaining that they don't have more. If it is not possible to furnish the full complement of resources that your people feel they need, help them understand what they do have to work with and why they may not have more at this time.

It is important for managers to understand the relationship between the allocated resources and the job to be done. If the task simply can not be done with the resources available, don't expect the impossible. Unrealistic demands will turn off good people and send them fleeing to organizations led by more reasonable employers.

When people are given all the resources possible, and enabled to understand the big picture, they can often "work miracles" in task accomplishment. Remember that the package of resources you give your team members includes information and perspective.

Strategy 3.14

Avoid rejection, raw criticism, humiliation.

Be sensitive to the way you treat your people. When you are not satisfied with their performance, let them know. But, convey your message with sensitivity to the feelings of others. Don't put other people down deliberately and maliciously. It's not good in the short run or in the long run.

People resent being chewed out by an angry boss, even in private. As much as possible, contain your anger and irritation, communicating with less emotion than you might really feel. Avoid personal attacks and damning terminology. Don't humiliate your people.

Criticize constructively, recognizing the positive attributes of your valued employee as well as the difficulties. Allow people to save face whenever possible. Build people up; don't tear them down.

When you are critiquing performance of a particular task, focus your remarks on the task itself. Don't allow yourself to be drawn into other aspects of the employees or their work. Talk about how the task could be done differently so your expectations will be met.

Strategy 3.15

Recognize that you could be part of the problem.

Sometimes the problem is not with the workers or the system, but with the boss. And that boss could be at any level in the organization. If you could be part of the problem, you need to discover that fact and learn how what you are doing isn't supportive. Then, and only then, can you make the corrections necessary.

To uncover problems or opportunities for your own improvement, assume that you may be more a part of the problem than part of the solution. Ask your people how you can do a better job of supporting them in their work. Challenge them to suggest ways you can improve. Ask for their help in a genuine effort to strengthen your effectiveness in supporting them.

Be open to suggestions. Build a collaborative relationship to enable everyone to more proficiently play their assigned roles of producer, coordinator, supplier, facilitator, director, etc.

Strategy 3.16

Provide effective communications systems.

High achievers become increasingly frustrated when they have difficulty communicating with other people as they try to get things done. If your telephone system, walkie-talkies, or other communications systems constantly provide irritating problems for your people, the situation could become counterproductive in more ways than one.

Your people know how they need to communicate. Give them the opportunity to present their ideas about how your systems should be designed. With the expanding capacities made possible by today's technology, you should be able to design and obtain the kind of system that will make sense for your people.

An increasing number of companies are using paging systems, often designing private systems that don't utilize outside commercial switching systems. Signals available include tone only, voice, and silent systems that vibrate to tell the person wearing the pager to follow some predetermined response procedure.

Strategy 3.17

Equip people to be productive.

Give people the tools and equipment they need to get their jobs done. Waiting in line to use a photocopy machine can inhibit productivity and build dissatisfaction. Not having the right tool to adjust a machine on a production floor can cost time, money, and people.

One of the problems in production facilities today, particularly in job shops, is the time it takes to get tooling prepared to run a job. Set-up takes too long; raw material is not available; supervisors or engineers are confused about what the customer really wants. Result, highly paid craftsmen in high demand in the industry become frustrated and critical of management. Another offer comes along, and they're gone. And their departure could have been prevented by having the right fixture or tool to expedite the job.

Good people want to work. They want to do a good job. Give them what they need to perform at peak performance and they will give you the results you seek. Make their work more difficult, and you may soon be replacing them.

Strategy 3.18

Be patient.

Many people in management positions, and even more frequently in ownership positions, are driven by a sense of urgency. There is always so much to do, and such a high awareness of the pressures to get things done efficiently, effectively, and quickly. And, of course, if an approach or system isn't working, the solution is to change it. Continual change has become a way of life in some organizations.

Some of the people working with you can easily adjust and respond to urgencies and changes. However, even more of your employees are not comfortable with uncertainty, unsettledness, velocity, and constant interruption of the status quo.

This difference does not lower the value of these people to the organization; quite the contrary in many cases. How happy would you be with someone who rushed through your financial statement just to get the job done in a hurry? Would you want your surgeon to operate against the clock?

Be patient with those who take a little longer than you would to learn something or to accomplish some task or project. Help them understand the big picture, why you are impatient. (Your attitude will probably be obvious, even if you try to hide your impatience.)

If you desire a behavior different from what you perceive you're getting, talk with your employee about your concern. Explain your impatience; help others view things from your perspective. Recognize that you won't always be right. People won't always do things your way. You may not want them to. If people can do things their way, and get the job done within the limits you have to work with, give them that freedom.

Look for ways you might be able to help people work more quickly or efficiently. Observe, ask questions, and be open to suggestions about how various tasks might be done better. Some changes in procedures, work assignments, or other factors may reduce or eliminate difficulties. If people are not comfortable in their work, they may well leave to find more suitable (for them) employment.

Don't expect overnight miracles. People take time to grow. If they're doing mental work, the creative inspiration might not come as quickly as you—or they—would like.

Some people will pace their work efforts to fill the time available. In these cases, it may be wise to have more assignments ready for those employees to work on as soon as the current project is completed. They may produce faster if they know more work is waiting for them. Good people need plenty of work to do. I know good people actively looking for new jobs because they don't have enough to do where they are.

Your good people will want to be productive, to make a difference, so give them that opportunity . . . in ways that work for them, as well as for the company.

Strategy 3.19

Encourage and welcome new ideas.

In the day-to-day operation of businesses, there will always be ways to improve how things get done. The people with the best ideas are usually those directly involved with the tasks that are targets for improvements.

Let your people know that you are receptive, even eager, for their ideas on how things could be done better. Show your interest in new ways to serve customers, earn a stronger market share, improve operating procedures, create a safer work environment, save money, or other aspects of your company's operation.

When ideas are suggested, give each of them your serious attention. Investigate them, consider them, and implement them whenever appropriate. When you move forward with an employee's idea, be sure to give credit where credit is due.

Give the suggesting employee a timely response regarding the disposition of the idea. If it takes extra time to do research before deciding to implement the idea, let the employee know what you're doing. If you can't use the idea, tell the employee and explain why. When people try to help and don't get any feedback, they naturally assume that management doesn't really care anyway. That's the kind of attitude that encourages people to consider leaving a place where they're not appreciated for their ideas and the contributions they'd like to make.

Many companies have active suggestion programs, with a wide variety of incentives offered to employees for making suggestions. These incentives include cash, certificates, inscription of their name on a plaque, a special parking space, dinner for two, a chance to manage the implementation of the suggestion. Consider what reward(s) might be appropriate and tell your people about the opportunity to benefit tangibly from their contribution.

Good people hove lots of ideas about how things might be done differently. Some of the ideas may seem "off the wall" and not really worthwhile. However, it's important to appreciate the effort, the thought, and the willingness to share to stimulate the offering of more suggestions. Be sure to thank people *whenever* they offer a way to improve what the company is doing. Their involvement is valuable . . . and so is their investment in the future of the organization.

Strategy 3.20

Define responsibilities.

Good people leave organizations when they don't have a clear idea of their responsibilities, or of their area of responsibility. Clear assignments and recognition are needed it people are to be comfortable with what they are expected to do. Ambiguity fosters uneasiness, which encourages people to look for opportunities with clearer definition.

Responsibilities can be defined at three levels: role project, and specific task. In order to perform as expected, people need to have their responsibilities clearly defined by their superiors, as well as by their coworkers.

There are responsibilities inherent in the roles we play in organizations. A manager has certain responsibilities that go with the job. To fulfill a role properly, one must establish and maintain certain relationships, behave in a certain fashion (sometimes on and off the job), and be concerned with certain aspects of the company's operation. The responsibilities of the role may not be obvious, especially to someone new to the organization or in the case of a developing organization. The responsibilities have to be explained and discussed.

Don't assume that someone joining your company from the outside will understand the responsibility allocation in your organization. Job duties vary from firm to firm, even when attached to the same job title. Be wary of the "baggage" your new employee brings along from previous employment(s). Learn how things were done at the former employment (there might be some good lessons to learn).Help the new employee let go of the old ways to pick up your ways.

When we work with others on a team, to accomplish a specific project or a stream of project-like task groupings, we assume responsibilities as part of that team. Usually a team effort involves a number of responsibilities that have to be assumed by the members of the team. The clearer the definition of those responsibilities, and who is involved with the discharge of those responsibilities, the more productive will be the team.

Project responsibilities are defined by members of the project team, by their designated and/or chosen leader(s), and by people or "forces" outside the team. Sometimes an outside person, perhaps a superior in the organization, assigns responsibilities on the project team. Those responsibilities must be accepted by the individual members, either as assigned or as reallocated internally by the team.

Regardless of the process involved, all responsibilities must be recognized by one or more members of the team. This recognition should be mutual, with those accepting responsibilities willingly agreeing to do so. If the responsibility is forced, resistance will cause you problems and may push a good employee out the door. Leave room for negotiation about responsibilities; be open to alternative designs that will still get the job done.

There are specific tasks to be accomplished in all organizations. Responsibilities for those tasks must be clearly defined and communicated to the individuals concerned. Be sure you are clear about who is to do what. If assignments and expectations are not clear, people will tend to blame each other, or outsiders, for incomplete or improper task completion.

To avoid finger-pointing and buck-passing, ask those accepting assignments of responsibility to explain to you what they understand their responsibilities to be. When you have conscious agreement, you have a significantly better chance of getting your desired results. At the same time, those charged with specific responsibilities will feel better because of their clear understanding.

Strategy 3.21

Define accountabilities.

Accountability is important in today's organizations. It's a concept we'll hear a lot more about in years to come. Not only are enlightened employers trying to push accountability downward in their workforces, but an increasing number of employees want to have a clear idea of exactly what they are accountable for.

People who produce (your good employees) want to be able to stand up and be counted. They want to be recognized, by their superiors, their team members, and/or their professional colleagues for what they accomplish. When they have done something worthwhile, when they have met a challenge successfully, they will want to feel legitimate pride that they got the job done.

When you assign a responsibility to someone, assign the accountability for results at the same time. Emphasize the agreement that the person accepting the *responsibility* also accepts the *accountability* for getting the job done correctly and on time. Define clearly what is expected and when it is expected. When you remove the ambiguity, the uncertainty, people are more comfortable and energetic because they understand their roles.

Good, dedicated employees are willing to accept the consequences, good or bad, of their efforts. If they do well, they want to be rewarded for their achievement. If they do not meet expectations, they are prepared to take the blame.

Realizing that their names and reputations are on the line, good people will perform to meet or exceed expectations.

Strategy 3.22

Define authority.

Employees need certain authority to get their jobs done. That authority may include access to information, control of budget dollars or other resources, or freedom to design how a job will be done. If you expect people to perform to their capacity, you have to give them the authority to do what is necessary.

Authority is power. People work best when they have the power to make decisions. They want the power to take a project and follow it through to completion. While they realize that superiors must be kept informed, they thrive when they have the control to use their best judgment to get the desired results.

Power, and thus authority, is carefully controlled in many organizations. Sometimes this control is justified; in other cases, the tight control is a consequence of an earlier non-participative management style or a byproduct of people not being able to handle the power. If employees lack the experience or the maturity to use the power properly, the company should monitor its use. At the same time, the company should train and develop its people so that gradually they can use power properly to achieve great results.

Define what power the employees have . . . as members of your team, as those assigned to a particular project, as the person responsible for specific results. Explain how the power is to be used, and any cautions that may be appropriate.

Ask empowered employees to check back with you in any situations that may be "borderline" or doubtful. When your guidance is requested, grant as much authority to them as you can. This authority will encourage and motivate people to stretch for you as you have stretched for them.

Strategy 3.23

Encourage initiative.

Initiative can be defined as people doing things before they are asked or directed to do so. It means operating independently without having to be told.

Most managers—in any kind of organization—would love to see their employees take more initiative. A few leaders may be concerned about the employees going overboard, but most would rather have to step in and set limits than worry about establishing parameters ahead of time or pushing people to take action on their own.

Good people want to take initiative. Unfortunately, they are often hampered by their employers, or at least by their superiors. Quite often, the people perceived as standing in the way are the same ones who say they want their people to take initiative.

So, where's the problem?

The answer is alarmingly simple. Managers unwittingly send messages to their subordinates telling them not to take initiative. No, they don't say it directly, but indirectly the message is received.

Three beliefs must be present before people will take initiative: they must believe they have the *responsibility,* the *authority,* and the *accountability,* to take initiative. If any of these elements are missing from the subordinate's beliefs, initiative will not take place.

People will be more likely to take initiative if they see that doing so is part of their responsibility. The leader must tell team members that they have a responsibility to take initiative. That responsibility must be explained if it is to be understood.

If the people take initiative on something and get negative reinforcement from you and/or others, the likelihood of further initiative is significantly diminished. It is vital to give people *positive* reinforcement when they do take initiative, to let them know that you want them to assume responsibilities for things that need to be done, that you appreciate their action.

Do your people have the authority to take initiatives in various aspects of their jobs? Do they know what authority they have, or don't have? Managers have to draw the lines clearly. If the lines of authority are fuzzy, some will opt to stay on the safe side, while others will overstep their authority and potentially cause problems for themselves and you.

Help your team members understand how much authority they have to take initiative without coming to you for confirmation. Let them know that if they come to you with an interest in taking initiative in certain areas, you will probably grant them some special authority to move forward.

A vital issue is accountability. Too many employees do not perceive that they are *accountable to take initiative* in their jobs. "I'm just supposed to do my job" and "They don't pay me to think" are heard too often. You probably need to tell your people, directly and clearly, that they are empowered and accountable to exercise initiative if they see something that should be done.

This taking of initiative doesn't mean that workers should go do the tasks assigned to others if they believe the others aren't doing so well. It doesn't mean they should stop doing what they're *expected* to do in their own jobs to assume a wide range of initiatives in other aspects of the company's business. Their energy needs to be focused.

It is appropriate to hold people accountable for taking initiative in their own areas of responsibility. And, if they see things to be done in other areas to communicate those needs to their supervisors—either for a go-ahead to take the initiative, or for the supervisors to follow through to see that the initiative is taken by other employees.

As an example, safety violations are ignored in many organizations because the workers who see them don't take the initiative to correct the problems. They don't see that as part of their responsibility. The supervisors or maintenance should take care of those hazards. Workers don't feel they have the authority to correct safety problems; they anticipate that their supervisors will tell them to get their own jobs done and not worry about other things. When someone gets hurt, the workers who saw the risks don't feel accountable; management should have done something.

Initiative, with its elements of responsibility, authority, and accountability, rest at too high a level in most organizations. They must be pushed downward so people directly involved with accomplishing the day-to-day work feel more a part of the results of their efforts.

Leaders would be well advised to share more responsibility with their people. Workers at all levels should be made more accountable for specific and general tasks and issues. Give more authority to those expected to get results.

Strategy 3.24

Inspire and enable creativity and innovation.

Good people thrive in environments where they are encouraged to be creative, to seek new ways of doing things. When such people have the freedom and the support to innovate on the job, they are more likely to remain with employers who provide those opportunities.

Creativity and innovation are not, by any means, limited to the research and development folks. People in accounting may see a way to gather and present information better than it is being done today. They may learn of some new technology and want to apply it to their work.

Truck drivers may see better ways to organize delivery routes to improve efficiency and customer service. Machine operators in production shops may have some ideas about tooling or material flow. Retail clerks may want to create special displays to promote some particular merchandise better. The list can go on and on.

An amazing proportion of employees believe that they are not supposed to be creative. They are not supposed to try new ways of doing things. Innovation is believed to be frowned upon by management wanting everything done the same way all the time. Procedures are seen as being more important than results. The perception is there, but you have the opportunity to change it.

Let your people know that you encourage new ideas. Ask for input from those on the front lines: they often see things more clearly from their perspective. They know what ought to be done, but don't think management wants them to do it. Your efforts can range from an active suggestion box program to giving your people the power to try new methods or approaches.

Many companies have aggressive programs offering cash awards, special parking spaces, recognition, and other incentives to employees making suggestions that are implemented. Actively looking for better ways becomes a part of the corporate culture.

Your suggestion program should at least have a response system so people know someone is seriously interested in hearing ideas. The suggestions made, and management's responses, can be posted on a bulletin board next to the suggestion box. It's important to explain why non-accepted suggestions can not be implemented. Without this feedback, employees may think no one is even reading what they write. If they don't think anybody cares, they'll soon stop submitting suggestions. It sounds silly to even mention it, but be sure there is an ample supply of suggestion forms available.

Whenever possible, allow and enable people to test their new ideas. This testing can be done on a formal, planned, budgeted basis, or it can also be done on an informal basis with *go ahead and try it* being the ongoing message.

When people try new ideas, there is always the risk of failure. As much as possible, give people *permission to fail* in trying something different. We learn a considerable amount from our mistakes. People don't want to fail, but they will take the initiative to be daring in a new venture if they feel they have support.

Your role as management is to monitor the innovative efforts to limit the risk and/or protect the venture from outside attack. There may be those in your organization who will not be supportive of experimentation. You may need to insulate your innovators from your overly cautious people. Great companies have been built by daring people; other companies have been ruined by them. Your challenge is to keep the efforts balanced, with an emphasis on the positive.

Do your people believe you encourage trying new and better ways to do things? Is your company interested in new products or innovative applications of technology? If there is a question in your mind, ask your people. Then, based on what you learn, communicate appropriately to send or reinforce the right message.

Strategy 3.25

Establish limits, parameters.

Good people can be extremely valuable, a positive asset. However, they can also become overzealous and overstep the bounds of sensibility. Unbridled enthusiasm can lead to inappropriate actions that may cause difficulties for the good people and their company.

One of the roles of leadership is to set limits. Let your people know how far they can go. Establish legitimate parameters and your people will operate within them.

The limits do not have to be tight; they can be very broad. They should still be there, so some sort of control is in place. You may never have to exercise that control, but your good people will appreciate knowing that there is some structure to what they are doing, to their environment.

The best approach seems to be to set wide limits, with lots of flexibility. Give people as much room as you can to operate and to stretch.

Two levels of "limits" seem most effective. The first is the area in which the employee may function without checking with anyone. The second level, beyond the limits of the first, requires the employee to check with management before proceeding.

People really do appreciate knowing their limits. It builds their confidence knowing what freedom they have, but they also like to know that organizational controls are in place.

Strategy 3.26

Know what your people are doing.

In the management of the various tasks to be completed by your organization, it's essential to know what your people are doing.

It usually isn't necessary to know every little detail of what people do each day or each week, but you should be aware of what they are working on, what progress they are making, and what results they are achieving.

There are several reasons for maintaining this knowledge. First, part of your role as a leader is to know what's happening in your organization. It's your job. Second, this awareness will keep you alert to opportunities for recognition and reinforcement. Third, you will be more sensitive to needs for you to lend support and to share your personal expertise. Fourth, your people will know that you are interested and that you really care about what they are doing.

This involvement doesn't mean that you have to be right on top of people all the time. You don't need to know every time they take a deep breath! Based on your people, and the circumstances of your situation, keep abreast of what's happening in ways that work for you and your people. While written or oral reports to you on some regular basis will keep you informed, your being personally involved with your people will be much more effective. Whenever you can reduce report writing time, allowing people to use those hours productively, you're ahead of the game.

Good people will usually not object to your wanting to know what's going on. If they resist your inquiries, their resistance may be a warning sign that something is amiss. Usually, good people will appreciate your interest and will want to share (brag?) with you.

Companies lose good people when those high performers don't feel management is really interested in what they are doing. Stay involved, but avoid getting in people's way. It's a fine line to walk; you'll probably make some mistakes. But, better to err on the side of caring than on the side of being uninterested.

Strategy 3.27

Respond when people ask for approval or guidance.

Another frustration for good people is the lack of response or direction they receive from their managers. Some managers believe that good people don't need the hand-holding and personal attention. They do. Your high performers may not need as much attention, nor the same kind of attention, but they need it just the same. They want your wind beneath their wings, rather than a warm blanket dropped over them.

Some of your top people will tell you they don't need to have your approval all the time. It's a matter of pride and self-reliance in many cases. While they may not want the frequent pats on the back, everyone appreciates at least an affirmation from the boss that they're on the right track.

People look for signals from others, particularly their superiors and their valued associates, that give them feedback on how they're doing. When they're doing well, they like to receive some indication of approval and support from others. Everyone does; it's a natural human need.

You don't have to make dramatic statements and heap praise to convey your message. A simple head nod, smile, a thumbs-up sign, or a few quiet words will often suffice. Be sensitive to the fact that different people will need more "stroking" than others, and tailor your communication to the individual. Additional helpful insight will be found in Appendix A.

Most of your good people can do quite well for a while on their own. Every so often, however, they need some guidance from their managers or other key players about what they're doing. If they are not able to gain clear guidance when they ask for it, dedicated employees can become frustrated and anxious. They want to move ahead with their work, but may perceive themselves to be stalled by a lack of responsiveness from someone else.

When high performers, eager to proceed with their work, feel a lack of support, they begin to feel like they are paddling upstream. If you don't respond with answers to questions, approval to move forward, budget support, or whatever is being asked of you, your good people will be more prone to accepting invitations to work elsewhere.

Encourage your people to assert themselves if you are not highly sensitive to what they need from you. Some managers are not as alert to these concerns as others and need some prodding. Build understandings of how you and your good people will work together so everyone's needs will be satisfied.

Strategy 3.28

Give clear direction.

One of the complaints heard from employees striving to perform well is that their bosses don't give clear directions. They don't explain well enough just what they want so the employees can meet (or exceed) their expectations. Do you fall into this category? At least some of the time?

If you're being totally honest with yourself, you will probably answer affirmatively. Yes, you are guilty of not always giving clear direction to others. Sometimes your team members have to struggle on their own trying to understand just what you mean.

Your team members are probably hesitant to come back to you for clarification. After all, how many people want to tell their boss they're confused? Overcome this natural organizational fear by encouraging people to come to you Explain that sometimes you have difficulty communicating exactly what you want and encourage your team members to ask questions, to challenge, to look for better ways to do things. Do your best to be clear when you tell others what you want them, or the organization, to do. Encourage questions and discussion of your mutual concerns to assure common understanding.

Avoid being patronizing when you give direction. Appreciate that more than one conversation might be needed to get your message across. Don't put others down for not understanding the first time. Remember, if they did not understand, you failed to communicate.

Giving direction, support, and guidance is an ongoing process. It doesn't just happen once and everyone lives happily ever after.

Strategy 3.29

Get people involved.

People want to feel a part of what's going on in their work function. They want to have a say in what work will be done, the sequence of the work, and how it will be accomplished. They want to have input into changes in their work environment, scheduling, and even the hiring of new employees.

More and more, people will want a more meaningful role on the job. This desire will apply particularly to your better employees; they will have a greater contribution to make and will be even more eager to participate in the decision-making process.

When people want to get involved, and they are not allowed the opportunity, they become alienated toward management and toward the organization. Obviously, this alienation can lead to people leaving the company. For some, being directly involved in the management of their work is very important.

Soliciting someone's opinion does not necessarily mean you will follow that person's advice or preference. You can show you care by asking for input, but the ultimate decisions are still yours to make. That's part of your job as a manager or executive.

Not every decision you make will be a popular one. You have to rely on your own judgment regarding the best choices to make. Even if you don't select the alternative recommended by your team member(s), your people will appreciate your interest and your receptivity to their ideas. In most cases, you will find they will have a greater tendency to support your decision, whether they agree or not, because they know you gave their input fair consideration.

When you invite your people to contribute their suggestions, ask for the reasons behind their proposals. This feedback will not only give you greater depth for consideration of various alternatives, it will also give you greater insight into the thinking of your people. You may open opportunities for coaching or mentoring, which in turn will generate closer relationships that bond people to your organization.

There is an almost unlimited number of ways to get people involved. Those methods range from deliberation on a major corporate decision to ideas on the rearrangement of furniture in the office. Take advantage of as many opportunities as you can to offer people a chance to put in their "two cents worth" when there is a decision to be made.

Strategy 3.30

Reduce reporting requirements.

Your good people are probably eager to focus their energies on accomplishing their objectives. They don't want to be burdened with excessive requirements for reporting their progress, their attendance, or the status of their paper clip supply.

The definition of "excessive requirements" for reporting will vary. The need for information is understood by most high performers, but the process is annoying . . . or even exceedingly irritating. Be sensitive to the attitudes people have about reporting and make the process as easy and non-interruptive as you can.

Some high achievers don't want to be bothered with any reporting at all. They insist they do not have time for such nonsense; they're too busy getting things done. When you ask for a minimal amount of data for project tracking, for instance, these people may get all upset.

"I don't have time for all this nonsense," they may argue. "Do you want me to get this work done or fill out your *@#!%# forms?" When such people have calmed down, help them understand why you need information from them. Don't ask for any more than you need; minimize their paperwork burden.

If you can find ways to make the reporting easy for your people, you will earn greater cooperation, more accurate information, and less hassle.

Many managers want to know where their people are and what they are doing. That is a perfectly legitimate expectation, from management's perspective. When you ask for such knowledge, anticipate such reactions as, "Don't you trust me?" and "Do you want me to get the job done or punch a time clock?" Answer these questions for yourself, then explain your position to your people.

Help people understand your position in having to monitor the resources of the organization. Emphasize, as appropriate, the need to know where people are or when they will be in . . . particularly when people must coordinate with each other in their work. Give people as much freedom as you can, but insist on cooperation in adherence to rules and procedures when you feel it is important for the organization.

Reporting is not limited to attendance, or physical presence in a particular work area. The more significant aspect of reporting involves sharing progress on projects or tasks undertaken. Good managers stay on top of what's happening in their organizations, but they avoid getting involved in a highly detailed tracking system. Keep it simple.

Many high energy workers don't want to take the time to fill out a lot of report forms. Paperwork is the bane of their existence. Limit the forms burden for these people, giving them the opportunity to report orally in staff meetings. Many managers hold weekly meetings just to provide a forum for all key people to share what they are working on, what progress is being made, coordination needed with others, and problems encountered.

Some of your good people will enjoy filling out forms or reporting what they are doing. Appreciate that people have different needs (*See Appendix A*) and work with them to achieve your best information relationship. You will have to re-focus some of these people from reporting as much as they want to.

For the best use of your time, structure your reporting systems to give you the basic knowledge you need to do your job. No more. Keep everyone focused on the productive nature of information-sharing, for you and everyone else in the organization.

Strategy 3.31

Don't look over people's shoulders.

Your job as a good manager, as a good leader, is to put the best people in the right positions, clarify your expectations, provide the needed resources, and get out of the way.

Your people need three things from you to stay focused on the task(s) at hand:

- trust
- confidence
- space.

Their jobs include taking care of the details. The only times you should be involved in their task responsibilities are when they ask for your help or when you are unsure of what they are doing. That uncertainty, which could indicate a lack of trust and confidence, is natural for concerned managers who aren't getting enough of the right kinds of information from their people (*See Strategy 3.5*).

If your people object to your looking over their shoulders, literally or figuratively, as they work, correct your problem. Back off.

If your problem stems from insufficient information about what people are doing, make necessary adjustments in your reporting systems.

If your problem stems from a lack of confidence or trust in people doing the job, determine why you feel that way. If you are concerned about their competence, provide the training and experience to build that competence. Don't expect miracles from people.

Your problem might be that you have too much knowledge about particular tasks, especially compared to your people. If you held that job before, you may be tempted to jump in and do it again. If you do, beyond an instructional period, your people won't be able to learn to fly on their own. And, you might get so bogged down doing their work for/with them, you won't fulfill your own responsibilities.

If your problem stems from having the wrong people in the job . . . take the steps you have to take to have confidence in your people to do their job, then give them plenty of elbow room to do it. Focus on their results, their accountabilities, rather than their specific task activity.

Strategy 3.32

Don't keep people overtime without previous notice.

The dedicated people who produce for your company all day long probably have plans after work. They have family obligations, social engagements, or other things they want to do. Their days are planned, with both work and after-work aspects clearly defined. If nothing specific is planned, they may just be looking forward to relaxing after work.

When their supervisors unexpectedly ask them to work over, past the normal ending time of the day's schedule, the change could be disrupting. If they had some advance notice, many of these same people could put in the extra hours happily, with less disruption of their lives.

You will find that a great many of your people will gladly work hard during their scheduled work time, but don't like to change their work hours without some advance planning. These folks do not like unexpected change and will react against it. They may refuse to work, be less productive or attentive, or just develop a negative attitude about management's lack of planning and organization. Whatever the actual expression may be, the feeling is against the company. This resentment increases the likelihood of these valued employees being receptive to employment opportunities elsewhere.

Plan your work, and the work of your people, to avoid or minimize overtime. This advance planning helps control your costs as well as manage the work schedule. If you are already running on a standard schedule of more than forty hours a week, maintain a fixed program as much as possible.

When you do have to extend working hours, to meet customer needs, better manage production flow, or accommodate a project, schedule those additional hours ahead of time. Last-minute, "I-need-you-to-work-over-tonight" arrangements should be the exception rather than the rule.

The more notice you can give your people, the more they will appreciate your consideration. They will probably be more responsive and, consequently, more productive, too. Your advance planning will demonstrate your planning and effective management, enhancing the loyalty and respect your people have for you.

Strategy 3.33

Appreciate routine work.

Workers who want recognition (all of us want to be appreciated) often think they have to do something extraordinary to get attention. Unfortunately, they are usually correct. Most supervisors seem to notice only when people do something exceptionally good or exceptionally bad.

Some of your most valuable people, frequently overlooked, are the folks who come in every day, don't bother anyone, and get their work done in a reliable, routine way. You can depend on them to be productive. They are probably the very foundation of your organization.

Other people on your team may be involved in some special assignment work, but are still counted on to take care of some routine tasks that "somebody has to do" to keep things running.

The performance of that routine work is important to your operations. If that work were not done, you could be in serious trouble.

Every once in a while, take time out to thank those people who usually don't get thanked. Show some appreciation for the routine work done by members of your team in addition to the more exciting parts of their jobs.

I vividly remember teaching a customer service seminar to employees of a bank a number of years ago in the early days of my consulting practice. During a discussion of face-to-face encounters with customers who appreciate good service, an accounting clerk exclaimed that what we were talking about didn't relate to her; she never had any communication with the bank's customers.

This declaration triggered my curiosity. In response to my question, this fine lady explained that she worked in a back room keeping records and never talked with any customers. In fact, she rarely had conversations with anyone other than the woman who shared the office with her.

I strode over to her table and, on behalf of all the bank's customers, gave her a little hug and said "thank you." This dedicated employee burst into tears! In all her many years with that employer, that was the first time anyone had ever thanked her!

Make a note: is there someone you want to thank?

Strategy 3.34

Enter into performance contracts with your people.

With the confusion and ambiguity about what performance we expect from our people, a wise technique is to enter into a sort of contract with each of your people.

This contract does not have to be written. We're not necessarily talking about anything formal. In performance contracting, you and your team member agree on what the employee will do "under contract" for you and the organization. In return for satisfactory performance, you will provide compensation in the form of wages/salary/commission, benefits, training and development, and various other kinds of support. Both parties agree to keep their part of the bargain.

The evaluation of the performance is a constant effort, but is formalized during the periodic appraisal of the employee. Wise managers seek other times to talk with the employee about how both sides of the agreement are being fulfilled. You have to do your part, too.

A number of employers encourage (or even require) managers to do various kinds of "contracting" with employees during the official performance appraisals. Both parties agree on performance standards, expected improvement, desired training and education, and career path opportunities. The more frequently you engage in this kind of coaching, the more your employees will feel your support and guidance. The optimal situation is for the performance appraisal to be a confirmation of what both parties already know to be true.

In some companies, Management by Objectives becomes a tool to establish and maintain performance contracts. This arrangement can, in its more formalized application, involve written plans and goals with specific objectives and timetables.

Whether you use an informal conversation, a formalized written program, or something in between, arrive at some sort of agreement with each of your employees regarding what they will do . . . and what you will do.

Strategy 3.35

Fight boredom.

Be sensitive to how your people are performing their tasks. Do they stay alert, attentive, interested? Some jobs can get downright boring after a while, increasing the risk of errors, accidents, or dissatisfaction.

Help your people fight boredom in the kind of work that can produce those feelings. One approach is to schedule more frequent breaks for people engaged in monotonous work. Play music with varying beats and sounds, such as that offered by Muzak and similar systems. Give people freedom to take a break away from the work as they may need to get away from a tedious job for a few minutes.

A machine shop client cross-trained a number of employees in each other's jobs. All of the tasks involved highly routine, boring work. Every couple of hours, the supervisors would have the employees rotate to another kind of work. Everyone shared together, building teamwork, and they relieved each other's boredom by sharing the load of the various routines. No one had to work more than a couple of hours at any job, so workers stayed alert and safe.

Strategy 3.36

Design tasks to meet personal needs.

Each of us has personal needs and preferences in the kind of work we do and how we do it. These preferences may be environmental, task-focused, or relationship-based.

Some people prefer to stand when they work; others like to sit. While some people prefer working outside, others want inside jobs. Travel is preferred by some, while others don't want to leave town if they can help it.

There are those folks who like working with their hands, and there are those who prefer work where they are thinking or communicating. Some people love to organize projects and make things happen, and they're different than those who want to follow someone else's lead and concentrate on task accomplishment. Working with people is just what the doctor ordered for many people. But, many other people prefer to work independently, perhaps with little or no contact with others.

As much as possible, tailor the tasks to be done, and the way they are done, to the individual preferences of those who will be performing the tasks. If you can not modify the job sufficiently to respond to the needs and wants of the employee, consider shifting the employee to a different type of work.

The better the match between the worker and the work, the greater the results.

Strategy 3.37

Give people a break.

This information may come as a surprise to some old school, hard line managers: people are not machines. They have limitations and they need to be treated differently.

When workloads are heavy and resources like extra people are slim. Some companies work their people for days and days without sufficient time off to enjoy a mental and physical break. This overwork can cause dangerous fatigue and stress. Even if your loyal team members want to pitch in to get the job done, don't let them overdo it.

I encountered a company recently that had a considerable number of orders to be filled. With the possibility that the production load was temporary, management did not want to hire more people. Instead, they worked their people as many as seventeen days straight without a day off. You can imagine how those people felt. They were proud, but exhausted. Safety and family relations were stretched to the danger point.

With a shortage of good people, these circumstances may occur with more frequency than in the past. Resist the temptation to work, work, work. Human beings need a break. They'll return to the job refreshed and more productive.

Strategy 3.38

Give specifics in performance feedback.

Good people want to know specifically how they are doing and how they can improve. Interestingly, many supervisors seem reluctant to be specific, offering generalized feedback and evaluations instead.

As you talk with your employees about their performance, include specific examples to illustrate what you like or dislike about what they do. With an understanding of what you want and don't want, your team members can make definitive modifications to satisfy you . . . and feel better about themselves.

The days of "gee, you're wonderful" performance appraisals are gone in excelling organizations. Today's enlightened managers give their people the information needed to meet expectations. Everyone working for these communicative leaders understands what tasks are to be done, how they are to be accomplished, and when work is to be finished. Employers, managers, employees—everybody wins.

Strategy 3.39

Provide flexibility in working hours.

People have all sorts of challenges—and preferences—that lead them to really appreciate some flexibility in their working hours. The motivations could be child care, transportation availability, a second job, a preference to avoid rush hour traffic, or just a desire to sleep a little later. Wherever possible, allow for variation and even full self-control of working hours. Some people may want to start earlier and leave earlier, take off in the middle of the day and work late, or work four long days and take off a fifth (not necessarily Friday). Give people as much flexibility as you can, with a clear emphasis on the critical importance of getting the job done.

With family and personal needs, some of your employees and potential employees may have some difficulty with traditional working hours. To attract and keep your good people, be sensitive to personal needs and make the adjustments you can.

People are placing greater value on life balance. Although they enjoy getting things done at work, they don't want to work all the time. They want a balance between their work and personal lives. Time with the family or just alone is treasured. Expect to hear more about "quality of life."

As an employer, you have a number of alternatives. Consider what is best for the employee and the company; seek those win-win solutions.

One alternative is to institute flex-time in your organization. This arrangement gives people freedom to choose their own working hours, as long as they work eight hours a day or forty hours a week. There are variations to this approach, but essentially you set the parameters and your people work within them.

Let's look at the eight-hour-day approach. If your official working hours are 9:00 a.m. to 5:00 p.m., you may require that at least six hours of an employee's workday fall between those hours. This schedule gives the employee freedom to work from 7:00 a.m. to 3:00 p.m., from 11:00 a.m. to 7:00 p.m., or any eight hour schedule in between.

On the forty-hour-week approach, employees design their own schedule of how and when they will work the forty hours. They may choose to work four ten-hour days. They may work four nine-hours days and one four-hour day. There are a lot of variations on the theme. Teams of employees negotiate their schedules, so the facility is adequately staffed from 9:00 to 5:00, or whatever your core hours may be.

One approach that is really appreciated is an arrangement of hours enabling a three-day week-end every other week-end. Other people prefer a weekday off, so they may run errands and take care of other personal business that can't be done on week-ends. See what's best for your people, responding to individual needs wherever possible.

Another alternative is to allow people to vary the hours they work based on childcare, eldercare, or other family needs. Many working mothers would like to start their work day right after the children leave for school. By the time the children return home, Mom wants to be there to greet her offspring. Many of your jobs will allow that kind of flexibility, especially in the office environment. You may find that some production lines can be scheduled with the same kinds of considerations.

Obviously there are jobs that don't lend themselves to as much flexibility as others. That's why flexibility can be a benefit, a valued "perk." If certain hours have to be maintained to serve customers or if a certain number of people are needed to operate a production line or work together on a job, the opportunities may be more limited.

Be careful to establish clear guidelines before beginning a flex-time program. Initiate this kind of program as an experiment, subject to adjustment or termination if things don't work out.

Strategy 3. 40

Encourage people to take time off.

Expect employees to take time off. Encourage employees to take time off. Take time off yourself to set an example Productivity is not about logging hours in the workplace. It's about achieving objectives and pleasing customers. People cannot perform well simply by occupying workspace. They need physical, emotional, and mental energy—all of which are sapped by a stressful work environment.

Employees need balance, time, and other kinds of support, particularly single parents. You might even want to create support groups for single parents, and for others who could benefit from some therapeutic moral support. Be sensitive that many people face obligations that exceed their capacity to deal with them, or at least seem that way. If their employer pressures them to work longer hours, they may reach a breaking point that causes them to quit. Working longer and harder isn't always the right answer; sometimes working smarter is really the best answer—if guided and supported by understanding supervisors.

Today's employees are emotionally drained. With the labor shortage and intensifying customer demands, many jobs today cry for non-stop cheerful, exceed-expectations service (while working happily and cooperatively with fellow stressed-out colleagues). The problem is exacerbated by bosses who are also under a lot of stress—over-wrought, poorly supportive, and not terribly understanding or sympathetic. Result: rampant stress, lower productivity, and violence in the workplace. Working to please-everybody-but-me drains emotional batteries quickly.

People, like machines, respond negatively to operating past safe tolerances—running harder and longer than they were designed for. They malfunction when they are put to uses they were not prepared for. People—just like machines—need downtime and preventive maintenance. Or they may self-destruct.

Review your work rules. Do your policies accommodate reasonable time-off from work when life unexpectedly intrudes into an employee's schedule? Are those policies fair to all employees? Do they allow for some flexibility?

Encourage people to take rest and relaxation time. Do not penalize them for using their available downtime. If necessary, be sure they know what time they have and find ways to get them more.

9

People Growth Strategies

Good people want to grow professionally. They want to learn and work with new knowledge and skills. Through this process of what Abraham Maslow described as "self actualization," people enhance their personal value. At the same time, they are increasing their value to their employers.

It's important to enable these key people to grow at as rapid a pace as they wish. Don't worry about them leaving you as they become increasingly competent. If people feel they are still growing, and you give them the room to do so, the chances are great that they will stay with you.

Recognize that as people grow, they will desire even more opportunities to apply their talents and expertise to help your company and their careers. They will be looking for challenges, new challenges. Give them those opportunities; everyone benefits!

It's not smart to simply "throw" education and training at your people. The growth process should be organized and structured in a way that makes sense—for the company and for the employees. Don't just rush into this learning system design experience. It takes time to explore where the needs are and the best way to meet those needs.

Some designs will suggest a heavy orientation toward a college degree program in some discipline. Others will lean in a different direction. The most effective will offer a variety of learning experiences to give the employee a well-rounded background. Consider both individual and group/team learning approaches, depending on your needs and desired results.

Strategy 4.1

Establish a learning culture.

To enhance employee learning—career-building growth, establish a culture in your organization that affirms that lifelong learning is a part of what the company is all about. Adopt a philosophy that everyone should learn something new every day. The learnings don't have to be big things; there are lots of little learnings that are valuable. Continuous improvement can apply to people as well as it can apply to systems and processes.

Emphasize learning throughout the organization. When people make mistakes, help them learn from the experiences. Encourage all of your people to gain the knowledge, perspectives, insights, and understandings that will enable them to become more wise, mature, and valuable—to the company and to themselves.

Strategy 4.2

Create individual learning plans.

Develop an individualized personal growth plan for each member of your team. Design each plan so that it is focused on achieving specific results that will support the employee's career, but keep it flexible as well. Creating an individualized plan for each employee enhances that person's feeling of importance—both in self esteem and in significance within the organization. These plans should be documented in writing and reviewed on a periodic basis by the employee and the employee's supervisor.

Strategy 4.3

Give people challenging responsibilities.

One way to enable people to grow is to give them increased responsibilities. Let them try new jobs. Allow them cross-training experiences to appreciate things from a variety of perspectives.

Recognize the expertise and experience of your people and find ways to tap that invaluable resource. When faced with a new job to be done, a challenging problem, or exciting opportunities opening up, invite input from your people. You would be amazed at what a little brainstorming can generate—even from people who are not directly connected with the particular issue under scrutiny.

Encourage people to use their minds. Those wonderful folks working for you have some terrific ideas, even if they "just" operate a machine or do some mundane work each day. They see things differently and have grown from different roots.

One company was able to solve a problem because a custodian overheard a conversation and was brave enough to offer an objective perspective. The executives, who had gotten too close to the problem to see the obvious solution, were flabbergasted, then highly appreciative. Every member of your team has something to offer.

Strategy 4.4

Support formal education.

Provide financial support to those employees interested in continuing their formal education. Their interest may be in a trade school, undergraduate college courses, or graduate courses at a university. While some employers limit their support to what they consider to be job-related courses, there are some other approaches to take.

You may want to offer a stronger degree of support for job-related courses than you do for courses that don't relate directly to the employee's work, but do contribute to a degree in the field. Be careful about being too narrow in your approach. While employees are learning about subjects that are not specifically job-related, they are also strengthening their self-discipline and self-esteem.

When they complete the curriculum and graduate, they may suddenly become more marketable because they have the degree. Be wise and keep their loyalty by supporting the achievement of their career goals.

There are a number of different measures of how much support to give employees who take recognized courses. Some employers simply pay for the course up-front. The concern here is that the company may pay for courses and books without the student being able to complete the course for some reason. One way to balance the concerns is to give the employee a pay advance to cover tuition, fees, and books. When the course is completed satisfactorily, the repayment of the advance is waived.

Most will reimburse the employee upon completion of the course. Reimbursements are done in several ways. Sometimes the full amount of the student/employee's cost is covered, regardless of the level of achievement . . . as long as the course is completed. In other cases, the amount of the award is based on the academic grade earned. Completion with an "A" would rate a 100% reimbursement. A "B" would earn

75%, a "C" 50%, and probably nothing below that level.

Some companies place a ceiling on the amount of money that will be disbursed per employee during any one semester or quarter. This limitation helps control costs for the company and guides the employee to limit the course load. While encouraging growth, employers must be careful to help their employees understand they are employees first and company-supported students second.

Strategy 4.5

Offer learning materials for personal growth.

Establish and maintain a lending library of books, audiotapes, videotapes, and periodicals. Make these learning materials available for the employee to borrow to continue personal and/or professional development.

Designate a room or some other area of your workspace at your company to be a library for your employees. Install some shelves and stock them with books, magazines, and other learning materials that will be of value to people working for your company. Set up a television and VCR and build a library of videotapes on your industry, your work processes, safety, and other topics of interest. Establish a collection of audiotapes that can be listened to in this learning center or in the employee's car during commuting time. For employees who don't drive to work, provide portable tape players that people can borrow.

Included in your library, which doesn't have to really be anything terribly formal, could be resource material on management styles and techniques, selling skills, and a wide range of technical topics. Books and tapes on personal skills such as listening, interpersonal relations, wellness, stress management, and time management are valuable to have on-hand. Include personal growth topics, not just industry-oriented themes. People will also benefit from motivational tapes, language tapes, and books that help them understand how to raise their kids, fix things in their home, or grow a garden.

Invite your employees to contribute books and tapes that they've purchased but no longer need. Post a list of new additions to your collection to show that the facility is dynamic and ever-changing.

Current periodicals, and even back issues, are valuable resource materials. Consider including local newspapers, business newspapers, and whatever trade publications and technical/professional journals apply to your field, adjacent fields, and/or your customer's fields of interest.

Some companies have extensive libraries, with the quantity of materials and the use strong enough to merit a full-time corporate librarian. You have to make the decision about what level of involvement and investment is best for your organization.

As young people enter and grow within your company, their mentors may want to spend some time in the library with them. These senior people can guide and encourage their protégés to read certain materials, absorb the knowledge from specific tapes, and follow applicable periodicals. Of course, by working with their protégés, the mentors themselves may find some things of interest to continue their own growth.

Encourage your people to use the library as a powerful resource to continue their growth. Include some introduction and how-to-use instructions in the orientation of new employees.

Strategy 4.6

Connect with outside resources for learning materials.

Consider developing a relationship with your community's library to give your employees access to even more resources . . . and to make your company's specialized industry-specific collection accessible to the general public.

Encourage your people to borrow learning materials from

community and university libraries. Interlibrary networking makes the collections of a number of libraries easily accessible. Booksellers will often give discounts to people buying books or tapes for use in business.

Contact booksellers located near your business location(s) to inquire about such discounts. They might be willing to extend discount privileges to any of your employees who present your company identification card. Such discounts could apply to any product purchased, not just business books specifically. This discount would not only be an employee benefit (at no cost to you), but would build more business for the bookseller. It's a win-win idea.

Strategy 4.7

Send people to outside seminars.

Your people can benefit greatly by participation in good quality seminars and workshops. The opportunities are boundless. These learning experiences, usually ranging from a half-day to a couple of days, are offered in central cities throughout the country. They are sponsored by commercial seminar companies, colleges and universities, and trade/professional associations.

Commercial Seminars

Beware that some of the commercial seminar programs pack people into a room and feed them a volume of information. Many of the opportunities available are quite valuable, but the actual learning experience may be relatively passive. Look for those seminars that will have a relatively low attendance, so your people will have a chance to interact with the instructor and fellow participants. Learning becomes much more effective when learners are personally involved in the process.

Even those seminars that simply load participants with information are helpful, especially if a number of people from the same company attend. If you only send one or a few people, require the attendees to share their new knowledge with others when they come back to work. This sharing not only inspires people to pay closer attention in the session, it reinforces the learning and enables others to share the experience vicariously. Emphasis should be placed on how the knowledge gained can be applied in *your* work setting.

The commercial seminar companies do a fairly good job of blanketing the countryside with promotional literature. In fact, you may find that your organization receives multiple copies of the same brochures. These companies use various sources to build their mailing lists, so your postal carrier will be bringing you all sorts of goodies.

You might want to arrange for one person or one department to be a central collector of these brochures, so there is a single resource for employees and their managers to learn of upcoming offerings. If you have all registration go through a single company approval process, coordinating attendance may produce greater savings from multiple registrations.

It's tempting to simply toss the brochures into the trash without even looking at them. Take a moment, even if you don't plan to send anyone, and look at what's being taught. The topic and the outline may give you insights into trends and suggest some topics you should address in your internal training sessions. Some of the national commercial companies will send trainers into your company for in-house presentations, if that is more economical and appropriate for you.

School-Sponsored Programs

Colleges and universities throughout the country offer both credit and non-credit educational programs that can help your people grow. Consider both kinds of opportunities in guiding the development of your employees.

The credit course alternative is discussed in detail in Strategy 4.4, so we won't spend much time on it here. If you have sufficient people and scheduling control, consider offering credit college courses on your company's premises. Many colleges will send instructors to you, making it more convenient for your employees and offering opportunities for focused discussion regarding situations in *your* company. When these courses are presented in-house, you'll have built-in, practical, meaningful case studies that will be of even greater value for your people.

Non-credit courses are offered by the continuing education departments of hundreds of universities and colleges. To learn what is offered in your vicinity, call the schools that serve your area. The schools are not as aggressive in their marketing, as a rule, as the commercial seminar companies, although you may receive their brochures from time to time. You'll be more effective seeking the information of your own volition.

Non-credit programs range from half-day sessions to multi-week courses. Topics include both "hard" and "soft" subjects, from relaxation methods to high technology or very technical classes. Sometimes these programs can also be brought in-house. They are taught by university instructors in some instances, but even more often by contract instructors with expertise in a particular topic. Quality will vary considerably, so don't hesitate to ask for outlines and references.

Many high schools offer programs for adults. The greatest effort in this area comes from vocationally oriented high schools, but there are many opportunities. Again, you have to take the initiative in most cases to discover what is offered. Some of these schools have outreach programs where they will send instructors into your company.

Trade and Professional Associations

An increasing number of trade and professional organizations are offering learning opportunities for members. The majority of these sessions are provided as part of the program at conventions or conferences, but some associations have established education departments to help meet member needs outside the convention environment.

Check to see whether your trade association is one of those offering seminars, workshops, or courses in various cities around the country. The programs range from retreats for senior executives to seminars and workshops for managers at all levels to skills training and technical updates for hourly employees.

Some associations present mini-seminars at their conventions to see which ones attract the most member interest. Those popular topics are then offered as one-or two-day seminars in central locations for member companies. If this sort of service is not available from your industry association, they might welcome your expression of interest and suggestions for topics to be addressed.

Many professions, particularly those with licensing requirements in various states, offer association-managed certification programs. Members must meet certain qualifications, usually including educational and time-in-service components, to earn the initial certification. Sometimes the educational opportunities are provided by the association or society; sometimes the member must submit validation of having met the requirements through alternative sources meeting sponsor-established criteria.

To maintain their certification, members holding the credential must show evidence of their continuing educational development by investing a minimum number of hours in courses, seminars, or workshops during each ensuing one-year or multi-year period.

Even if the membership organization does not provide the actual learning opportunities, the certification programs may provide a structured design of recommended education and training to offer in-house. This design will provide a course to follow in working with employees to support their professional development.

Strategy 4.8

Have learners pass their training along to others.

As your people participate in various learning experiences, under the sponsorships described in the previous section, encourage them to share the knowledge they have learned with other members of your team. You'll find that, while not every topic lends itself to this kind of pass-along, quite a few will.

The method of sharing will depend on the people involved, the nature of the material, and your company's facilities. Don't try to make every learning opportunity fit the same procedure. Some knowledge will be best shared on a one-to-one personal basis; other information will be communicated more effectively in a seminar or lecture mode.

When your company is paying for an employee's training outside the organization, establish the expectation that a condition of payment is that the knowledge gained be shared with others. Don't expect your employee to present the seminar verbatim. Most seminar participants don't have the combination of knowledge and presentation skills that professional seminar leaders do.

Instead, invite the employee to share highlights or key points with his/her manager and others who might benefit. As much as reasonable, let the means for communicating this knowledge be determined by the employee. Some people are *terrified* of standing up to give a speech. Don't force people into doing things that aren't comfortable for them.

To assure worthwhile transfer of the material learned, give the employee the time and space needed. An extended lunch hour, a conference room, a chalkboard or flip chart, or other support will enable the employee to communicate the knowledge effectively.

When learners know that the knowledge shared in seminars or workshops will have to be taught to others upon returning to work, they pay closer attention and absorb more in the sessions they attend. Everyone benefits more when the learning is made a part of the job, rather than just something extra that is done without relation to achieving better results in the work environment.

The people who come back from seminars to share what they've learned will gain two additional benefits: they'll gain experience in presentation skills and they'll get reinforcement of the seminar learnings from teaching it themselves.

Strategy 4.9

Help people grow into bigger jobs.

While the Peter Principle (postulated by Dr. Laurence J. Peter) suggests that people can be promoted to their level of incompetence, I assert that many people are held back from achieving their full potential.

In too many organizations, people in management and supervisory positions invest an inordinate amount of time protecting their own positions. This effort includes guarding secrets such as details of particular projects, puffing-up one's own importance, and not sharing information about how or why things are done.

Unfortunately, some people believe that holding back subordinates from professional growth may strengthen their own positions. These misguided folks think that if their people become too good, they might be promoted . . . even perhaps beyond the boss' positions. This leap frogging would certainly not look good—subordinates shouldn't be better than their superiors, the protective bosses muse.

Actually, quite the contrary is true. One of the measures of leader effectiveness is how well their followers perform. If followers are trained and developed well, followers will be able to do their jobs more competently. They will also be more prepared to take on other assignments and other opportunities in the organization.

As these people move into positions where they can accept—and perform—new challenges, the boss becomes known and appreciated as a people-builder. Those kinds of bosses are most valuable, because they have proven ability to teach and empower people to grow. As the bosses move into more responsible positions, coworkers will be confident of their ability to develop a productive teams in practically any situation. Everybody wins.

Many supervisors and lower-level managers dampen their own opportunities for advancement because they have not developed their people to be able to take their place. If you want to be promoted, train one or more people to succeed you. There are many stories of people being passed over for promotion because no one was prepared to take their place.

As you prepare your people for jobs with a wider scope, more responsibility, or a higher position in the company, their enhanced capacity will enable them to perform better as members of your team. You can derive both short-term and long-term benefits by investing your time, interest, energy, and other resources in growing your people.

Your good people's appreciation of your interest and support, will inspire them to stay with you as loyal members of your team.

Strategy 4.10

Enable people to discover the wealth of talents they have.

Over the years, people develop a wide range of talents, abilities, expertise, experiences, and aptitudes. All this capacity adds up to a tremendous amount of potential.

How much do you know about the real potential of your people, let alone yourself? If you're like most people, you are so busy with the many challenges of getting things done and leading people toward high achievement, there is a tendency not to look deeply enough.

Some of your better people are involved, or have been, in activities that helped them discover, develop, and practice new skills and talents. While some of the personal and professional development may have been on the job, a significant portion of this growth takes place in non-work settings.

Are your people involved in community activities such as Scouting, Little League, church groups, civic clubs, or fraternal organizations? Are they in leadership positions or other positions of responsibility? Does the experience they gain in those activities strengthen their capacity to perform for you and your organization? Would the skills and background they have gained make them eligible for a different kind of work and/or a leadership position on-the-job?

Quite often, people active in their communities develop a high potential for leadership and accomplishment they are not able to apply at work. They put in their time on-the-job, eager for the end of the work day so they can return to the fulfilling work they really enjoy. Their focus is gradually more on their non-work activities. Result: They become less loyal to their employer and more apt to leave to accept positions where their talents are appreciated and useful.

I personally experienced this phenomenon early in my career. My work assignments were nowhere near as exciting, challenging, and rewarding as the higher level of involvement I had in civic activities outside of work. After a frustrating 18 months, I resigned my position in a fast-track executive development program with a Fortune-500 company to accept a turn-around opportunity with a much smaller employer. I might still be with the major corporation today if that company's managers had recognized what I had to offer.

Not everything your people try will be successful. Some of us have mechanical aptitude, some have fine abilities to reason and think logically, others are great organizers or smooth persuaders. Testing your people's capacity, in non-threatening situations, will give them—and you—a chance to discover and apply their talents in satisfying ways.

The enhanced level of self worth, enmeshed with their work accomplishment and development, will build people's confidence and loyalty. Their personal growth will be part and parcel of their work with you.

Strategy 4.11

Encourage intellectual growth.

Much of the training and development being offered in corporate America is directed toward technical skill building, management and leadership, sales and marketing, customer service, application of technology, and personal growth topics such as time management, coping with stress, decision making, and dress for success.

Few of these topics inspire learners to stretch intellectually. Your good people could benefit from growth opportunities to learn to think more clearly and rationally. Experiential courses in logic or creativity might strengthen your organization's problem-solving capacity.

The THINK sign has become commonplace in the workplace, but we still encounter numerous difficulties in the business world because people just don't think. Television programming, fast-food restaurants, quick-read shallow-coverage periodicals, and other trends in our lives have made it possible to survive quite nicely without thinking very deeply. Leading edge employers will find ways to help people reason better. The power of greater thinking and understanding is good for everyone.

Organizations striving to gain the strongest possible return on their investment in human resources create opportunities for people to talk with each other. They have discovered that their good people have a considerable amount to share with each other, that they have quite a bit of power in their own ranks.

Usually, everyone is so busy accomplishing the work of the day, no one has time (or takes time) just to sit and talk.

When a piece of time is set aside for people to discuss issues and concerns, especially with the help of a professional facilitator, an incredible amount of growth and progress occurs. It's amazing what can happen during a retreat. We've seen significant results with our clients in only a day or two, even before constructive follow-up. Retreat experiences can be valuable for all kinds of employees, not just executives.

There is a real need for people to learn and practice the basic skills of thinking and cooperating. A surprising number of people are actually afraid to think for themselves. It's a threatening trend that must be overcome if people are to function to their full potential. Interestingly, we've responded to specific requests from some of our clients by providing workshops on Common Sense!

Strategy 4.12

Assign special projects.

To give your people opportunities to broaden their knowledge, perspectives, and experiences, offer them special projects that are beyond their comfort zone. These should not be "make-work" assignments, but legitimate work that will contribute to the forward movement of the organization.

Furnish the resources, including time, for the appropriate dedication to meeting the challenge. Provide access to needed data, people, and expertise so your shining stars can learn, grow, and achieve. People want to make a significant difference; give them that opportunity and you'll see bountiful returns for the employee and the company.

The assignments do not have to be earth-shaking projects that will change the direction of the organization's progress, although some of your people might benefit from such a study. One of our clients asked middle managers to assess whether the company should remain in several facilities, consolidate into the existing plant, or move everything to an entirely new building. Those involved learned quite a bit about the corporate world beyond their functional areas.

An increasing number of companies take hourly production line employees along to industry trade shows. The selected employees learn about the latest technology, what other companies are doing, how buying decisions are made, and how various components of the industry relate to each other. They return to work with a whole new perspective. In some cases, the employees who make the trip are expected to share their new knowledge with their coworkers. (*See Strategy 4.8*)

For other ideas, how about having machine operators gain some experience in set-up? Your customer service people might benefit from going on some sales calls, then critiquing the process. And sales professionals will learn from spending a day in customer service. Have you sent production supervisors or quality control people on visits to your customers' sites? How many of your retail employees have shopped the competition, then reported and discussed their findings?

Be creative! Get people involved in new product design, market studies, public relations events, and industry associations. Expand their vision, then watch that new insight and energy go to work for you, the employee, and the organization! It's a win-win-win situation.

Strategy 4.13

Invest in career planning.

A growing number of companies invest time and resources in career planning with their employees, especially the people identified as the rising stars. It's a valuable practice to engage in with all your people.

In counseling interviews, explore career options for each of your employees. Concentrate first on opportunities within your company. As necessary or appropriate, consider options outside your organization. When your people see that you really care about them—as individuals, they will look more seriously at their career development. As much as possible, focus them on learning and growing within your company. Build their dedication to their continuous improvement.

Consider having the counseling done by a professional in the career planning field, someone not employed by your company.

Be careful not to make any promises about future positions to be held by any employee. It's fine to talk about how people can prepare themselves to be eligible for consideration, but don't make promises you may not be able to keep. Concentrate on growth and keeping options open, rather than locking onto any particular career path.

Strategy 4.14

Build competency deliberately.

As you identify the competencies needed for each person to move ahead in his/her career, start making a list. Measure the employee's current capability against what will be required for future opportunities with the organization. Prioritize the needs as you both see them. When will they be needed: a month, a year, three years from now?

From this list, develop a plan to enable team members to expand their professional capacity through deliberate, organized plans of competency-building. Indicate who will be responsible for each component of the plan. Will the employee be expected to take a course or gain some specific skill? Will the supervisors make training or experience available? Will arrangements be made jointly, with the supervisors and subordinates learning together?

What resources will be needed to implement the plan? Personal or paid time for the employee to learn? Funds to pay for training programs or college courses? Time off from normal duties for growth experiences?

After you have established a realistic timetable, initiate the development process. Meet with the employees periodically to review progress and make any needed adjustments in the plans. Maintain written records in the employees' personnel folders for permanency.

As your people advance themselves, be sure to recognize their achievement. Letters of congratulations or praise from superiors, public announcements in house organs or even in local newspapers, and interim promotions or special assignments are alternative methods to mark growth.

Strategy 4.15

Provide incentives for growth.

If you encourage and enable your people to learn and grow without some sort of payoff, you may encounter a couple of risks.

One risk is that the employees may become disillusioned. They are hoping for promotions, opportunities to put their new knowledge into practice, or at least some enhanced status in the organization. If those avenues are closed to them, they may lose their enthusiasm for personal growth. You don't have to promote people or pay them more because they've learned, but it is important to give them an opportunity to use their new knowledge.

Another risk of strong investment in development is that you may help people grow professionally to become fine, highly productive employees for someone else. Be prepared internally to utilize the new knowledge and skills your people will gain. Help them put their new strengths to use in viable efforts in your organization. Make the whole experience, learning and application, meaningful. If they are able to apply their talent working with you, there is a greater chance they'll stay to continue that experience.

Yes, it is worthwhile to learn merely for the sake of learning. However, the judicious use of corporate funds suggests that monies invested in employee development should have a positive return to the company. Your people feel the same way: the investment of their time and energy should reap a reward.

As much as possible, establish in advance your process for response to opportunities for employee growth. Clarify what you expect from the employee, and what the employee can expect from you. Unless extenuating circumstances make it impossible, fulfill your part of the bargain. If you fail to keep your promises, especially without an explanation to the employee, you will lose credibility. And you may lose a valued employee.

Follow through to achieve the maximum benefit for all concerned.

Strategy 4.16

Operate a mentorship program.

Mentoring has proven to be a highly valuable learning experience for people of all ages, backgrounds, and experience levels. A mentor is someone who can help you learn, understand, plan your career, become more effective. Sometimes a mentor is someone who is older and wiser. In other situations, the mentor may be younger, with a particular expertise. A mentor can be another employee of the same company, come from another company in the industry, or not even be affiliated with the same industry as the protégé. Mentor and their protégé can enjoy a long-term relationship, or the interaction can be relatively brief. There is no set method or system of mentorship, though contact is usually initiated by the protégé.

If each member of your organization has a mentor—from inside or outside the company, everyone will have someone to turn to for guidance, for learning, or just for talking and reflection. You can facilitate this growth opportunity by maintaining a list of people interested in serving as a mentor and requests from protégés for mentors meeting certain criteria. This connection system can be a passive activity; you don't even have to get involved in assigning people to work with each other. The easiest, and sometimes most effective, approach is to simply offer an availability/interest listing much like the personals column in the newspaper. When people freely select each other, the relationship and results are much more effective and rewarding.

It is also wise to offer workshops on how to serve as a mentor. The emphasis is on how to listen, ask challenging questions, provide guidance without direction, and share experiences as lessons for growth. The protégé learns in similar sessions—how to ask for advice and insight, what life planning issues should be considered, and how to optimize relationships with mentors (it's OK to have more than one). A key here is to avoid calling the mentor every day; make calls and visits special experiences. Frequent expressions of gratitude should be encouraged, so the mentor knows he or she is making a difference that's appreciated.

Strategy 4.17

Establish a corporate university.

If your company is large enough, setting up a corporate university might be a good idea. An in-house university or training academy can begin with as little as a couple of courses, then expand to offer literally dozens of courses of various lengths, levels of difficulty, and topic orientations. The sessions can last from an hour to several days, taught by company employees and/or outside resources.

Over the years, our consulting firm has created a number of corporate universities. There is no one formula for success—except to design the learning opportunities to respond to the needs of the organization and its people . . . both learning needs and the time available to learn in a classroom setting. If you don't have enough people in your company or in a particular location to justify mutli-session, multi-topic education, look into creating a consortium of companies in your area.

Together you can accomplish what none of you can do alone. Look to trade associations, local schools, and professional contract trainers to help with instruction.

Our experience shows that the greatest success comes when you have the senior people of your company on your faculty. Their involvement builds their commitment to the corporate university concept . . . and to the support of the application of the knowledge gained throughout the company. Even just teaching one course once in a while will help your top executives keep in touch with operational concerns and corporate community issues.

A good resource to learn more about what's happening in this field is Corporate University Review, published by Enterprise Communications in McLean, Virginia. Call 703-448-0336.

Strategy 4.18

Initiate an exchange program.

Your valued workers can learn quite a bit working with your company. They can learn some different things in another company's environment—visiting, observing, even working for the other company. And you and your people could learn things from someone employed by another company who came to work with you for a while. This sharing and learning can result from an exchange program.

With your trade association contacts, you may develop a friendship with your counterparts in another company in your field located in another part of the country. Through this relationship, arrange for one of your employees to spend some time at the other facility. You'll incur some travel costs, but this investment in learning will probably be very worthwhile. There are many factors that would influence how long your employee should be at the other location, but a week is often a good time frame. After your employee has learned and returned, invite that employee's counterpart—or another member of the other company's team—to come visit you.

There are probably enough firms in your field that you could arrange annual exchanges with a number of different non-competing companies throughout the country . . . and maybe even in other countries. Don't overlook the learnings that will come from doing visits or exchanges with companies that are in other fields. Imagine what *you* could achieve through familiarization visits or exchanges with customers and suppliers.

Strategy 4.19

Provide cross-training and cross-experience.

There are countless ways for people to learn new skills, strengthen old ones, and practice and polish their abilities in the work environment. Give your employees special assignments, cross-training and experience, and other opportunities to gain new knowledge and capacities. Enable them to experiment, to get their feet wet with something new.

Train people to perform a number of jobs within the company. The jobs can be similar or related, or totally different from what the employees normally do. Participating workers will build their skills and their value to the employer, while gaining deeper insights into the kinds of work other people do. Career building is a positive benefit, of course, but so is the greater understanding and appreciation that results from learning how others do their jobs.

Don't stop with the training; give learners some actual experience performing the new jobs. The actual performance of the work will give employees a greater sense of confidence about really being able to function effectively in more than one job. This increased proficiency builds career security for the worker. The company gains from having greater flexibility in job assignment, back-up when someone is ill (or has left the company), as well as having greater capability if the workload is heavier in a particular job category. If you want to engage in some reorganization of your corporate structure, you'll have more multi-talented people to assign to newly created or newly designed positions.

Strategy 4.20

Conduct personal assessments.

A valuable experience in personal and professional growth is to gain focused, practical, and insightful feedback about perceived behavior, leadership style, organizational effectiveness, and learning opportunities. This information is gathered for employees through assessments. Such evaluations of aptitude, attitude, effectiveness, strengths, and weaknesses can be performed in the company setting and/or off-site. Some of the survival courses, ropes courses, retreats, and external learning environments can include this input for your people.

Behavior style assessments are very valuable in helping people understand how they interact with others. They can learn what kind of environments are most motivational for them, so they can create the optimal conditions for high achievement and satisfaction. As people get to know themselves better and discover ways to fully self-actualize with your company, there's a greater potential for them to stay with you.

In recent years, more attention has been given to the process of 360 assessments. In this process, the individual being evaluated completes a questionnaire indicating how he feels he's doing. The same form is completed by his superior, several peers, and several subordinates. The report that accumulates the responses gives the individual a tremendous amount of information about style, effectiveness, and opportunities for improvement. Done in a positive way, this sort of assessment opens doors for wonderful growth.

There are a number of evaluative instruments on the market. We use one with our clients that gathers input on two dimensions: how the individual is seen to function today and, in the opinion of the respondent, how the individual should function. Comparing the two types of answers with a process known as "gap analysis," we're able to see the difference between how the individual is operating today and how others would like to see him operate. Action plans can be developed in this process, putting ideas and opportunities into concrete steps for improvement.

Strategy 4.21

Engage in organization-wide succession planning.

When companies talk about succession planning, their scope is usually limited to the top tiers of the organization. In today's volatile labor market, where people can—and do—leave their jobs in all levels of the company, a deeper scope of succession planning makes sense.

You should designate at least one candidate for succession to every position—from Chief Executive Officer to front-line supervisor. Some employees may be possible successors eligible to move into several different positions. Emphasize your preference to promote from within, but state clearly that you'll extend your search outside the company if suitable internal candidates can not be moved into the new position.

Establish a requirement that employees can not move into another position unless there is a qualified successor ready to move into the position that would be vacated. This qualification makes it imperative that all employees prepare their successors. This preparation may include company-provided training, outside education, shadowing, actual experience, and open-book briefings that assure that all #2 and #3 people in various departments know what's happening.

Strategy 4.22

Arrange for external growth experiences.

In your community are all sorts of opportunities for people to gain enriching experiences in leadership. Support your people—at all levels and in all kinds of jobs—to become more active in community organizations.

There is much to be learned sitting on the board of directors of a not-for-profit organization. Serving as a loaned executive for a period of time can be a fascinating learning experience. Elected public officials, such as state and local legislators, gain invaluable insights into how our self-governing society operates. There are plenty of positions available on boards and commissions in local government. Volunteer organizations always need people and supporting teachers in schools can be a rewarding and eye-opening experience.

Your people can acquire or polish their skills in negotiations, management of subordinates who don't have to do what you tell them to do, research into emerging ideas, interaction with people who zealously represent emotional positions on issues, problem-solving, creative design of new solutions, and operating with limited resources.

Support your people to gain this special kind of learning by giving them time to participate in these activities. Discuss with them on a regular basis what they're learning from their experiences . . . and how those learnings help them do a better job for their employers. Support them with funds, as necessary, and allow reasonable use of photocopy machines and other company resources.

Strategy 4.23

Sponsor internships.

College and university students are eager for opportunities to learn in real-world environments. Their active involvement with your company reinforces your dedication to learning. A side benefit is that your employees will supervise those interns, learning themselves from the mentoring experience. The interns, being current with the latest teachings in their fields, will probably help your people learn some things they didn't know.

To invite interns into your company, contact the colleges and universities in your community. Many of them will have an internship office specifically charged with finding and coordinating internships for the school. If there is no separate office, contact the head of the department that specializes in the field of interest for which you seek an intern. For instance, the chairman of the business department or marketing department, depending on the size of the school, could arrange for a marketing intern to work with your company.

Most internships will be for a semester, although some may have a longer or shorter duration. Much depends on the student's needs and interests. The students usually get paid for their work with your company—the people at the school can give you an idea of the range of pay you could offer. There are, however, still a number of interns who will work at no charge for the experience and contacts. In many cases, these "free" interns will work with you as part of their curriculum requirements . . . actually paying tuition and fees for the opportunity to learn from an internship monitored by a professor.

You can extend this internship concept to working with high school students, as well. School systems around the country have co-op arrangements where students can take classes part of the day and then work part of the day. Their work is supervised by visits by instructors who monitor what the students are doing and what lessons are being learned.

Hiring high school or college students during the summer is another option. Assign prospective supervisors or managers to oversee the work of the students. With guidance from an experienced manager, these young employees can practice their leadership skills as they work with the co-op students and interns.

Strategy 4.24

Take advantage of Internet learning.

The increasing use of the internet for educational purposes will open more and more opportunities for training and education. Electronic universities offer degrees on-line. Research can be done with a greater depth, breadth, and speed than ever before.

Arrange for your employees to access the internet for learning purposes. Structured courses will be available and the World Wide Web will offer a broad range of unstructured learning opportunities. With the right kind of support, your employees could—with help from superiors—design and implement a independent self-learning program. The knowledge gained will enable the employees to take initiative for their own growth.

Remember that the key to attracting and keeping good people through personal and professional growth is to support every employee on a path of continuous growth and development.

10

Compensation Strategies

One reason people leave one employer to join another is to gain improved income and/or benefits. This motivation has existed for generations and will continue to be an influence. However, research indicates that the desire for increased compensation has become less of a motivator, in favor of other factors that are more meaningful for workers.

Money will always be a motivator. Few people want to earn less money. Everyone can always use more money, regardless of how much is earned already.

Working people at all levels of achievement and experience want to have something to show in return for their investment of time, talent, thought, and energy. People want money to spend, money to save, and the security and comfort of a reasonably strong benefit program. A large proportion of American workers has become more conscious of conspicuous consumption—showing achievement through the acquisition and display of material wealth.

Some of us equate "more" with "better," focusing on the quantity of compensation, rather than the quality of the position we hold or the work we perform. Compensation is the overriding issue for fewer and fewer people. Many workers are more concerned about being fairly and reasonably compensated while enjoying a positive work environment and a sense of satisfaction from getting things done.

Some people look at compensation from a competitive perspective. The level of wages, salary, commission, and bonuses becomes a measure of personal achievement. The comparisons may be sibling-sibling, neighbor-neighbor, employee-employee, or a variety of other relationships. Some even compare today's compensation package against what was received last year or in a previous job. It's important to be sensitive to how people feel about the competition/comparison issue and enable them to hold their own in the race.

Financial compensation is emphasized by many workers because it is their only means of recognition. Too often the cash in the paychecks is the only thanks for all their hard work. If people get no other feedback, the amount of money they earn becomes the only measure of their value and level of appreciation from their employers.

With varying tax treatment of differing methods of receiving income, cafeteria benefit programs, and a wide range of combinations of compensation elements, employers have a great deal of flexibility. The costs are still there, but today there are more ways to create compensation packages that are practically custom-tailored to the needs of individual employees.

The key to success in this arena is to assure that the ways you put things together are both legal and fair to all concerned. Most importantly, from the perspective of keeping good people, is that the arrangements be good for the employees . . . *in their perceptions.*

Change

The field of compensation is changing, some would say, rapidly. Flexible financial packages, combined with creative benefit offerings, are heavily influenced by an ever-changing tax structure. What works today may not even be legal tomorrow . . . and what's not legal today may be tomorrow's new compensation idea. Today, we need compensation specialists to stay on top of the situation. It's a real challenge for generalists to keep up with all the changes and their ramifications.

Because of the speed and complexity with which the compensation arena is changing, we will not deal in depth with specific plans and options. While we can talk in general about deferred compensation, salary/bonus ratios, and other approaches, it would be a disservice to our readers to be definitive about compensation issues. What follows in this chapter should not be construed as financial or legal advice. Use these ideas as a foundation for conversation with your advisors to determine what's best for your company.

In addition, although compensation is important, the thrust of this book is in a different direction. The philosophy of ***Keeping Good People*** is that if the non-monetary strategies are employed, there will be much less need for emphasis on the compensation area. And, if all employers do is throw money at their people, they'll soon hear "you can't pay me enough to stay here!"

The wise approach to follow in compensation management is to work with professional advisors who stay current with this complicated field. Your accountant, benefits broker, compensation consultant, and attorney will be helpful.

Strategy 5.1

Present the full value of compensation.

Show your employees the full value of their compensation package. Most employees do not really understand the full costs of the monetary and non-monetary rewards they receive for their work. Enlightened employers now provide their employees with detailed information explaining the value of the employers' benefit programs—and make sure the workers grasp the information.

A typical technique is to list all the benefits available to the employee. Next to each one, show its equivalent dollar value on an annual basis. For example, if you provide health insurance coverage, paying all or part of the cost of this benefit, show the dollar amount you contribute each year. For sick leave, show the amount of money you would have paid for the days available if the benefit were fully used.

Be sure to show the dollar value of your contributions to government-mandated programs such as Social Security, Workers Compensation, and Unemployment Insurance. These vary from state to state, so be sure to adjust your figures to account for differences affecting employees in various locales.

Some companies showing their employees the cost breakdown even go so far as to include administrative costs for processing health insurance claims. The rationale is that employees would have to perform this task themselves (at a time-dollar cost) if individually insured. There are obviously many ways of computing value.

This individualized report can be presented annually, distributed to all employees at one time. Another approach is to prepare the report on each employee's anniversary date of employment. It can be given to the employee by a supervisor, human resources professional, or senior executive. Use your imagination to see how this process can be facilitated most effectively in your unique organization.

Strategy 5.2

Pay for performance.

Linking pay with performance has long been an objective of compensation plans, but by and large, it has not been well executed. One of the main reasons that "performance-based" plans have failed is that the expectations of employers and employees have not been well matched, measured, or managed. To avoid problems with performance-based reward systems, whether they are incentive- or merit-based, a few sound ground rules should be followed:

- keep the plan simple
- develop realistic objectives that can be legitimately measured
- define the level of *expected* performance for each objective
- develop a performance array, i.e., what is unacceptable performance, what is expected, and what constitutes outstanding or exceptional performance
- get employee "buy-in" or ownership with each objective to insure commitment
- focus on key issues which truly impact operations, the employees, and the company (usually three to four objectives are sufficient)
- thoroughly communicate the reward system to employees, describing how it is calculated and how they can impact the outcome of their rewards.
- ensure a positive correlation between level of performance or result and level of reward (a $25 gift certificate for a $250,000 result is incongruent).

Approaching performance pay design with this methodology will insure that there are no reward surprises and that rewards are equitable and motivational. Those employees who don't receive higher levels of compensation will do so by choice, since the qualifications are abundantly clear.

Strategy 5.3

Provide linking incentive opportunities to all employees.

Intensifying competition dictates that employees fully understand the roles of their jobs and how these roles affect the success of the organization. One method of focusing the attention of all employees on maximizing their performance levels is through providing incentive opportunities—at all levels of the organization and in all jobs, commensurate with the employees' levels of responsibility or contribution.

Typically, incentive plans will be of different design or emphasis for various levels and job functions in the organization. Some recognition should be based on the achievement of key strategies. Other should be based on productivity or task accomplishment as appropriate.

Rewards should be based on measured results that have been communicated to employees and understood by them. Incentive plans should be designed in such a manner that the incremental reward opportunities link together and are logical, equitable, and challenging. Provide outstanding total compensation for outstanding performance.

Designing incentive plans on a universal basis insures that no segment of the organization is ignored and that all employees feel part of the team.

Strategy 5.4

Leverage the total cash compensation package for maximum effectiveness.

Establishing the basic components of total cash compensation, and the relationship between them is a critical element to the success of any performance-based compensation program, whether that program is intended to be for executives, salespeople, staff, or hourly workers. The two key components, base salary and incentive opportunity, must be set in proper relationship for maximum performance and cost effectiveness.

Base salary levels should be established on the basis of competitive labor market conditions, industry comparisons, internal equity, ability to pay, control of fixed labor costs, and the extent to which incentive opportunities are available.

In some cases an employer will provide only a "living wage" for base salary, but provide an opportunity for a very high level of total cash compensation through incentives. This strategy may be a function of the industry in which the company operates; the way operations are structured, the level of profit margins produced, the amount of labor available, the ratio of material costs to labor, or the degree to which the organization's pay philosophy impacts employee earnings.

In other cases, the employer will provide a higher ratio of base salary to incentive opportunity. This higher ratio is more appropriate where the labor force is tight, the product and market more mature, or the margins higher.

Incentive compensation's pay focus today and for the foreseeable future will be on reducing or containing fixed labor costs, while encouraging retention. For the employee, this focus means reduced opportunity for guaranteed increased earnings, but greater opportunity for self-driven income increases based on performance. For the employer, this focus means a better control of payroll costs, a paramount issue in our turbulent times. The solution to this dilemma is performance-driven incentive opportunities. Both employer and employee win.

The establishment of the level of available incentive opportunity (leveraging) is critical. If the employees are to accept a reduced level of base salary, then the incentive must be perceived as a sound, achievable opportunity. It must be seen not only as a replacement for higher base salary, but as a real opportunity for substantially greater total compensation as performance objectives are achieved. Without the proper leveraging, the motivational intent and potential effectiveness is lost.

The level of incentive opportunity should be based upon at least the following factors:

1. Age of company (i.e., new, highly leveraged companies in start-up mode may wish a ratio of lower base, higher incentive)
2. Competition
3. Industry practice
4. Motivational stretch required
5. Organizational culture
6. Pay philosophy.

Again, a caution: Developing a performance-based pay program is not as simple as it seems on the surface. You'll be wise to work with compensation professionals to analyze the best approach for your company.

Strategy 5.5

Design reward systems to stimulate employee involvement.

Competition, mergers and acquisitions, cost reduction, organizational structuring, technology, and work methods have made it imperative that organizations rethink how they utilize their employees. These imperatives, when directly faced, demand workforces that are more flexible, responsive, productive, knowledgeable, efficient, and more able to deal with and solve problems at their own work level . . . without a lot of hand-holding from upper management.

As a result, more and more employers are approaching this dynamic with strong emphasis on employee involvement (EI), self-directed work teams, and matrix organizations. For many companies these changes mean not only cultural and organizational shock, but substantial changes in their pay schemes to address the new work methods and to retain employees who have become more valuable as a result of these methods.

Group incentives most effectively address the employee involvement concept and will emerge as a significant component of compensation. Group incentives basically fall into two categories: profit sharing and gainsharing.

Although profit sharing has been around for a number of years its popularity and effectiveness as a compensation tool is growing rapidly. The concept is simple, its measures are understandable, and it is popular with employees from the standpoint of motivation and retention. Profit sharing plans can be of an immediate cash type or can take the form of a deferral program which has tax advantages for the employee and can be used as a retirement supplement. Whether the plans are of a cash or deferred type, the mechanics operate in a similar way. (Note: these thought-provoking ideas are not the only ways profit-sharing can be done. These approaches are shared to stimulate your thinking, not be inclusive.)

First, before the plan begins to operate, a threshold amount of profit must be achieved, or specific profit reserves achieved. Next, a set percentage of profits is "banked" or set aside to generate the profit sharing fund. At the end of the performance period, the fund is distributed to employees either directly in cash as a fixed or escalating percentage of base salary or deferred into an employee's account.

If the plan is a deferred type, it may allow for employee deposits as well on a pre-tax and/or after-tax basis. The deferred assets are normally invested in one or multiple funds such as diversified funds, guaranteed interest funds, bond funds, company stock funds, real estate funds, or life insurance for participants.

Cash plans, which may have a shorter life than deferral plans, can be designed to pay off as the company meets certain profit objectives on a quarterly, semi-annual or annual basis. These plans may have formulas or certain individual performance criteria as elements which help determine individual profit sharing awards.

The idea behind the profit sharing concept is that all employees have a hand in helping the organization and should be rewarded in direct relationship with how profitable (or unprofitable) the organization is. In reality, most employees have little influence on the overall profitability of the company.

Gainsharing plans are increasing in their popularity as a means for rewarding employee groups or employee involvement. Gainsharing plans, profit sharing plans, and all their variations fall under the category of nontraditional reward systems. Gainsharing, broadly defined, is any corporate or unit-wide pay plan or system designed for rewarding all participants for improved performance. "Gains," or measured real-dollar earnings, are shared with all employees in the work unit according to set formula(s).

In the past, incentive plans have focused on specific segments of the work force. Gainsharing, however, is often based on involving all employees in the unit under the plan. The most prevalent reasons for implementing a gainsharing plan are to improve productivity, improve quality, reduce costs and improve employee relations.

Recent experience with gainsharing plans has indicated that, in order for them to work most effectively, employee involvement and information sharing are critical. The most prevalent type of payment under gainsharing plans is cash in the form of a separate check. Other organizations include the gainsharing payment in the basic earnings, while still others defer the amount. The separate check serves to emphasize how much the employee earned in addition to the regular paycheck.

As a strategy for keeping good people, gainsharing is an excellent choice, providing the organization's culture promotes employee participation. All employees have a higher stake in the organization and its drive for success. There is a heightened employee commitment to achieving that success and a managed expectation regarding eventual reward. The majority of gain-sharing plans today are customized to the company.

Strategy 5.6

Compensate high potential/low skill employees with a skills-based system.

One of the dilemmas we will face during the balance of 1990s and through the first decade of the 21st century is the scarcity of skilled workers. This situation dictates that companies will have to seek out those people entering the workforce who have high potential, even though they have no demonstrated skills. Once companies have identified and hired workers of this type, they must immediately begin the process of training them in the work ethic and then building their skills.

The compensation strategy must yield more than just a paycheck. It must yield an understanding of the relationship between performance and reward, then stress the element of reward and how it can grow in relationship to the accumulation of skills and abilities. This type of goal in a compensation strategy suggests that some form of skill-based pay or competency-based pay will be effective. This kind of program recognizes both the issues of quantity/quality and the improvement of skill levels, while at the same time lending itself as a basis for participation in incentives as the skill base grows.

Skill-based pay systems work best in participative environments and have their roots in the thought that the more employees know about their work, the more productive and valuable they are. Therefore, the greater the accumulation of skills workers have, the more they should be paid. Obviously the per-capita earnings under this pay system are high, but are offset by high productivity, high quality, and worker flexibility. Translating this type of system to employees who need skill building presents some definite advantages:

1. There is an opportunity to learn, be productive, and be paid for it.

2. The list of skills to be acquired is clear with a direct link between skills acquired and pay.
3. Employees understand what they must do to acquire new skills.
4. Role models and training are available in the workplace.
5. Once a particular set of skills is acquired and the learning process and work ethic established, employees can acquire new skills and move through the organization more quickly.

Skill-based pay programs are now being tried in office settings as well as on the factory floor. They should prove valuable to attract, train and retain high potential, low-skill employees.

Some compensation consultants argue against using this skill-based pay approach. Their arguments include that this approach is one of the most complicated, expensive, and unsuccessful compensation options. Tread carefully, but consider how it might work in your environment.

Strategy 5.7

Use flexible benefits to respond to a changing workforce.

The change in the composition of our workforce and escalating employee benefit costs has caused employers to take a serious and critical look at the type of benefits they provide, how they provide them, and how the costs for these benefits can be better controlled. Companies generally spend in excess of 40 percent of payroll on employee benefits (including statutory benefits), with health care expenditures comprising a significant portion of recent growth in benefit expenses.

Thirty years ago, benefit plans were designed to meet the needs of the "typical employee" –a man with a wife and children at home. These benefit packages usually included a retirement plan, medical, disability and life insurance, and perhaps some ancillary benefits.

Today, however, that once-typical employee comprises less than 10 percent of the workforce. The remainder is composed of working couples, with or without children at home, and singles, some with children. At the same time, there is a much higher percentage of females in the workforce. Each of these "non-traditional" employees and family units has different benefit needs.

These lifestyle changes during recent decades have caused employers to reevaluate the need for certain traditional benefits, as well as consider what other benefits might be appropriate. Traditional benefit packages often do not meet the needs of the majority of employees. Working couples may have duplicate medical insurance, but lack desired coverage for child care. Single employees may have life insurance they do not need or appreciate, but lack disability income protection they wish they had.

Recent data indicates that only slightly more than half of all employees feel positive about their total benefit packages. This dissatisfaction is a continuation of a downward trend that began during the late 1980s. Much of this drop is due to the fact that many benefit packages have not kept pace with the myriad demographic changes and resulting shifts in benefit needs.

Although most companies have incorporated cost containment provisions into their benefit programs, and the percentage of companies requiring employee contributions to some of their benefits has risen dramatically, these changes have not achieved significant improvement in cost control.

Cost containment has become a major issue for employers as costs of benefits, which they have committed to provide their employees, have risen higher and higher. Some companies have reacted to the increasing benefit charges by reducing benefits; some start-up companies are simply not offering them. A 1998 study by Dun & Bradstreet (first quarter

1998 Small Business Hot Topics Research Report on employee issues) revealed some startling information. Only 19 percent of the firms surveyed offer retirement benefits, down from 28 percent in 1996. Only half provide paid vacations for full-time employees, 46 percent pay for holidays, and just 36 percent pay for sick days.

Even with these somewhat surprising numbers, the survey results indicate that small business employees remain highly motivated. Sixty-nine percent of business owners gauge employees' motivation by their willingness to work overtime, improve job skills, and enhance job performance. Sixty-three percent of owners surveyed said their workers do more than expected and want to move up in the company.

The companies surveyed are small businesses (1–100 employees), representing a large proportion of all businesses. The vast majority of American workers are employed by small business.

Employers are faced with the dual dilemma of wanting to offer the right mix of benefits to attract the workers they want and reward them appropriately while controlling the costs that can spin out of control. For many companies, the solution is giving employees options from which they can design their own benefit package.

This approach puts the employer in a position to control spending. As benefit costs increase from year to year, the employer can decide what portion, if any, of the *added* cost will be absorbed by the company and what portion will be paid by the employees (usually on a before-tax basis).

In addition to medium-sized and large companies, employers with fewer than 100 employees can now successfully design and implement a flexible benefits program. While a flexible benefits program may not be suitable in every environment, employers can ask themselves some important questions to help make the right benefits decision for their company:

1. Does the company's benefit package provide coverage that some employees do not need or want?
2. Would some employees would rather have other benefit coverage?
3. Do employees really understand the current benefits plan? How would they rank their benefits compared to those of other companies? Compared to what they want and need?
4. Is the current benefit package a plus in recruiting and maintaining good employees?
5. Is the company interested in containing and managing benefit costs?
6. Does the company believe it is getting the most value for the dollars spent for benefits?
7. Would the company be willing to commit to an aggressive communications effort to inform employees about a new program?
8. Is the company willing to explore new ground in the benefits area and be a leader among its competitors?

These and other questions should be examined by every organization making an effort to integrate management's objectives with employee needs and desires.

Flexible compensation programs are spreading fast. There are indicators that more and more employers are either considering or in the process of implementing flexible benefit plans. Indeed, a trend is in motion. Besides being an expression of reward and appreciation for your employees, benefits can be used as a means to attract and hold good people. How competitive is your package? Flexibility in offerings can be a competitive advantage.

The changing demographics of the workforce in the years ahead will require a more flexible strategy and approach to employee benefits if this form of compensation is to be meaningful to both employer and employee.

Strategy 5.8

Consider ESOPs and employee stock ownership.

Having some ownership in the enterprise for which one works is a compensation feature which fosters strong interest in the organization's success and growth, as well as commitment on the part of the worker to help it happen. Employee stock ownership plans (ESOP) were introduced to enable employees to acquire an equity interest in the employer organization, while at the same time providing them with a source of retirement income. As a compensation feature, ESOPs really have a double benefit. They provide a source of accumulating retirement funds with tax deferral advantages, and an opportunity to share in the company's growth and success.

From an employer's standpoint, there are also a number of positive aspects to ESOPs. These include tax incentives, improved employee morale, better employer-employee relations, and improved productivity.

There can, however, be negative perceptions of ESOPs including employees perhaps not wanting a substantial portion of their retirement income tied to the company's performance. ESOPs are complex and sometimes difficult for employees to understand and trust.

ESOPs may not have the investment diversity of a qualified, defined contribution retirement plan. ESOPs can provide compelling reasons for employees to remain with a company. An analysis of a number of factors should be conducted before a decision is made to implement such a plan:

1. What is the employer-employee relations climate?
2. What are the short- and long-range business prospects?
3. What is the impact on financial considerations such as cash flow, earnings per share, and the balance sheet?

In view of all the considerations, it is extremely important that the company conduct a feasibility study before making the ESOP decision.

Strategy 5.9

Offer stock options.

The stock option benefit has been featured increasingly in the news media recently. Once a benefit available only to high-level executives, it is now offered to all employees in some companies. This benefit offers the employee an opportunity purchase company stock at a reduced price. This advantage effectively gives the employee a bonus without the company having to take cash out of its bank accounts.

The perceived value of the stock options will be influenced by employees' feelings about the value of the company's stock—to them and to others—and the money they have on hand to purchase it. Public companies will be in a much different position than privately-hold organizations. Talk with your attorney about related approaches, such as "phantom stock" and gifts of company stock.

Employees who own stock in their company generally have a different sense of loyalty toward the employer . . . and, indeed, that's a motivation to provide such a benefit. One hopes that owning stock in the company will be an incentive for the employee to be more dedicated—in performance and in longevity. This expectation may be overly optimistic, however, since employees can hold or sell their stock and still move on to other employment. Restrictions on the options may be designed to counter this departure tendency, but may also dilute the perceived value of the benefit.

Strategy 5.10

Offer creative benefits.

Many employers are experimenting with tangible and intangible benefits that go far beyond the traditional hospitalization and major medical insurance. Being able to bring your pet to work is an important benefit for some employees. A company in North Carolina has a handyman who provides service for workers at their homes—for the cost of materials only. A company in California pays for employees' lunches on payday . . . and the day before payday. The same company gives workers a day off on the day *after* their birthdays. How about a bonus for bicycling, skateboarding, or walking to work?

Talk with your employees. Engage in some fun out-of-the-box thinking. Create benefits that make sense for your people, for your organization, for your culture.

Strategy 5.11

Consider sabbatical leaves.

Colleges and universities have been offering sabbaticals for years. Now the practice has entered the business world. There are several ways to design sabbaticals, ranging from totally non-paid (take some time off, then come back to us) to fully funded with the employee's salary and benefits continuing at 100 percent during the sabbatical period.

If you really want to be generous, you could even go beyond the 100 percent level by paying for the costs of the employee's travel and at least part of the cost of taking the family along. This seemingly outrageous approach might make sense if you mixed the employee's time off with some time invested in research along the way—checking out competitors, visiting other company facilities, looking at new product ideas or technology, or exploring new markets.

The length of a sabbatical can also vary. This time away from work could last from a few weeks to as much as a year. Anecdotally, we're hearing terms typically ranging from a month to about four months as an average.

Strategy 5.12

Explore non-financial compensation.

When we think of compensation, we usually think of money. There are other ways to recognize and reward performance, particularly performance that is above and beyond the level for which people are paid in cash.

For special behavior or exceptional performance, consider non-financial compensation using tangible and non-tangible rewards. Here are some possibilities.

- Tickets to movie theaters. Don't just give one ticket; give two or four. Going to the movies is usually a social event, not a solitary experience in our society.
- Tickets to sporting events.
- Time off with pay. Or even time off without pay, depending on your industry and how people are typically compensated.
- Flowers, delivered to the workplace or to the employee's home.
- Letters of commendation for jobs well done, with copies to the employee's personnel file and to the employee's family.
- Picnics for employees and their families.
- Turkeys or hams at holiday times . . . or at other times of the year.
- Thank-you cards placed at the employee's work station. Even a hand-written note on a Post-It stuck to a computer is appreciated
- Candy bars.
- Articles of clothing (like ball caps or gym bags) with your company logo. Some companies use logo key rings, pens, coasters, or similar premiums.
- Certificates or plaques. Or a variation on this one, an inscribed item like a pen holder or paperweight that can be placed on the desk.
- Ice cream delivered to work stations as a surprise on a hot day. (Our employees get surprises like warm homemade apple pie every once in a while.)
- Special parking spaces or rides to work. A company in Virginia recognizes long-term employees with a ride to

work on their anniversary date—in a chauffeur-driven limousine hosted by the Chief Executive Officer.

- Visits to a beauty shop or a spa.
- Subscriptions to work-related magazines and memberships in professional societies. Some companies provide this support as part of their employee growth programs. Being able to join with colleagues from other companies—locally and at state or national conventions—with time-off support and funding from their employers is a significant benefit for many employees.
- Long distance telephone privileges. A company in Ohio gives its part-time telemarketers permission to make one 10-minute call anywhere in the country each day.
- Oil change and lubrication of the employees' cars. We fill our employees' gas tanks the day before they leave on a vacation trip.
- Just saying "thank you." You'd be surprised how many people just want their bosses to say "thank you" once in a while!

Strategy 5.13

Offer retirement plans or employer-paid pension.

This benefit has been around for a while. In larger companies it's considered as an expected part of the compensation. Support for retirement planning and funding is shifting toward plans recognized under Section 401 (k) of the Internal Revenue Code. These plans are more portable, so workers can take the benefits (and their own contributions) along with them when they change companies . . . presuming they are vested in the program. This feature appeals to people who expect to move, at least a few times, from one employer to another, rather than staying with one employer for their entire career—which is most of today's workers.

Consider the best approach for your workers. Explore the possibilities of designing similar programs, funded by contributions from both you and your employees, that permit earlier withdrawals to fund employee-initiated sabbaticals . . . perhaps between jobs. (As a Strategic Business Futurist, I forecast that more people will want to take some serious time off between jobs—after they've been working for a while—just to take a break. I describe this deliberate career interlude as a "mid-career" retirement.) There may be significantly more interest in options for using the accumulated funds to finance breaks during employment than to support a no-work retirement option in later years.

Strategy 5.14

Provide an employee assistance program.

The everyday challenges of life sometimes become overwhelming. An employee assistance program (EAP) offers counseling through the rough stages, provided by trained professionals working for firms that serve employers as outside contractors. Included in their services are counseling for drug abuse, stress, family problems, emotional difficulties, and smoking cessation.

Even if they're trained, it is not recommended that employees of your company—managers or not—provide this kind of special support for your workers. Your employee assistance program should be out-sourced, with confidentiality maintained. EAP companies usually give billing reports to their corporate clients that indicate how many hours of service were provided for how many employees, but without revealing any further details.

Strategy 5.15

Give away lottery tickets.

If your company is located in a state which operates a lottery, you can have some fun with lottery tickets. Purchase a quantity of tickets and give them as tokens of appreciation to deserving employees. If there's no value ("thank you, please try again"), the employee hasn't lost anything, has enjoyed the anticipation and a moment of fun, and knows that your heart was in the right place (near their wallet). However, employees also stand to win at least small amounts of money, if not some serious prizes.

A client in Ohio awards lottery tickets to employees who catch a mistake that might have cost the company or a client time, money, and aggravation. Another gives the tickets to employees with perfect attendance each week.

Caution: some of your employees may consider playing the lottery to be a form of gambling . . . an activity which is contrary to the teachings of their religion. You may feel that the lottery is in conflict with your company's Statement of Guiding Principles. Or, there may no problem at all. It would be wise for you to conduct a reasonable due-diligence investigation before implementing this strategy. Talk with your people; listen to their feelings.

Strategy 5.16

Provide childcare.

Childcare benefits can be provided in a number of ways. Here are some ideas.

- Subsidize the cost of childcare for eligible employees. This benefit is paid with before-tax dollars and is thus of high value to both employer and employee. Checks are often written directly to the childcare provider.
- Collect information about childcare services throughout your community and make that information available to your employees as a reference service or a referral program. Employees make their own choices, but you have given them valuable comparative data about what services are offered, how they're priced, and how they're evaluated.

- Contract for childcare services for your employees' children using one or more established service providers in your community. The company pays all or part of the cost and negotiates a special rate for its employees with the provider(s) in return for the volume of business. Everyone wins.
- Create a consortium of employers in a commercial neighborhood, like an industrial park or a retail mall area, to provide childcare for the employees of all participating employers in the area. The consortium contracts with a licensed provider to deliver the childcare service in a facility owned and operated by the provider or by the consortium.
- Develop an in-house childcare facility for the exclusive benefit of your employees. Contract with an established provider to set-up and operate the service in your building or in a nearby structure which is very convenient for your employees. Some of these operations have become so sophisticated that they offer closed-circuit television connections so employees can observe their children using the computers on their desks. Others have one-way glass for walk-by parent observation or arrangements for parent-employees to have lunch with their kids.
- Another variation is to provide the in-house service with staff paid directly by the company. This option would probably require state licensing, the extra obligation of handling trained specialists in childcare and early childhood education, and would make the employer liable for a service which could generate some highly emotional challenges regarding children. With all the challenges employers have already, it is not recommended that you select this option. Leave this one to the professionals.

Strategy 5.17

Establish a charter school.

Many states now permit employers to establish schools to educate the children of their employees. These schools, usually housed on-site or near the company's location, are funded by the employer but operate under the auspices of the local school district. Teachers and administrators are paid by the employer, who also has some influence over the curriculum.

The quality of education in charter schools is usually measurably better than that available through the public school alternative, so parents are eager to enroll their children in such a program. The extra advantage of being able to take your kids to school at the same time you're going to work is a convenience, and the system usually provides after-school care for children until their parents are ready to go home.

An exciting advantage of charter schools from the employee retention perspective is that it is a powerful motivator to hold employees. In fact, a well-known computer hardware company reports 50 percent less turnover among employees who send their children to the company's on-site school. Parents serious about their children's quality education don't want to change jobs and have to pull their kids out of the really good school. They'll stay with the employer for the benefit of their children.

Strategy 5.18

Provide childcare for sick children.

When children are sick, their parents usually want—or need—to stay home and take care of them. With this obligation, the parents are forced to miss work . . . often unexpectedly when they haven't had an opportunity to make arrangements to cover their work responsibilities. Their absence may cause a ripple effect of problems in the company as long as the child is ill.

To counter this risk, some companies offer sick child care. The usual arrangement is to contract with a hospital or clinic that is set-up to provide this kind of service. If the company has a nurse on staff as part of its safety program, it may be possible to establish a sick child service in your facility. The options are worth investigating if it's important for you to have people at work.

Strategy 5.19

Provide eldercare.

Eldercare comes under the same umbrella as childcare, except the bodies are bigger and older. An increasing number of workers will have parents or other older people in their care. These folks may not be in such condition that they must be placed in a long-term care facility, but they may also not be able to completely care for themselves while their caregivers are working. In such cases, companies that provide eldercare will have a competitive advantage in attracting and holding the employees who have the caregiver obligation.

Depending on the need, you might explore opportunities for similar arrangements to what was described for childcare in Strategy 5.16.

Note: The Family Medical Leave Act may have some relevance to this strategy and Strategy 5.18. Since laws change, it is not appropriate to explore implications of this law. When you anticipate providing (or denying) benefits that may relate to care of the family, it will be wise to ask your attorney to look into the impact of the FMLA and other similar legislation and Supreme Court rulings.

Strategy 5.20

Provide petcare.

Mention doggie day care and most people will chuckle with disbelief. Yes, it seems outlandish, but it's a very real concern for some of your employees. The demographics of pet owners are quite broad, including large families, couples, and single people. Some single people or couples have pets instead of children and tend to treat their pets as if they were children. They take their pets along when they travel, spend a lot of time with them, and are concerned about their pets when they're away at work. (I've talked with employees who prefer to work at home so they can be with their pets.)

Some companies invite their employees to bring their pets to work, with some caveats, of course. This option is not practical in all work environments.

Pet care can be offered in similar ways to childcare. Pets must be house-trained and, of course, well-behaved. There are not currently as many providers of petcare as childcare or eldercare, but the market will grow.

Believe it or not, there are also companies that offer veterinary care benefits and pet burial benefits. If you have a lot of employees with treasured pets, these ideas may not seem so far out. Their value in attracting and keeping good people certainly suggests in certain circumstances that these benefits be explored.

Strategy 5.21

Provide hospitalization and major medical insurance.

This benefit has been around for a long time, but it is still important. The Dun & Bradstreet study cited earlier in this chapter revealed that only 39 percent of small businesses even offer healthcare benefits, down from 46 percent in 1996. There are a lot of variations in the type and level of benefits that you can offer your employees. Today we have HMO, PPO, and a plethora of other initials in an alphabet soup of alternative managed care options.

In this book, particularly considering the complexity and pace of change in the healthcare benefits field, it doesn't make sense to go into more detail. If you don't have healthcare benefits expertise on your staff, consider engaging a benefits consultant to increase your understanding of the many alternatives available to you.

Strategy 5.22

Provide vision care insurance.

Eye care can be expensive, whether people wear glasses or contacts . . . or just want to have their eyes checked periodically. Employers can provide vision insurance that covers eye examinations, treatment, and prescriptions—including glasses and contact lenses.

You might also negotiate a sort of managed care arrangement with a nearby optician. Your investment may be quite reasonable, enabling you to offer another benefit for your employees . . . one that will be appreciated without costing too much. Remember employees' families, too!

Strategy 5.23

Provide dental care insurance.

Several companies, like Delta Dental, offer good dental insurance packages. Some hospitalization insurance programs offer a dental insurance coverage option. This benefit is worth investigating to support employee health and peace of mind. The incremental cost of adding dental coverage to your group health policy might be well worth the investment to differentiate your company from the competition.

Strategy 5.24

Provide life insurance.

Life insurance is usually offered as a part of group hospitalization and major medical policies. You can purchase life insurance under separate group plans and/or your insurance agent will be happy to write individual policies for your employees. You could pay the entire premium or a portion, even arranging a payroll deduction service to make the process easier for your employees.

Strategy 5.25

Provide disability insurance.

Your employees can be covered by short-term and/or long-term disability insurance. This coverage is available under a group plan or individual policies. As with the life insurance, you can share the premiums with the insureds or pay the entire cost from company funds.

For some of your valued employees, the peace of mind engendered by this coverage is priceless. They will appreciate your attention to their security.

Strategy 5.26

Provide personal time.

In many companies, employees (and supervisors) have to count how many days have been taken for sick time, vacation time, and holidays. The rules are rather rigid, and the number of days varies from company to company. In some companies, employees can take portions of days as vacation time, perhaps to go to a doctor. In other companies, time must be taken in full-day increments. If a child is sick, the employee is forced to lie (I'm not feeling well today.") in order to get a day off to stay home with the child. Many employers don't take kindly to employees who take time off to care for children or run personal errands.

To overcome the problems with the complications of how time can be taken away from work and still be paid for, enlightened employers have come up with an interesting alternative. All the days off—sick days, holidays, vacation days, mental health days are all lumped together into one package. The days off are described as "personal days." Employees can take them one at a time, multiple days together, or in portions or a day.

Under the personal day plan, employees can extend their vacation time using unused sick time. If a child is sick, the employee simply takes a personal day. When friends come in from out of town, workers may take personal days to spend time with their friends. If stress is high on a rough project and employees just want to sleep late and take a break, a half personal day will do the trick. Errands to run? Well, you get the picture.

Relieve the ethical pressure. Shift to personal days and make the whole process easier.

Strategy 5.27

Fund college educations.

A college education benefit can be viewed from three different perspectives. Each or all of these options can be incorporated into your compensation program.

The first type of employees who can benefit from a program that pays college costs is recent college or vocational school graduates. Their loans have to be paid, and the sooner the better. A company contribution to paying off at least a portion of those loans relieves great stress on young employees facing the seemingly insurmountable challenge of paying off their deferred education cost.

Employees of all ages choose to return to college to earn an initial education or to take more courses and perhaps earn additional degrees. For this group of workers, some sort of tuition payment program is a great help. One idea is for the company to pay on a sliding scale: 100 percent of all costs if the employee earns an "A." Earning a "B" grade generates reimbursement of 75 percent. If the grade is a "C," the company pays 50 percent of the costs. No payment is granted for courses in which the student earned a "D" or and "F," providing an incentive to take every course seriously.

To fully support your employee/student, agree to pay for all legitimate courses, whether or not they relate to the employee's current assignment.

A third group of employees are those workers who are looking ahead with a sense of fear and trepidation as they consider how they are going to pay the college costs for their children. For them, a tuition savings plan would make a lot of sense, especially if employee contributions are matched to any degree by the company.

Strategy 5.28

Arrange for services of professionals.

Each of us, from time to time, has a need for the services of professionals like accountants, attorneys, or even engineers. These professionals may already be on retainer to the employer or be available under a pre-determined arrangement. Their services could be made available to employees at no charge or at a discounted or subsidized fee level. This benefit, paying for the cost of preparing employees' tax forms, for instance, may be offered to a group of employees (like managers or high achievers) or to everyone.

Strategy 5.29

Serve meals on-site.

Tax laws permit deductions for some company-paid meals. Check with your accountant. Pay for employees to enjoy a free lunch on payday and/or the day before. When the paycheck runs out before the week does, that little bit of help can make a big difference. If the lunch is served to employees as a group—in a cafeteria or a buffet set-up in a conference room, for instance, eating together provides another opportunity to build the camaraderie that strengthens those all-important emotional bonds.

Pot luck meals can also provide opportunities to eat together, but may or may not work on the day before payday. Talk with your employees and see what makes sense for them. Perhaps you could host a pot luck one week a month (providing beverages and maybe other foods) and pay for everything on the other weeks. You could even have a prize each week for the most unusual dish, awarding a modest amount of much-appreciated cash for the winner of the most votes from their co-workers.

Strategy 5.30

Arrange discounts on purchases.

Does your company manufacture or distribute products or services that would be of interest and value to your employees? Why not make that merchandise available to your employees at a deep discount? Employee stores are very popular, though they are usually limited to the company's own products.

Expand the opportunity by purchasing merchandise manufactured by other companies in your community. Buy their goods on consignment at a very low price, then re-sell it to your employees at a price that is still comfortably below retail. Resist the temptation to make this benefit a profit center! Cover your costs, but don't get greedy.

Reach out to retail stores in your community. Arrange for discount coupons or recognition of a company discount card that would be carried by your employees when they shop. Look into the possibility of using merchandise catalogs in the same way. Give your employees as many opportunities as you can to purchase at a significant discount. Arrange for discounted tickets to amusement parks, sports events, and cultural programs. Employees will appreciate your arranging discounts to things they use around town—like car washes, movies, and video rentals. Offer fellow merchants whatever kind of reciprocation can. Make the arrangements as much of a win-win as you can.

Every once in a while you can offer a special deal like tickets to a community theater production, rodeo, or circus at a group discount price. Sometimes free tickets can be negotiated—a wonderful benefit for loyal employees.

Strategy 5.31

Coordinate special visits or outside events.

Ever have special people come through town? Take advantage of these opportunities whenever possible. Quite often sports figures, politicians, visiting businesspeople, touring international executives travel through communities to meet people and see what businesses are doing. Invite these people to visit your company. Your employees will appreciate the exciting and unique opportunity to meet and chat with these luminaries.

Example: One of my consulting clients was a distributor of music recordings to retail stores. Whenever a recording star would come through town on a tour, the company would arrange for a visit to the warehouse and offices. You can imagine the thrill the employees felt as they were thanked personally by all those big name-stars!

Strategy 5.32

Arrange laundry service.

All your employees have laundry to do . . . continually. If they don't wash their clothes personally, someone else in their family has to do the chore. And then there's the dry cleaning that someone has to take to the cleaners and pick-up when it's done. How can your company help relieve your employees of this routine burden?

One company we know actually bought washing machines, dryers, folding tables, and other equipment and hired some people to run an in-house laundry. Employees can bring their dirty laundry in when they come to work and take clean, folded clothes home at night. The cost to the employees is $1.00 a load.

A hotel that offers on-site dry cleaning services for guests makes the service available to employees, as well. Workers pay significantly less than they would off-site and enjoy the additional convenience of proximity.

This level of service may be out of reach for your company, but there are alternatives. Talk with the laundry and dry cleaning services in your community and see what you might be able to put together. A discounted pick-up and delivery service could enable you to provide this benefit.

Strategy 5.33

Pay for transportation or parking.

Getting back and forth to work can be a hassle. Employees who have to find spaces to park in downtown areas, often at exorbitant rates, are stressed by the time and cost factors. And driving or taking public transportation through rush hour traffic isn't an experience that most people cherish. Faced with the choice of working for a company where travel and parking will be a hassle or working in a location where the challenge is less stressful, many employees will opt for the less difficult situation. If you want to retain people with commuting issues, look for ways to reduce the problems.

How about arranging van pools? Look at modifying working hours so people can avoid the rush. Explore opportunities to rent parking spaces for your people. If people have reserved spaces to use, the stress of finding a space every day evaporates. If the company is absorbing at least part of the high cost of parking, that will inspire people to stay with you instead of moving to a work location where parking is not a problem.

Some employers are subsidizing commuting costs for their employees. (Some state and local governments offer tax incentives to employers who do so.) This benefit can be quite valuable in attracting and holding the people you want, regardless of your location. Such support might be a strategic advantage in attracting people who live in the central city to commute to work in suburban jobs at hotels, restaurants, retail stores, manufacturing plants, and other venues.

Strategy 5.34

Pay bonuses based on performance.

A strong emerging trend in compensation is to pay for performance. One interesting approach is to pay a base wage or salary that rarely, if ever, changes. In other words, pay rates no longer change with the turn of a calendar page just because another year has passed. The emphasis is placed on paying for performance, for results.

The assumption underlying this concept is that every job can be measured in some way—from a process and/or results perspective. Supervisors negotiate with employees regarding how their performance will be measured, similar to the Management by Objectives process. Bonuses, over and above base pay, are paid based on individual, team, department, or company-wide achievement. Employees all know what is expected of them, what return can be expected for various levels of performance, and when they'll be paid.

Strategy 5.35

Give spontaneous bonuses.

In addition to these pre-planned bonuses, employers can also reward individual high performers with spontaneous or "spot" bonuses. This recognition is usually in response to an employee doing a good job with a customer, showing some great results on a project, helping a fellow employee, or something else that's worthy of a special salute. The amount of the cash bonus, paid on-the-spot, is not as important as the act of giving it. (We've seen bonus amounts range from one dollar to $50. Accountants tell us that a cash payment of up to $50 is allowable without writing a check and calculating all the deductions. If you're concerned, check with your accountant to be sure.)

A nice benefit of those spot bonuses is that the employee is getting some extra cash that the family won't know about—cash that can be used for something personal, a special gift, or some other purchase that's outside the family budget.

Strategy 5.36

Award special prizes.

When people have done an exceptional job, they deserve exceptional rewards. Again, these prizes can be given to individuals or to groups . . . or, if your company is small enough, to all your employees.

If you check around for some deals, it's not difficult to put together a reasonably-priced package for a holiday trip for those special people. How about an all-expense-paid trip to the Ka'anapali Beach Hotel on Maui, described as the most Hawai'ian hotel on the islands? Or a trip to one of the European capitals? Or to a bed and breakfast in the Shenandoah Mountains of Virginia? Even a week-end at a resort that's relatively close—with reimbursement for babysitters for the kids—would be most welcome.

Let your imagination run wild with the possibilities. The ideas suggested above are often selected as incentive trips for high-performing salespeople. Other types of employees can be rewarded with similar incentive packages. Some of your employees may not be interested in this kind of reward. Be flexible. Design a prize that is responsive to the preferences of those who will benefit.

Strategy 5.37

Match donations.

College graduates receive solicitations from their alma mater to contribute money to help the school continue its work. Alumni fund raising is big business for most schools. Matching contributions from employers are encouraged and often recognized in college publications. The extra support enables employees to provide even more support for their schools, an important motivation for many grads to stay with employers that have donation matching programs.

Some of your employees may be involved with other organizations that are as deserving of your support as those colleges and universities are. You might consider matching donations your people make to non-controversial not-for-profit groups like a community parade committee, civic beautification group, Little League, Scouts, 4H, and others. With a broader policy, you will be fair to all your employees—including those who did not graduate from college but feel they should be able to enjoy the matching donation benefit.

Caution: It is wise to establish a limit of how much money will be donated in support of any one employee. This policy will maintain fairness and will also protect the company from having to pay out extraordinary large amounts in support of overzealous givers.

Strategy 5.38

Contribute time.

To encourage those employees who are motivated to contribute their hours, talent, and expertise to support community endeavors, you can give the gift of time. Arrange for the employee to take some time off, with pay, to support the civic activities. An employer in Virginia permits one of its employees to leave work early each Friday in order to get to his church in time to teach a Bible class that starts at 4:00.

You can combine the time contribution with a growth opportunity by providing interested workers on loan to United Way organizations for a set period of time. Loaned executives learn a tremendous amount from the experience, including how to lead people who don't have to take orders from you. The gentle art of persuasion is learned well as a survival skill in the non-profit sector.

Strategy 5.39

Fund fitness club memberships.

The wellness fad is significant for a lot of people. Health clubs and gyms around the country are popular and sales of fitness equipment are strong. Keeping in shape is important for many of your employees. You can recognize this personal investment—it takes a lot of time, energy, discipline, and dedication to stay fit—by subsidizing the cost of membership in a fitness facility.

To be sure of the employee's commitment, you might want to fund all or part of the second year of membership during the employee's time with your company. Arrange for the membership to be company-owned, so it can be transferred to someone else if the employee leaves your company. The membership benefit should not extend beyond the member's employment with you.

Strategy 5.40

Arrange direct deposit of paychecks.

This benefit is rather easy to arrange, and is greatly appreciated by a wide range of employees. Instead of physically presenting your employees with their paychecks each payday, you arrange for their paychecks to be deposited directly into their accounts electronically. The funds are instantly available for grocery shopping or any other need, without the time-consuming trip to the bank. Direct deposit of checks is a welcome convenience for employees who already have enough to do in their lives. A time-saving convenience like direct deposit is a real boon for working parents with child-care, carpool, and similar responsibilities that begin at almost the same moment that work ends each day.

Strategy 5.41

Pay for bereavement days.

The typical benefit in this category is to pay for 2 to 3 days away from work in the event of a the death of a member of the employee's immediate family. Included in this category are the employee's parents, children, and sometimes siblings. The benefit can be expanded, reasonably, to include grandparents. With people living longer, chances are greater that people will experience the death of grandparents or close older aunts and uncles during their working lives.

Strategy 5.42

Award use of a car.

Some workers are highly motivated by a new car . . . or use of a fancy car for a year. If your company is financially strong enough, you might be able to give away cars to high performers or employees with perfect attendance records . . . or those who meet any other criteria you want to use. No, you don't have to give a car to each one; use a lottery method to determine who gets the car. Eligible employees are entered into a drawing to select the winner(s).

Instead of a purchase, you can lease a car and award use of the car for a particular period of time. This idea is particularly exciting if the car is a sports model or other vehicle which turns heads. (I've heard of employers awarding use of expensive models or classic cars which they own, if employees achieve specified goals.)

11

Tactics for Implementing Strategies

In the pages preceding this chapter, you have read about over 195 different strategies for keeping good people. We have seen how doing things to keep good people will also keep them productive. Being productive encourages people to want to stay on the job. It's a win-win cycle.

Each of the strategies can stand alone. Each can be applied to make a positive difference in your organization. The strategies can be applied by managers at any level, in any kind of functional position.

When the strategy is applied, there will be an impact at all levels beneath the manager who implements it. In some cases, the effect will be direct and immediate. In other cases, it may be less direct and less immediate, depending on a variety of circumstances.

The quickest and most apparent results will be seen among the manager's direct reports. If nothing else is done by any other members of the management team, the impact will diminish as the implementation of the strategy moves down through the chain of command. The influence on the way the organization does business will depend on how far the implementing manager is from the front line, where the action is.

There are four ways to enhance the effect of the manager's efforts:

1. involve subordinate managers in a vertical implementation,
2. involve peer managers in a cooperative implementation,
3. involve higher level managers to increase the strength of the intervention,
4. research, plan, act.

Vertical Implementation

Making the strategies work requires concentrated, consistent effort by the implementing manager(s). The further down—and up—the chain of command you go, the more potential you have to get the results you seek.

If you are a first-line manager with direct responsibility for hourly workers or salaried employees on the firing line, you have a considerable amount of influence over the attitudes and behavior of your people. Your team is composed of the people who are the hands-on, get-the-job-done folks, who accomplish the real work of the organization.

In many companies, these front-line employees are highly sensitive to meeting the demands of the customers as well as fulfilling your expectations. Whether in a retail or service environment, in distribution, in manufacturing, or in research and development, their focus is on doing what the internal and external customers need and want.

These people are usually among the most valuable human resources in an organization, although sometimes senior management acts as though this relationship is not the case. The application of the strategies is important with these folks to keep them happy, productive, and loyal. What they do—or don't do, how they perform, and the attitudes they display, directly affect customer satisfaction . . . and thus the bottom line.

Because of their limited exposure to more senior members of your organization, front-line employees have an especially strong relationship with their supervisors. Over time, those relationships become bonds. To the employees, their supervisors *are* the company.

If the first-line supervisors perform well, implementing the strategies in a deliberate and organized fashion, members of the front-line teams will probably feel satisfied, valuable, and productive. There will be less chance of them leaving to accept other positions. They will feel a part of the company and will probably remain in their positions of comfort.

If the first-line supervisors do not perform well, do not implement the strategies well, there will be friction between management and labor. Workers will transfer their feelings about their supervisors to the company as a whole, building a dangerous animosity. Productivity will drop, and so will feelings of loyalty.

After a period of time working for supervisors who are not focused on keeping good people, employees become restless and dissatisfied, ready to jump ship at the slightest provocation. Their attitudes of disloyalty and irritation can be highly contagious, poisoning even those who had been outstanding employees prior to the development of negative feelings. They will seek out others with similar opinions, eventually blowing the difficulties out of proportion.

When you have this kind of a situation, and it may have already developed in your organization, you must apply the strategies with a higher level of intensity and dedication. Plan your actions more carefully to gradually get results.

As was brought out in Strategy 1.20, when you have a difficult situation, your best solution may be to terminate the employment of the "infected" people. This house-cleaning is always difficult to do, especially if some of the people had been good performers in the past. However, the longer you wait, the more difficult the task becomes . . . and the higher the risk of further damage. To hold your good people, sometimes you have to remove the bad ones surgically.

Be alert for any "bad apples" in your organization. They are those people who demonstrate negative attitudes and/or won't go along with the program. We're not saying that everyone has to conform and march along like toy soldiers. Nonconformity can be healthy in organizations. That's what inspires innovation and leadership. Just be sure the nonconformity is directed in positive ways, and not into activities that could have a negative impact.

If the implementing managers are at a higher level, more removed from the day-to-day action, the direct impact of strategic intervention on the front line will not be as strong. To achieve the desired results, the higher level manager must work vertically. Working down through the chain of command, the leader must persuade each lower-level manager to support the efforts to implement the strategies successfully.

If there is a missing link anywhere in the chain, the process will not have maximum effect. In fact, if there is resistance or even just apathy on the part of any manager in the vertical chain, the results could be negative. Vertical continuity is vital to convey the message throughout the organization so the leader's actions actually result in stabilizing the workforce.

I observed this phenomenon recently in a company where a senior-level manager demonstrated the approach described in this book. The first-line managers felt the same way he did, and liked what he was saying, but were virtually powerless because the middle managers didn't support the process. The middle managers were more concerned with protecting their own positions than they were with the business of the company. In reality, the first-line managers were disenfranchised in their efforts to turn the company around and make a significant positive difference.

Implementation of the strategies works best when the implementing managers, at any level, have the sincere commitment and support of their superior *and* subordinate managers.

Managers without support from their superiors may feel practically powerless in the implementation of many of the strategies. Subordinate team members need to feel that their leaders have the support of the next higher level, or the words sound empty. Without having that support from above, some managers are afraid to attempt even a small strategic effort for fear of being caught out on a limb. Others just opt out and do nothing.

This need for support goes all the way up the organization. It's not just at the operational level.

Good, worthwhile results can be seen from unilateral implementation of the strategies, but the power just isn't there. Managers at any level should apply the strategies as best they can, but everyone has to be involved to really make it work.

Powers of persuasion work well going up the organization ladder, not just down. The more successful you are in gaining the visible, involved support of your superior and his subordinate managers, the more chance you will have of making a difference as an implementing manager.

Cooperative Implementation

Department managers, or a vertical chain of managers in a particular functional area, can make a positive difference. Most organizations of any size will have a number of managers at each level. Cooperation is needed among these people.

To succeed in your efforts to keep good people, and keep them productive, your policies and their strategic implementation have to be as consistent as possible. You'll have some differences because of differences in personalities and styles of managers. The more consistent you are, the greater will be your results.

Your objective is to help the managers, in all areas of the organization, to speak with one voice. If profanity is frowned on in one part of the company and not another, for example, the "mixed signals" get confusing. People aren't sure just what the company wants.

With widely varying approaches, you may also generate an overt or unconscious competition between supervisors. Sometimes this rivalry is healthy; often it becomes counterproductive, especially for the manager whose people want to transfer to another department.

Teams of managers at each level should meet regularly to examine how they are working with their people. What "messages" are they sending by their actions, by their application of the various strategies? How are the various functions of the company working together, or not, and how can implementation of some of the strategies make a difference?

The cooperative process will be more difficult to initiate in some companies than in others. Your ease of cooperation will depend on past practices, experiences of the managers, and the way senior management handles the situation.

One way to start is simply to have a meeting of all the managers you want to cooperate. Explain the concept and your expectations. Emphasize that these people are a key team in building and maintaining the organization's strength . . . and in keeping good people. Be open to questions, resistance, and skepticism.

Introduce this book to them. It will be valuable for each member of the management team to have a personal copy of ***Keeping Good People*** for individual study and reference. Encourage them to highlight, underline, make marginal notes, and discuss strategies with each other and with you.

In subsequent meetings, discuss particular strategies you want to implement across departmental lines. Talk about how the application of each of those strategies might affect each manager and that manager's team. Strive for consensus—about the value of the strategy, the commitment to implementation, and the way it will be done. Remember consistency *is* important.

During this introductory phase, in particular, it will probably be wise to use the services of professional trainers to build a sense of "teamness" and to sharpen management and leadership skills. Unfortunately, many people in management positions, at all levels, are sadly deficient in the skills and knowledge needed to do their leadership jobs properly. In some industries there has been an increasing emphasis on management training and development, but we still have a long way to go.

Professional trainers and consultants, especially outsiders who have not been a part of your organization, can serve as facilitators of discussion in your management meetings. Sometimes, participants in such meetings will say little. Individually, they don't "buy in" to the program, so they become those counterproductive weak links.

You need to get *everyone* involved, bringing out ideas, feelings, perspectives, and reactions. The sharpened skills of experienced facilitators enable them to build the involvement and the interchange that could significantly increase your chances for success.

If you do use an outside facilitator, that person's role is to stimulate the discussion and decision making of your people. The role is *not* to determine your policy or to "force" people to go along with something if they're not comfortable with it.

Your leadership role should be responsive to, and interactive with, your facilitator. The outside professional is there strictly to help you do your job better, not to do your job for you.

Consider your people and your organization, then take the steps necessary to build commitment and consistency among peer groups of managers. As they collaborate more, you'll see positive changes among each of their work teams and in the operation as a whole.

Involve Higher-Level Managers

It should come as no big surprise that the higher you go in the organization, the greater power and impact the manager has on the behavior of people and the direction of the overall team.

To keep good people, and keep them highly productive, the leadership for this initiative needs to come from as high in the organization as possible. The higher the source of commitment, the greater will be the results.

Ideally, the chief executive officer of the company will assume an active leadership role in the confirmation and implementation of the strategies. Even if the senior person sees the strategies as "of course we should do that here," subordinate managers may not hear (or accept) the message.

You can't assume that "everyone does it" in leadership today. Too many people set their own direction or just float waiting for the next pronouncement from "On High." To build consistent implementation of these strategies, to really have the kind of organization-wide impact that builds corporate reputations, top management *must* be involved.

The involvement can not be mere lip service. Saying, "I think this stuff is all on target, so go do it," won't work. People are looking for an active commitment. They want to see that senior executive actually practicing the strategies . . . and supporting those subordinate managers who do the same.

I remember my frustration talking with the president of a manufacturing company a number of years ago. I was trying to emphasize the critical importance of using outside professional trainers and facilitators in his company. He didn't think he needed help. He viewed consultants with disdain, figuring he had all the answers.

This company president bought copies of ***In Search of Excellence***, the stimulating book by Tom Peters and Bob Waterman. The book was getting a lot of media exposure back then, not long after it had been published. He gave the book to all his managers on a Thursday morning, asking them to read it over the weekend. "We're going to start doing this Monday morning!" he exclaimed forthrightly.

The managers read the book with enthusiasm and came in Monday fired-up and ready to go forth and excel. The president praised them and encouraged them to go forth and do something. However, he explained that he was pretty busy. He would have to stay in his office to get his work done and would not be able to join them.

About a year later, the company went belly-up. The bankruptcy put the company out of business and put several hundred people out of work.

What happened, obviously, is that the bankruptcy began in the president's office. Remember that your people need active and visible leadership. You can't influence people vicariously. Leadership is shared, not delegated or assigned. When you have someone lead in your stead, you are abdicating your position.

The more the organization's leaders work together as a team, speaking with a single voice that is backed up by consistent action, the better your results will be. You'll have a more productive workforce with greater stability, satisfaction, and pride.

You'll be on the exciting cutting edge. You'll have the power to excel in a stable environment where people stay with their employer because they want to.

Research, Plan, Act

A key to keeping your good people is to understand what they want . . . and how those desires compare to what they perceive they get from employment with your firm. To conduct that research, you may want to use a survey process to assess perceptions and expectations. The knowledge you gather will enable you to move forward with the most needed strategies first.

To support this process, we designed a corporate culture assessment survey around the concepts of this book. Essentially, it allows you to begin applying what you've learned in ***Keeping Good People*** in a powerfully targeted approach. With the help of a trained professional consultant, you administer the *Best Practices Profile* questionnaire to all employees. The completed forms are computer-scored and results are usually produced within a week.

The fresh report is presented to the company's leadership team in a day-long intensive briefing. An amazing volume and quality of information and insight is shared, discussed, and interpreted. Using a gap analysis process, company leaders explore the levels of dissatisfaction and congruence to gain a clear understanding of the organization's culture as it relates to employee retention. As part of the briefing workshop, the consultant guides the management team in the development of a focused action plan to address the issues raised.

The leadership team is then charged with taking deliberate action to resolve key issues and make specific improvements—as the employees indicated in their responses—to build higher levels of workplace satisfaction. As this tool has been applied by companies in a number of fields, some needed shifts in attitudes and methods applied by managers have also been uncovered. As more people become involved in the improvement process, a productive bonding begins among all members of the company team. This approach produces long-term results that show up clearly on the bottom line.

Whether you use our instrument and process or some other approach, you will be wise to measure attitudes and beliefs to evaluate your culture. Your culture must be supportive of workforce stability or you'll be working against yourself. Keeping good people—workforce stability—is now a strategic issue. Workforce stability will be your company's competitive advantage in our turbulent environment.

12

Combining Strategic Approaches for Optimum Results

The format of this book has presented strategies in individual and, for the most part, independent sections. This design was used to call attention to each strategy as an approach unto itself and to make the book more readable and usable as a reference work.

As you implement the strategies, it is important to appreciate the interdependence of these techniques. While many of the strategies can be tactically implemented as tools by themselves, they become most effective when related to other strategies.

In fact, many of the strategies depend on other strategies being in place or being implemented concurrently. There are close linkages connecting many of the strategies that were included. It is advised that you read through all the strategies before trying to work with any of them to any great degree. Gain an appreciation for the *comprehensive* approach.

In leading people, and inspiring them to stay with you, it is helpful to appreciate the complexity of their environment, especially from your people's perspective. If you concentrate on making one aspect better, while ignoring a related aspect, you may get results that are different from what you expect.

Management gurus and evangelists urge corporate leaders to leap into making changes in structure, policy, procedures, and people. Some of these self-styled experts exhort managers with rash pronouncements like, "Don't just stand there, do something!"

I encourage you to take a different approach: *"Don't just do something, stand there."* Look before you leap. What is it that you are trying to accomplish? What strategic approaches will enable you to achieve your objectives? How can they best be implemented? By whom? When, and how quickly? What resources and support will be needed? What are the implications of what we are about to do? How will you measure your results?

Strengthening one area of your operation may weaken another. Or, your efforts may point out weak areas with to which you had previously not been sensitive. You may become aware of some vulnerabilities that you hadn't seen before.

As you deliberately apply the strategies for keeping good people, consider *all* the aspects of your organization. Try to anticipate the reaction/response of your people as you formally introduce a strategy and strive to make it work. Even when you try to gradually slip into enhancing a strategic approach, your people will have a pretty good idea what you are doing.

Don't try to sneak in with these strategies. They should be applied overtly, deliberately, with the full knowledge and solicited cooperation of everyone involved. Your efforts will be appreciated by your good people, and they will support your efforts. This support may be longer in coming than you would prefer, based on past history with the employer and present company. circumstances.

A number of the strategies presented in ***Keeping Good People*** may already be in place in your organization. Even if you believe they are part of the way you and your people do business, you should confirm the belief for yourself. Quite often, managers (especially senior managers) honestly believe that their people have certain understandings that they simply do not have.

To confirm for yourself, talk with—and listen carefully—to your subordinate managers and their people. Ask open-ended questions that will put them in the position of telling you what they think, what they believe, what they do. Comparing that input against your desired situation will give you a more realistic idea of what strategies people perceive to be operating in your corporate environment.

Once you understand the reality of your situation, you can plan the tactics you will follow to integrate the strategies into your organization. Build on the strengths you already have, gradually folding in commitment to the new strategies.

Note, please, my use of the word, *gradually*. Changes will not come as quickly as you might like or expect. The old habits have taken a long time to become part of your people, part of your culture. They won't just, *poof,* change overnight. Be happy to make a little progress each day, but strive for conscious improvement continually.

Make your improvements conscious in your own mind, and also in the minds of your direct reports and their people.

Share with others that you expect people to excel, that you expect the organization to excel.

As you implement the strategies, you will probably discover that some of them are compatible. When you have the opportunity, implement companion strategies together. One may well support another.

For example, Strategy 1.17 talks about promoting a healthy working environment. As you implement parts of Strategy 1.36 to maintain the best atmospheric conditions, you'll support a healthy working environment. Reducing stress, Strategy 2.31, might also fit right in. Some sort of a wellness program might be a sensible answer for you. Using Strategy 4.10, you may assign development of a program to one or more people (a task force?) to give them some valuable research and organization experience.

Talk with members of your management team to learn their perspectives of the various strategies and how they "fit" in your organization. Discuss where you and/or the organization are falling short, in lip service or follow-through, to see how you can improve individually and as a team.

Some of your fellow managers might be somewhat skittish about applying these strategies. People like to stay in their comfort zones, and using these strategies consistently and continually will create some discomfort . . . at least temporarily. Relate what you are trying to do in terms these people can understand and deal with. Meet people where they are; know their positions. Then, gradually, move them toward your position . . . that is, where you would like them to be.

Force yourself, and your colleagues, to always look at your people and your organization as a *system*. Everything is interrelated.

13

Focus on Individuals' Needs

Your organization is composed of individuals. A variety of individuals. Each person striving for his/her own goals . . . in work and in life. To gain the most from your people, and to inspire them to remain part of your team, it is vital that you recognize them as individuals.

As long as being a part of your organization fills their particular needs and is compatible with their values, employees will probably stay with you. Most people seek what we might describe as a "comfort zone" in their careers, where they can feel challenged, useful, productive, empowered, and appreciated. When they find jobs that have such comfort zones, they usually settle in for an indefinite period of time.

If their jobs do not include a complete and satisfactory comfort zones, if all needs and values are not met, employees will be restless. The degree of restlessness varies from person to person, based on the importance placed on fulfilling unmet aspects of the desired comfort zone.

The key, then, is to learn all you can about what motivates each individual member of your team. What are each person's personal career goals? How well can your group respond to the fulfillment of those goals, now and into the future?

What kinds of challenges does your rising star seek in the working environment? Are the desired challenges more of a project nature, or does this individual want the challenge of the increased responsibility that comes with assuming new positions of leadership? Is the interest more in narrow, task-focused challenges, or in wider position-focused arenas?

How fast does the individual want to move along the career path? Is this person a fast climber or a steady-as-you-go type? Should the path be fairly well chartered early in the employment relationship, or would this rising star prefer a less structured reactive arrangement in which career moves are determined by emerging opportunities?

Job Satisfaction

We use "job satisfaction" as an all-encompassing term to describe how people feel about their positions of employment. A number of factors enter into the measurement of job satisfaction, most of which have already been covered in this book.

Our concern at this stage must be to investigate and analyze the job satisfaction level of each individual. What factors define job satisfaction, and how does the individual worker measure them? It does not matter how *you* measure them; what matters is how *each employee* gauges his or her own personal level of job satisfaction.

The level of job satisfaction significantly influences an employee's stability with a particular employer. If the job satisfaction level is low, the roots are very shallow. They go deeper as the level increases. Setbacks are always possible; the fragile, volatile equilibrium must be monitored and maintained.

If satisfaction with most aspects of a job is high, an employee may overlook the areas that aren't as high as desired. The positive can offset the negative. If the balance starts going the other way, the negative aspects take on a new significance and the process of disequilibrium can occur very quickly.

Attention must be given, therefore, to discovering what weights the employee places on various parts of the personal job satisfaction equation. Then, take concrete steps to meet as many of those elements as possible, as *well* as possible.

Be careful you don't go overboard meeting the needs of any one employee, particularly if your support might be at the expense of others. If you don't maintain your focus on the big picture, you could easily invest more in keeping one employee happy than it is worth to keep that employee. Hard as it is to accept, especially when you are in the middle of an emotional campaign to hold an employee, everyone is replaceable.

Useful, Productive

Today's employee wants to feel useful. Each individual member of your team wants to feel a high level of productivity, that results are being achieved because of his/her personal effort.

In every way that you can, help each of your people see exactly what he/she is contributing to the accomplishment of the organization's mission. There will be a contribution, of course, because without any contribution to desired ends there would be no reason to even employ that individual. Most employees never appreciate the personal contributions they really do make. When is the last time you talked with your direct reports, those who work directly with you, about their personal contributions to your team effort?

People know when they are productive. They also know when they are not. Part of this judgment is measurable; part of it is a feeling that people have about their real value to their employer. People don't want to be parasites on society, when the opportunity is there to earn their own way.

Some of the jobs to be done in your organization might involve people waiting for what seems to be a long time for the next piece of work to be ready for their contribution. That's just the way some systems work. Appreciate that the waiting time may become agonizing, especially when others around them are productively occupied.

With your sensitivity, help those affected accept the waiting gracefully without losing esteem. These job predicaments are becoming fewer in manufacturing as a result of process reengineering, but workers in retail and service jobs spend a lot of their time just waiting for the next customer. Whenever possible, find other work for them to do so they don't get bored during the waiting time.

I remember earning part of my way through school at Hiram College in Ohio setting up and serving banquets. There was always a period in our work, after everything was set, when we weren't needed for a little while. I felt that I should be doing something, other than sitting, to earn my pay during those long stand-by moments. My supervisor and mentor at that time told me something I have never forgotten: "they also serve who only sit and wait." Help your people put things in perspective, so they'll always feel that they are serving.

Empowerment

The concept of empowering workers is relatively new, at least in its current definition and conscious position in the workplace. It's not revolutionary; there are employers who have been empowering their people for years. Empowerment is a vital aspect of today's working environment and is unquestionably important in your efforts to keep many of your good people.

Historically, during the 20th century we spent most of our management time *directing* the efforts of others. That's what managers were expected to do: tell others what to do. In carrot-and-stick fashion, if people did well what they were told to do, they were rewarded with better jobs, more money, more authority over others. If they didn't perform, they were punished with discipline, lower incomes, dead-end jobs, and diminished social status.

Moving away from the management styles of telling everyone what to do, how to do it, and when to do it, we began to emphasize enabling workers to do things on their own. Providing varying levels of support, we gave up some of the managerial control over everything employees did. The techniques of definitive reward and punishment were replaced by less obvious approaches of motivational management.

The concept of leadership wrestled with the concept of management in an often uncomfortable effort to transform the way we worked with people to get things done. The shift inspired managers to become "facilitative leaders"—facilitating the high performance of individual workers. Truly empowering people, with confidence in their capacity, enables leaders to take a quantum leap into making employees responsible and accountable for their own performance.

As people gain more real control over the way things are done and over the resources needed, a significant change takes place. Workers begin to determine *what* should be done, and in what order of priority. They're taking control of their own work. With this higher level of responsibility and accountability, there is often a deeper commitment to stay with the company. The involvement is more palpable; the sense of significance is more evident.

The message heard by empowered employees is that everything is in their hands. They have the power to do things their way, but with an even higher expectation that the objectives will be met. Much of the reward and punishment motivation from the autocratic approach now becomes intrinsic.

People want to be empowered, both as employees and personally in other aspects of their lives. This empowerment has become critically important in an age where people feel practically powerless to influence the events in the world around them. At the same time, the idea of having so much power over their own destiny is intimidating for some people. They just aren't ready to handle it. Empowering people has to be done gradually, accompanied by sufficient training and reinforcement to build confidence.

Appreciation

All of us want to be appreciated. Each person seeks that appreciation in a different form. Some merely want an affirmation, others want you to bring on the brass bands and the parade. Some folks prefer a quiet recognition, a one-on-one personal communication from a supervisor or some other significant person(s). There are those on the other extreme who want "the whole world" to know you appreciate what they do. And, of course, there are many variations in the middle of that continuum.

For maximum effectiveness, tailor your expression of appreciation to each individual employee. Learn enough about the people on your team that you can understand their preferences, then meet those personal expectations.

The two important points are: first, that you must show appreciation for work done, for knowledge gained, for skills applied, for attitudes shown. But, second, you must also show that appreciation in ways that are wholly appropriate for the individual with whom you are dealing.

If you neglect to show appreciation, or if you express your feelings in ways that are not befitting to the individual or to the situation, the negative response will be the same. Your actions must be genuine. They must be sincere. If they are not, your efforts to praise or reward someone may backfire. Always be appropriate for the specific individual in question.

You can't win 'em all

No matter how hard you try, you will not be able to keep all your good people. There are various reasons for this, some of which are completely out of your control. Put things in perspective and know that some people you would like to keep are going to leave.

Beyond the five reasons presented in Chapter 5, there are other reasons for people's departures. One is some sort of dissatisfaction with the kind of work assigned. Another reason relates to the way work is done in your organization. Some folks will leave because of their fellow employees. Others won't see the opportunities they seek working with you, and you may not be able to offer them what they want.

Still other people move on just because it's time to move on. There are those who don't want to work for any one organization for too long. Any organization. It's nothing against you, personally, or against the employing organization. It's just an inner drive to keep moving, to keep growing, to keep trying out new experiences. I lost one of the best employees I ever had, a fine woman in her early twenties, because she wanted to move to another city to improve her social life. Her work life was fine, but she wasn't getting the balance she needed in other aspects of her life.

Many of the people in today's workforce, and many of those entering the workforce, are restless by nature. Part of their value system tells them not to stay in one place for very long. "Gain some experience, then move on" is the message they hear from their inner voices—and society. They tend not to put down roots in any aspect of their lives, acting almost like modern-day nomads.

In researching this book, I talked with some of these people who were perfectly satisfied with their jobs. Their employer could do nothing more to satisfy them any further. They just needed to move on. There are new things to see and do, new horizons to be seen, new dragons to be met and conquered.

When it's time for people to leave, wish them good luck and get out of their way. Begging on bended knee for someone to stay with you is not appropriate. It is viewed with disdain by other employees, and will cloud your thinking as you search for the right person to succeed your departing star.

Know that, even though you might give them the world and promise them more, some people will leave anyway. As my friend and speaking colleague, Joe Charbonneau, is fond of saying, "Of all the people who will never leave me, I'm the only one." Be true to yourself, and everything else will work out.

You can't keep all your good people. It's unrealistic to expect to. Not only are you training and preparing them for greater opportunities, they themselves are seeking new horizons for themselves. As a balanced, mission-focused employer, you can not be all things to all employees.

Part of your role as a leader is to contribute to the development of people. Some will stay, some will go. All of them will give you something back. Enjoy those "somethings" you receive, and pass them along to the new people eager to join your team.

Enjoy working with all those wonderful individuals who comprise your unique team. Help them become more of what they are, and what they want to be.

14

Retention as a Strategic Business Issue

In today's turbulent workplace, a stable workforce is a significant competitive advantage.

If your competitors have unstable workforce conditions, they're forced to invest thousands of dollars in recruiting, orienting, training, overtime, and extra supervision. Those dollars come right off their bottom line. Without continuity, they don't have ongoing close relationships with their customers; customer loyalty is fragile. Their managers are more stressed, as are their other employees. Conflict is more likely; efficiency is hampered. Such challenges will make it more difficult for these other companies to compete with you.

Arguably, your most valuable (and volatile) asset is a stable workforce of competent, dedicated workers. Employee longevity gives you a powerful advantage. Depth of knowledge gives you strength. The priceless treasure of knowledge and experience rests within your people.

If you lose a competent employee (and it's always the good ones who leave), it will be increasingly difficult to replace that asset with someone of comparable competence. Even with an effective succession plan, you'll need to hire someone—at some level—to keep your staffing levels where they need to be. (Note: critically examine your staffing levels. You may not need so many people.)

With a tight labor market and tight competition for good people, your chances of hiring a qualified replacement are in jeopardy. Result: you are forced to hire a person with less competence. If this scenario repeats itself enough, the aggregate competence and capacity of your workforce will gradually diminish . . . along with your ability to meet customer expectations. Unhappy customers leave, and take your cash flow and profit with them.

Selecting new employees carefully, then holding on to practically everyone you hire makes good sense. Acquiring and maintaining a productive workforce is similar to acquiring tools, machinery, and buildings in an earlier era. Today, and tomorrow, people are, and will be, your company's greatest asset.

Everyone's Watching

A number of important stakeholder groups watch workforce stability and capacity carefully. Workforce strength, capacity, and dependability influence the confidence of customers, suppliers, creditors, investors, and employees.

Customers are increasingly concerned about the quality and service levels they get from their suppliers. They want to have confidence that their suppliers can perform for them, especially in situations that call for specialized knowledge, fast response, or appreciation of the customers' history with the company. If customers aren't comfortable with their vendor, it's usually very easy for them to change to a different supplier. Alternative resources are probably already seeking the business. Customer relationships are stronger when your workforce is stable and customers can depend on your people—the continuity of their product knowledge, industry experience, and proven performance. It's a comfort issue.

Suppliers are eager for new business, but not at the risk of losing their investment in goods, services, or relationships with customers. Companies are reluctant to grant credit to other businesses when they have questions about the overall strength and financial stability of the customer. Credit worthiness reviews are done more frequently during shaky times. Diminished or closed credit capacity can cripple or kill a corporate customer, especially in today's world of tight margins and cash flow challenges. Suppliers have more confidence in companies with stable workforces—people who can get the job done for their customers so their business continues to do well.

Creditors continually watch the stability and performance of their clients. Any hint of potential problems of non-payment of obligations, and creditors become very uneasy. Even if they don't tighten controls, creditors will likely monitor the situation much more closely. This oversight means that representatives of the creditor might consume a lot of your time to stay on top of their risk . . . and that's time you need to run your business more proactively. Those creditors will look closely at the stability of your workforce.

Investors are understandably very concerned about a company's capacity to perform in ways that will positively influence the value of their stock. When they detect an unstable situation, they start asking questions. If they're not comfortable, you can expect those investors to move their funds to ventures that are more stable, more strong, more likely to produce the desired return. High turnover raises red flags that warn investors to be extra cautious.

Employee morale can be seriously affected by unhappy people. Whether they leave or not, disaffected workers can damage the attitudes of other workers. Negative feelings are highly contagious and can dangerously infect an organization. Low morale affects the quantity and quality of work, absenteeism and tardiness, cooperation with supervisors, and a company's ability to attract desired applicants. Instability of the workforce, often caused by insensitive or ineffective supervisors, can cause far-reaching problems. When dedicated workers have difficulty getting their jobs done, they quite naturally look for other employment opportunities where they can achieve the satisfaction they seek from work.

Tight Labor Market: A Strategic Concern

The combination of our expanding economy, and a drop in the birth rate a generation ago, have caused a serious labor shortage throughout the country. It's actually a global problem as more good jobs go looking for fewer qualified people to fill them. This problem will continue. There's no way to "manufacture" more adults; cloning is not an accepted way to build a workforce. There is a finite supply of people coming into the workforce through traditional channels. No more are available.

To meet staffing requirements, astute employers will be deliberate about seeking to hire the caliber of people they need. Employee retention levels will depend, in part on the people who are hired, why they are hired, and how they are hired. Employers who establish firm standards for employment qualifications—and stick with them—will be much more successful.

Bringing in the right people for the right jobs is essential. Effective selection and hiring—all the interviewing, testing, and background checks—must be focused on acquiring the right people. To accomplish this task, and it's not easy, wise employers use people who have training to do this kind of work and they apply the tools to do the job right.

Assure that all who are involved in interviewing, from the human resource department to front line supervisors, is trained in conducting hiring interviews. Help them learn what questions to ask, what not to ask, and how to probe and explore conversationally. Their vital role includes evaluating the applicant and selling the opportunity at the same time. Yes, sales training is appropriate so your interviewers can help persuade qualified applicants to join you. Retention begins even before the applicants are hired. You're setting the stage for how that employee will feel about your organization.

Welcoming new employees with a thorough orientation will help assure that they will understand your company, your mission, your objectives, and their place in the organization. When they really "get" their value to the flow of work and the service to internal and external customers, you begin to build the commitment to stay for longer than a week or two. Helping them feel comfortable at this stage will avoid the quick resignations (you'd be surprised how many employees quit within the first 1 to 4 weeks).

A critical transition occurs when your new employees move from the comprehensive orientation program into relationships with their supervisors. If the supervisor doesn't clearly exemplify what the employees have just learned about the company, you have a high risk of losing your new hires. Supervisors and managers must fully comprehend everything that is said in the orientation, and why. The leadership style demonstrated in the early encounters with new employees, as well as through the continuing relationships, will influence whether the workers will stay . . . enthusiastically.

The Competitive Environment

There is no question that the labor market is tight. Just look at the unemployment rate in your community and you'll get the picture. The numbers do vary from city to city, from state to state, but not by much. Whatever the actual numbers are, it's clear from trends in employment and the labor market that job demand for qualified workers will remain high.

In this kind of operating environment, business leaders should pay close attention to trends in their fields, in their industries, in their regions, and in their communities. Watch the numbers so you have a clear understanding of your circumstances. Learn from research conducted by your trade association, by pollsters, by universities, by the government and by other organizations that monitor workforce and workplace trends. Subscribe to publications that will keep you attuned to trends and how employers are responding. See information about the *Workforce Stability Alert* newsletter in the section about The Workforce Stability Institute at the end of this book.

Survey after survey confirms that the most critical concerns for leaders of all organizations will be finding and keeping competent workers. The serious importance of this issue must be conveyed to your entire workforce, especially your front-line supervisors. Everyone should be cognizant of the vital link between your retention strategy and your business strategy. Simply put, you can't meet your business objectives without people who can get the job done.

It's a "given" that businesses compete for customers, whether they operate in the business-to-business or the business-to-consumer arena. Companies compete for customer attention, dollars, and loyalty. Astute leaders aggressively promote their company, its fine reputation, its quality, its service, its pricing policies. Frequent shopper programs reward customer loyalty. Now employers must compete similarly for workers.

For most employers, competing for workers is a new phenomenon. The balance in the number of jobs versus the number of people to fill them has only recently shifted. The labor market is now a seller's market. Employers compete for workers in their own fields and in their local communities, but this reach is rapidly expanding. Workers can—and do—switch career fields at the drop of a hint. In some of my speeches I tell the stories of a fine chef who decided to become an over-the-road truck driver, and of the CEO who gave up that life to become an airline flight attendant.

The playing field has changed. The rules have changed. To compete effectively for the workers you need, new approaches must be designed and employed. Strong leadership must come from the top of the organization. Workforce stability has suddenly become a crucial strategic issue . . . for survival as well as for growth.

The competition for good people will intensify. Employers hungry for talent to sustain and to grow will increase their recruiting—their poaching. Every good employee now has a metaphorical bull's-eye painted on his—and her—chest. The vulnerability is palpable. Loss of key people can interrupt expansion plans or special projects. Shortened tenure and severely reduced operating knowledge send productivity into free fall . . . perhaps never to recover because of the dangerous lack of people with training and institutional savvy.

The Cost of Turnover

Measuring the cost of employee turnover can be a real challenge. What costs should actually be included? Hard costs? Soft costs? Indirect costs? Do you only measure uncontrolled (voluntary) turnover, or do you also account for the replacement costs for people you have to terminate because they weren't working out? Bad hires can be expensive.

Regardless of what components you include in your calculations, it's clear that most business leaders have seriously *underestimated* the cost of turnover. As they discover the hemorrhaging on their bottom line, and realize the relationship to their top line, employers

are often astonished at how they have to drive sales just to stay afloat. Calculations by one large corporation I consulted worked with recently revealed that their turnover cost was larger than their bottom line!

The Saratoga Institute, a strong research firm in the human resources arena, says, "Losing an employee, even a lower level one, often costs the equivalent of from six months to one year's pay. Highly skilled technicians, professionals, and managers typically cost as much as twice that to replace."[1] A study by The Corporate Advisory Board[2] suggests that the cost might easily reach 2.4 times salary, if not higher. The shock of this reality becomes even stronger when you recognize that employers may re-fill some positions several times during the year, driving the per-position cost even higher.

This list of costs of employee turnover, while not at all complete, will give you some insight into the components.

- Loss of productivity
- Cost of overtime or temporary help
- Lost efficiency, including the smoothness of employee interaction and the lost institutional knowledge (Where is that tool stored? How do workers make this adjustment?)
- Lowered morale of co-workers left behind
- Increased supervisor stress
- Accrued vacation
- Recruiting costs (advertising, time to place ads, development of promotional materials, management of web sites)

---

1. Retention Management, Saratoga Institute and the American Management Association (January 1998).
2. Workforce Turnover and Firm Performance, Corporate Leadership Council of the Corporate Advisory Board, Washington, DC, 1998.

- Screening (time to review resumes)
- Interviewing time (How many people interview each applicant?)
- Hiring costs like testing and background checks
- Orientation
- Training, assimilation into work team
- Lower productivity during learning period.

The list goes on. For further information, see "Calculating the Cost of Turnover," a white paper produced by The Workforce Stability Institute.

Staying in Balance

There is no question that uncontrolled and unexpected employee turnover can damage a company deeply. If enough of the right people leave, the loss can cripple and even kill a company. The difficulty of hiring an equal replacement, combined with the time the critical position will be open, can make recovery practically impossible.

This vulnerability doesn't mean that you should protect yourself by favoring certain employees with compensation packages that can't be ignored. They may still leave; job satisfaction now comes from more than money. The wiser approach is to build a strong cadre of competent workers who are cross-trained and cross-experienced to reduce your exposure.

It's important to strike the right balance. If you pour too many resources into stabilizing your workforce, your sales efforts may never be able to generate the gross income you need to meet your over-extended obligations. But you need people to get the work done.

Consider all alternatives. Outsourcing may be a smart strategy for you. Maybe you need to spin off part of your company? Often you can modify the way you get work done, eliminating steps or changing the process. Perhaps there are things you are still doing just because “it’s always been done that way.” Should you even be doing all those things you’ve done in the past? (In one of our client organizations, many hours were consumed researching and preparing reports that no one was even reading anymore.) Eliminating such wasted endeavors enables reassignment of work to create a more balanced, stable work environment . . . the kind of place people want to go to work . . . and stay.

15

Beyond Retention: Workforce Stability

As you've proceeded through this book, you've explored how to reduce employee turnover. Uncontrolled and unexpected costly turnover.

Now turn this concept upside down. Instead of looking at turnover and all its horrible effects, look at the positive picture. Employee retention. Shared commitment between the employer and the employee. A stable, happy workforce. That's the goal. Express concepts in positive language and you can inspire supportive behavior. A company with 25 percent turnover still has a 75 percent retention rate. Look at the bright side. More people are motivated by positive outcomes than fear of negative consequences.

There are considerable benefits to maintaining a stable workforce. Your organization is more stable, so it is better prepared to meet—and exceed—the expectations expressed by customers, suppliers, stockholders, and . . . arguably the most important, expectations of employees. Competitive positioning is much stronger. Everybody wins.

Benefits of a Stable Workforce

Increased applicant interest is seen in more stable organizations. Good employees typically don't want to join unstable and insecure companies. Employers with good reputations of stability attract higher caliber applicants, as well, making the hiring and growth process much more enjoyable and productive.

Reduced recruiting and staffing costs are a highly valuable advantage. Having a stable workforce means fewer resources have to be diverted to maintaining staffing levels. This advantage of less recruiting expense means that more gross revenue can be driven right down to the bottom line without being diluted along the way.

Higher employee morale means happier, more confident, more productive employees. High morale means fewer problems and conflicts to be resolved, so managers can concentrate on results instead of trouble-shooting.

More family involvement is enjoyed in companies where the workforce is stable. People know each other and are comfortable with each other. The employer has resources to invest in family events like picnics, parties, and trips to amusement parks. Family involvement fosters greater work/life balance, further stabilizing the workforce.

More response to surveys, like employee attitude studies, is practically automatic. The results may not always be exactly what management wants to hear, but the willingness to respond, contribute, and make things better will be stronger in a more stable environment. Trust is higher.

Internal promotions are often more prevalent in stable organizations. People are staying around long enough to be promoted, to grow with the employer. Fewer managers have to be brought in from outside, so the priceless institutional knowledge remains with the company and the human capital grows.

Employee longevity is better in stable organizations. People are able to find what they're looking for—rewards and recognition, long-term relationships with co-workers and supervisors, an established pattern of activity and work. As they stay longer, the dedicated employees become a storehouse of company knowledge about products, history, and relations with particular customers.

Improved efficiency is a wonderful benefit. The reduction in learning time required with new hires is a powerful benefit. The long-term employees already know what to do and how to do it. Inefficient loss-of-time start-ups become a thing of the past.

The number of former employees returning is greater in stable organizations. These returns bring knowledge and experience back into the company, seasoned by perspectives gained working for other firms or agencies. And those who discover that the grass isn't necessarily greener on the other side of the fence will serve as a stabilizing influence on other workers who have thought about experimenting with work for another company.

Reduced absenteeism results from the long-term relationships and the strong emotional obligation workers feel toward each other . . . and toward the work that has to be done. The workers find a way to get to work, even if it involves going to the employer to ask for help. A number of companies operate buses or vans to bring employees to work from home or from the closest bus stop.

Productivity is typically higher at companies with a stable workforce. People are more accustomed to working together, so things run more smoothly.

Response time and effectiveness in customer service are much better in stable companies. Employees who take pride in the jobs they do, communicate that pride to customers. As a result, customers are happier, sales are more steady, and the need for higher sales and marketing investments is diminished. Again, this condition pushes more money to the bottom line, enabling bonuses and other rewards for the loyal workers.

Reduction in turnover rates—voluntary and involuntary—is a natural experience in more stable environments. The existing stability motivates new employees to adopt the same attitudes and behaviors around building their longevity with the firm.

Reduction in need for temporary employees to fill-in is sometimes seen. Experienced and dedicated long-term employees find a way to pitch in and get the job done. On the other hand, the stable core employees can serve as fine coordinators, monitors, and supervisors of temporary workers brought in to help relieve overloads or assist with special projects.

And, of course, the list of benefits can go on and on. Stable companies have tremendous advantages in acquiring and holding customers. They usually have greater expertise, capacity, and dependability because they enjoy a greater proportion of employees who know what they're doing. That value is becoming more scarce as turnover rates increase.

Stable companies are healthier and more profitable, which of course makes their owners and stockholders happy.

Stable employers are often viewed as "employers of choice." This stature generates better applicants, but also gives the company a coveted image in the community. The firm is often perceived in a more favored position in civic endeavors, zoning issues, and other matters where a positive influence provides a sort of power that can have many advantages.

People who work for strong, stable companies feel better about themselves, as well as their employer and their community. That higher self-esteem is reflected in many ways—through church and civic involvement, continuing education for self-improvement, support of public schools, and similar values that tend to add strength on many levels. The enhanced confidence is evidenced in performance, reduced stress (and the need for expensive employee assistance programs), and greater life balance.

People who work in stable organizations know each other well enough to provide mutual support during difficult times. In this era of constant and rapid change, life can seem exceedingly difficult. Stable organizations are better able to weather substantial change because of the resiliency of a tough team that finds unity in staying together.

Stability builds cohesiveness, competence, and confidence—essential ingredients to creating and maintaining a powerfully successful organization. The company does well, respects and rewards the people who make it possible, and affirms a win-win relationship.

The Workforce Stability Model

Our firm has developed a model of the various components of workforce stability. It is a comprehensive model, taking into consideration all the aspects our research suggests are fundamental to workforce stability. The components apply to any kind of organization. Even in entities that have been around for a while, some remedial work may be appropriate.

Mission and Vision. Before determining its staffing needs—how many of what types of people are needed . . . and when, leaders must inspire and lead the creation of a mission statement and a vision statement. What is the organization's purpose? What will its future be? This process should also explore how progress and achievement will be measured.

Strategic Staffing. Armed with a clear vision of the company's purpose and future, leaders can now ascertain what levels of staffing will be needed to achieve desired results. In this phase, you explore how many people will be needed, what skills they should possess, when they will be required, and what kind of work they will be doing. Included in this effort is succession planning—from the chief executive officer down to the front line. The company must be prepared to fill any position that opens . . . quickly.

Marketing and Recruiting. To attract applicants—to fill existing vacancies and to build a resource for future hiring—an aggressive marketing effort must be mounted. Activities will range from soliciting referrals from current employees to campus recruiting, job fairs, advertising, and targeted outreach campaigns. This marketing emphasizes the inherent value of the employer—describing the attributes that make the company an "employer of choice." Those qualities are used in broad marketing, as well as in the one-on-one interviews that will "sell" the applicants on the idea of coming with the firm.

Specification and Selection. You don't want to hire just anybody; you want people who are qualified to perform the specific kinds of work that have to be done. You want to hire people with the desired qualifications that relate to the job to be filled . . . and you want workers who will be able to grow into other positions that may not be open for some time.

As you list the specifications for the people who will fill the jobs, look carefully at all parts of the job duties. Good evaluations of the collection of talents is needed, list criteria required of those who might be chosen to fill the jobs in question. Selection tools (see appendix) are used to assess the applicants in terms of the open jobs . . . and future positions with the firm.

Hiring and Orientation. Applicants are interviewed carefully and deliberately. They are tested and background checks are conducted. A comprehensive orientation process begins with at least a full day of introduction to the firm, its mission and vision, goals and objectives, procedures and culture. New employees become familiar with all aspects of the company. They get a tour of the entire operation so they can appreciate the importance of their entry position—and the opportunities available in other departments.

During the hiring process and during the orientation program, company representatives emphasize expectations of long-term employment. Longevity is understood to be a core value of the organization.

Compensation. There are many ways to reward people for a job well-done. Wages and salaries are just one part of the picture. Performance-based compensation, stock options, and a wide variety of fringe benefits are integral parts of the package—sometimes uniquely designed for individual workers. Surveys in this field confirm almost universally that money is not the prime factor in attracting or holding good workers. Money is important, but it's no longer the largest factor. Non-financial rewards like time off, theater or sporting events tickets, direct deposit of paychecks, and even thank-you cards are becoming more prevalent.

Internal Marketing. If you ignore employees once they are in place and performing, you risk losing them to competitors in the blink of an eye. Everyone needs to be reassured that they've made the right decision by selecting your company to work for . . . even if the decision was 10–15 years ago. Internal marketing—applying the proven principles of external marketing to build employee loyalty can include frequent, substantive interaction with senior executives, newsletters (or e-mail or intranet), posters, and a host of other approaches to support worker comfort with the company, its direction, and its progress.

Training and Development. Recent surveys have revealed that a majority of employees are hungry for personal and professional development. Endeavors in this arena include the standard classroom learning experience to external training, additional college or university education, an opportunity to learn other jobs, and a library of books and tapes for employee use. Mentoring and sponsoring workers is also highly valued as retention tool, as well as a means of increasing worker strength. As part of this element, it is recommended that each and every worker have a personal development plan—formalized and supported by the worker's immediate supervisor.

Retention. All the above aspects fit into the workforce stability model, supporting retention. There's more that can be done—much of the power resting with employees' immediate supervisors. Command-and-control management styles evolve into genuine inspired leadership. Cultural issues, interpersonal relationships, support of the workers are all important and should be supplemented by training and compensation appropriate for the specific jobs.

All of these aspects must be solidly in place—and working well—before you are able to fully realize your workforce stability objectives. It doesn't come easy or all at once, but like every journey, it begins with a single step. So stop worrying about only retention and/or recruitment and concentrate on the big picture of workforce stability.

16

A Perspective on the Future

Some folks say it's impossible to predict the future. Others emphasize that the past is a prologue to the future. Historians caution that those who do not study the past are doomed to repeat it. Economists tell us that everything moves in cycles. Futurists talk in terms of trends.

In reality, we can't predict the long-term future with certainty. Nothing is definite. Forecasting is more an art than a science. We can join our fellow futurists and study the trends, while we accept input from the historians about what formed the foundation for the fate that awaits us.

Based on today, and our recent past, we can predict with a fair degree of confidence, our immediate future. Ten years, a decade, seems like a long time. Yet, studying trend indicators, at least we can see the tendencies that will influence our lives in the years ahead.

People

Considering what we can predict for the balance of the historical decade of the 1990s and the first part of the 2000s, it is obvious that people will continue to be the most vital resource for practically every kind of organization that produces goods or services. Some jobs will remain pretty much the same as they have been, but others will change dramatically with the gradual introduction of new technologies in the workplace. Technology will drive the creation of many new jobs that don't even exist today.

The knowledge and skill base required of tomorrow's employees will change in response to both technology and the need to produce more with tighter resources. A somewhat smaller workforce, with a changing composition, will be called upon to keep the machinery of our economy moving. Doing more with less will present a frustrating challenge for business owners and managers as they compete for people that will have to be trained to perform the tasks asked of them.

A new generation of college graduates with teaching degrees will find jobs in industry, teaching basic literacy skills to high school graduates who lack the knowledge to meet minimal requirements. Companies will have to provide this educational support to bridge the gap in employee availability. They'll have to grow their own "good people."

Attitudes

Attitudes will regain their importance in the workplace and in other aspects of our lives. Attitudes will spell the difference between "good" employees and also-rans. Employers will offer attitude training in an effort to help marginal employees become the kind of workers that will be needed to meet increasing competitive challenges. This "attitude training" will be a combination of motivation and inspiration, mixed with a greater understanding of what kinds of attitudes and behaviors are expected in the workplace.

The attitude training will make a difference for many employees, as they discover more of their real potential. For others, it just won't work. It will be too difficult for them to overcome the counterproductive attitudes and habits learned so well over the years. Some of these folks will wonder ignorantly why the world is passing them by.

Those employees with the right "stuff" will be highly successful, enjoying rewarding and satisfying careers. The demand for such people will practically assure them fulfillment in their chosen endeavors. They will have a wide range of exciting opportunities to join the teams of people working for different employers. The next ten years will be active years for recruiting firms–"headhunters" searching for talented executives, operational managers, supervisors, and technicians in all fields. The companies that comprise the burgeoning staffing industry will do very well in the years ahead, supplying both permanent and temporary (contingent) workers.

Leadership

Managers will adopt and apply *leadership* skills in the workplace. The old hard-line management techniques, the autocratic approach, simply won't work in most environments anymore. There is no question that participative management is here to stay.

Unfortunately, precious few people in management positions today really know how to be leaders. They've been well-taught and reinforced in the methods of command and control, when the need in the future will be facilitation and empowerment. A whole new set of skills will have to be learned and practiced to enable people and organizations to excel. In response to the need in the marketplace colleges and universities will add more human relations classes to their offerings.

Organizations of all kinds will provide remedial and skill-sharpening training and development, focused on helping their managers and executives understand how to work more effectively with people. This training will focus on team leadership, sales, and customer service.

Sales and Service

Selling goods and services will become more consumer oriented. Sales will be made on the basis of long-standing relationships in which professional sales counselors help customers buy what is best for them. Service after the sale will become increasingly important for salespeople in all fields as competition strains to earn the right to modify buying patterns. Salespeople who become proficient in this changing style will be in high demand.

Customer service will become an integral part of corporate strategy. The concept will extend far beyond "smile training" and slogans. Consumers at organizational and personal levels will expect higher quality in both merchandise and service. A resurgence of consumerism will emphasize service, providing wonderful opportunities in the growing field of customer service for people-oriented employees.

Roles and Structure

To get the jobs done, people on the front lines will be expected to accept greater responsibility. Accountability along with increased authority, will extend beyond senior management levels right down to the hourly employees. We will expect more from those "on the ground floor" of our organizations as companies thin their management ranks.

Corporate structures will change as middle managers are replaced with computers, other technological tools, and new leadership methods. More people who now hold management titles will become functional specialists, providing support to fellow team members. An enhanced sense of cooperation will displace the fiefdoms that many staff and line departments have become.

Employees will have more freedom in determining how their work will be done. The emphasis will be on results and collaboration, rather than on activities and departmental independence. The trend toward managers having the choice of purchasing needed resources in-house or from outside vendors will continue. Leadership, relationships, quality, and service will become key ingredients for survival.

While good people will be hard for some employers to attract, others companies will have their pick. The difference will be in the hiring company's reputation about how they work with people. Issues of concern in that reputation will be how people work together, opportunities to make a difference (which means a significant degree of control over one's destiny), corporate responsibility to employees and to society, meaningful work, growth potential, and both intrinsic and extrinsic rewards. See an in-depth exploration of this next generation of corporate culture in ***Lean & Meaningful*** (Herman and Gioia, Oakhill Press, 1998).

Changing for the Future

The changes will be comfortable for some organizations, painful for others. Some employers are already well on their way, operating to a significant extent according to the strategies presented in this book. Unfortunately, some companies will not change. Many are already having difficulties. Most of the inflexible organizations will disappear. They just won't be able to survive in our ever-changing world. Flexibility, responsiveness, and agility will spell success in the years ahead.

The late 1990s and early 2000s will be exciting times. Employers who attract and keep their good people will become magnets for more high quality employees. Working together with a common vision and dedicated leadership, these teams of conscientious people will enjoy being on the leading edge . . . having a competitive edge.

Eventually, other elements of society will follow the pattern. We'll see a gradual improvement of standards and performance in all sectors of our economy. A trend of increasing acceptance of responsibility and accountability will strengthen our educational system, the management of our environment, and a whole host of other aspects of our lives.

We're on the threshold of a resurgence! Each of us has the potential to enjoy the thrill of riding the wave successfully into the next century. The knowledge we need is already here. We know what we need to do to keep people productive and part of our team.

The future belongs to those who *do* what needs to be done.

17

The Corporation of the Future: A Sneak Peek

As you work diligently toward stabilizing your workforce, a peek at the corporation of the future might be helpful. The following chapter from ***Lean & Meaningful***, co-authored with my wife and partner, Joyce Gioia, will give you some insight into what's coming. The table of contents of this idea-packed book follows this chapter.

What will the corporation of the future look like? How will the corporation of the future differ from what we've seen in the past and what we experience today? How will it be structured? What kind of a workforce will we need to staff the corporation of the future, and how will people work together?

These are all valid questions. And they're just the start of the inquiry into how we might expect corporate life to be in the years ahead. Anyone who is a leader in business, government, education, or a not-for-profit organization must be concerned about what the work environment will be in the future. Aspiring leaders have the same concerns—what are they working for, what will they inherit?

When we have a clear view of the future—one design or alternative scenarios, we can better manage today. How we manage today will influence what our tomorrows will be. These are strategic issues—on an organizational level and also on a personal one. What role do we see ourselves playing in our future work environment? How can we best prepare for the future we want for ourselves, our families, our colleagues, our enterprise?

Futurists

As futurists, we observe trends and consider what scenarios may develop in the foreseeable future. It's fascinating work, particularly when you let your mind stretch to imagine possibilities that are "on the fringe" of what we see in today's world. In the past few years, we've seen a considerable amount of progress—moving us dramatically into a different kind of world. The velocity of change is increasing at a rapid rate; we're all having difficulty keeping up.

To do a thorough job as a futurist, it's necessary to watch the trends in a wide range of arenas. These trends interact with each other, causing reactions that are sometimes clearly predictable . . . and sometimes more elusive. Since most of our work as consultants, writers, and speakers revolves around the corporate world, we pay careful attention to trends that influence the continuing evolution of corporate structures, cultures, strategies, people, operating systems, relationships, and environments.

A Transformation

The corporation of the future will be substantially different from the corporation of today. Trends in organizational structure, operating technology, workforce availability, strategic relationships, and economic development suggest that tomorrow's company will be much more streamlined and simplified. Leaders will concentrate on the entity's core business, valuing characteristics such as agility, nimbleness, responsiveness, and flexibility. They will have a tighter structure, emphasize efficiency, and build strength through outsourcing, contracting, alliances, and creative approaches. A nucleus of collaborators will drive the corporation's success, drawing in outside resources as needed to accomplish work for customers.

This new design, this new organizational culture can best be described as "lean & meaningful." The driving strategies will be to do more with less—and to have the work done by highly productive employees who are all well-qualified, find meaning in their balanced lives, and genuinely enjoy their work.

Counterbalancing the streamlining will be a new focus on building the meaningfulness of work and the work environment. The future corporation will be concerned with providing meaningful work, offering a meaningful career characterized by personal control, an enhanced sense of family centeredness, dedication to community involvement, social consciousness, environmental awareness, spirituality, and similar issues.

Leaders will be both forced and motivated to create new, more meaningful cultures to attract and hold quality employees. This organizational design will be easy for some employers, almost impossible for others. The future of our corporations and what is described as "corporate life" could easily be threatened by the influence of social and financial trends. The key today is not just how people treat each other, but in whether there is enough inherent strength in the organization to sustain it through the inevitable shift to the corporate design of the future.

Where We're Heading

Corporations will not change dramatically overnight. The move into the future is an *evolutionary* process, not a *revolutionary* one. The shift will be gradual.

The transformation to a lean and meaningful culture will be led from the top of the organization in almost every case. People at lower levels will be understandably reluctant to rock the boat of tradition. Inertia will be overcome only through the enlightened, assertive, and visionary leadership of company owners and senior executives who know how to think and lead far past the bottom line at the end of the next reporting period.

Lean Machine

We know the corporation of the future will be lean. The movement toward reducing fat, streamlining operations, concentrating on core businesses, and achieving strong results for stockholders in a turbulent world are "given," to use a term from geometry.

The effort to tighten-up is a driving force in the business world, as well as in government and non-profit organizations. The evolution is marked by what seem—at the time—to be revolutionary events. Processes are improved. Facilities are reduced. Workforces are down-sized. Product lines are limited. Inefficient operations are closed or sold. Expenses are controlled. While it is dangerous to go too far with cost-cutting measures, there's plenty of fat to be trimmed in most enterprises.

As this crusade continues, executives will re-design, reengineer, re-shape their companies to do more with fewer resources. In recent years, we've seen some dramatic examples of such campaigns. Practically every corporate leader in America is familiar with "Chainsaw Al" Dunlap and his board-applauded reputation for slashing costs. That's lean—no question. But it's also *mean,* in the eyes of most people in management and non-management positions. Many people agree that cuts have to be made; the issue is *how* the cuts will be made and who they will affect.

Less Hierarchical

Multi-level corporate hierarchies will experience a dramatic metamorphosis. With apologies to Max Weber, intricate bureaucracies will become creatures of the past. They'll be replaced with matrix organizations which are not just flatter, but multi-dimensional in their multiple connections with collaborative work groups both inside and outside the company.

Much more responsibility will be placed on each member of the corporate team. We'll see considerably more autonomy for employees. Each work group will have more opportunity to have an impact on the decision making of the organization, more authority to implement decisions, and more opportunities for learning and personal growth.

Self-directed work teams, ad hoc task forces, and all sorts of new designs will emerge as people work with a higher focus on achieving desired results . . . then moving on to the next thing to be done. No longer will we see people sitting around waiting for their next assignment. Everyone will be a lot more tuned-in to what's happening . . . in the whole organization.

Performance Driven

Performance of the organization will be tied to the performance of the employees. Employees will understand how their jobs and responsibilities fit in attaining corporate goals and be rewarded based on their contribution to the success of the company. No longer will employees be put in dead end jobs that have no value to the organization just because of longevity. Employees will need to demonstrate how they enhance the profitability of the organization. And if the organization is to enlist the support of these highly mobile employees, it will need to provide a clear set of goals that support a strong mission.

Agility

The competition will demand that organizations be agile and flexible, able to switch markets or make design changes to meet customers' needs in days, if not hours. To keep this agility, organizations will need to optimize the collective intellectual capital of their employees. Companies will need to include employees from all levels in decision making roles, using the collective knowledge to remain competitive. Only when employees have a meaningful role in the organization will they be optimally productive.

Customer Focus

Not only is the workforce changing, but customers are making decisions based on more than successful advertising campaigns. Customers are becoming more sophisticated in the methods they use to determine which product to buy. They now take into account the way a company responds to the local and global environment; the relationship of the company to the community and to its employees; the values the company stands for and how it demonstrates those values publicly.

Successful companies know that to compete in the current marketplace they must be customer-focused. They must be able to respond quickly with a quality product or service. Companies are also learning that the linchpins to this customer-driven cycle are employees. The people who provide the services, build the parts, answer the phones, send the invoices, etc., are, individually and collectively, the keys to the success or failure of the business. And that is precisely why, after all the chaos of the past decade, companies must change their relationships with their employees. Finding, keeping, and motivating good employees is the key to a successful business future.

Stable Workforce

One of the lessons learned after all the downsizing was that customers value stability in the workforce of the companies they do business with. As we've seen in banking over the last few years, customers are becoming increasingly dissatisfied by the lack of service. Dissatisfied customers soon leave a bank, profitability declines, and investors are less interested in the company. The impact of employee turnover is particularly evident with companies that have significant customer contact, but even in a manufacturing environment, absenteeism and turnover will always impact product quality. Poor quality always impacts customer satisfaction. The cycle is the same.

A recent study of 275 portfolio managers by Ernst & Young's Center for Business Innovation showed that 35 percent of investor decisions were driven by non-financial information. The ability to attract and retain talented employees ranked high on the list of factors to be considered when making investments. Investors are increasingly including employee stability and motivation as part of the analysis process.[1]

As the workforce becomes more fluid, companies will be increasingly concerned about recruiting and retaining good employees. Not only will companies need the knowledge and

---

1. Shellenbarger, Sue, "Work & Family" *The Wall Street Journal,* March 19, 1997

expertise of these employees, but they will also need to keep close tabs on the costs associated with employee turnover. Recruiting and hiring costs can amount to as much as 2 to 7 times the annual salary of the employee being replaced.[2]

In our changing global economy, which is becoming more competitive every day, companies have recognized that their employees are the key element in overall profitability. So how's a company going to develop a loyal, stable workforce under this new "employment contract?" The first step is to understand what employees want and need. The second step is to design programs to meet those needs. Let's examine some of the most important issues for workers in the corporation of the future.

Meaningful Work

Employees want to know that what they are doing is meaningful—to the organization and/or to the world at large. There's a strong sense of personal and corporate responsibility rising—a drive to do something to make a positive difference . . . something beyond self, beyond profit. Wise employers in the future will emphasize the intrinsic value of the company's work for the various stakeholder groups who benefit.

More than just a paycheck, employees in the future will want a stake in the success of the employer organization. They'll look for reward through stock options, incentives, training, perks, and bonuses. Few employees will remain in dead end jobs without significant potential for personal growth or contributions to the betterment of our planet. This expectation will present some serious challenges for a lot of employers in the years ahead. Too many of today's companies simply don't think in these terms.

---

2. Herman, Roger E. "The Cost of Turnover." A White Paper published by the Workforce Stability Institute, Greensboro, North Carolina, 1997.

Career Security

Employees also want to develop a meaningful career path that makes them more marketable both internally and externally. To accomplish this self-development, they want opportunities to learn, to increase their responsibility, and to create and implement solutions. Learning opportunities include both academic and experiential methods and apply to both work and personal skills. They also want health care and retirement benefits to be portable, so that they can care for their families now and in the future, regardless of where they work.

Tomorrow's employees will assume responsibility for managing their own careers. In so doing, they'll deliberately seek opportunities to strengthen their knowledge, experience, and marketability.

A Values-Based Organization

Employees want to know that they are working for an ethical company with a mission and a clear set of values they can believe in. Workers are more likely to leave an incompatible work environment than ever before. Generation X workers are much more motivated to support the mission more than the process.

To keep these employees of the future, a company will need to stand for something more than a profit. Generation X employees are more interested in the mission of the company than the stock prices. Older employees have put in their time under the pressures of the old system and the overwhelming changes of the last two decades. They are more cynical and less inclined to give their all to a company they instinctively mistrust. To keep good employees in the future, companies will need to maintain a values-based culture. How a company is perceived by society will have an impact on its ability to find and keep good employees.

Balance Between Work and Family

Employees are looking for balance in their lives. The quality of their work and family lives is becoming more important. Child- and eldercare issues are not just women's issues any longer. Increasingly, men are making career decisions based on family matters.

What employers have to gain by addressing these issues is a motivated, stable, productive workforce. To remain competitive in the marketplace, companies cannot afford to ignore these needs and expectations.

Companies will need to demonstrate that they understand the work *and* personal needs of the employees and be willing to act on that understanding. Employees are increasingly more concerned about quality of life issues. The need to find a balance between work and family is a prime motivator for many workers. The companies who fail to take this into account will lose the best and brightest, either to another company that meets those needs or because employees are willing to downsize their lifestyle to achieve balance.

As we look at how some companies are meeting the diverse needs of their employees, it will become obvious that the cost/benefit analysis produces a favorable outcome. In many cases, the family-centered programs adopted by companies, both large and small, return benefits far in excess of the cost.

Corporate Citizenship

Customers, shareholders and other stakeholders will look for more than just profitability. Companies are being held more and more accountable for being good corporate citizens. In purchasing decisions, buying a consumer product or investing in stock, consumers are choosing to learn about a company's policies and standards and vote with their pocketbooks.

The Relationship Between the Company and Its Employees

The ways companies handle diversity, harassment, hiring and firing, profit sharing and any number of other employee issues are used as criteria for evaluation by consumers. A number of companies recently in the news can vouch for the impact of their internal decisions on their image. AT&T lost huge image points when it laid off thousands of workers in a year of profits; Texaco's failure to handle discrimination within its own ranks will remain in the public consciousness for years to come. And these are only two examples.

The expectations of employee populations will be big challenges for employers. If companies are to be successful, they will need to create an environment that will attract and keep good employees. Concepts like "It's just a job" or "It's a paycheck" will no longer suffice to keep employees motivated and productive. Meeting the needs of the "internal" customers, the employees who *are* the company, will be the only way to succeed in meeting the needs of the marketplace.

The Relationship of the Company to the Environment

The level of environmental awareness is a growing influence on a corporation's image. Whether the company uses environmental considerations in the planning stages or ignores the issues unless it gets caught, can make a difference in the loyalty and marketability of the organization. A company that is aware of environmental issues and takes an active role in protecting the environment, either through its own product or through community involvement, will have a stronger position with its constituencies.

The Relationship to Society, Both Locally and Globally

Companies are judged on their actions in the community at large. Customers and employees prefer companies that look beyond today's profits to opportunities for giving something back. The process is similar to the agricultural investment in crop rotation.

Workers and consumers seek companies that have a demonstrated commitment to the future of society, not just to marketshare. How an organization invests its time, its people, and its resources in activities that impact the greater good of society will be an important factor in the future.

Companies will become more involved in their host communities, making a positive difference for their surroundings and for their employees. Enlightened companies will contribute resources to support activities in which their employees are involved. This tactic supports the community *and* the employees—attracting and holding workers who are involved in local activities (community leaders who can also assume greater leadership at work).

Moving Toward A Different Design

How companies operate relates in large part to the way people are treated in the corporate environment. They can go along with the "lean," but resist the "mean" aspects of the "lean and mean" company. The emphasis—based on attitudes in corporate America, societal trends, expectations of the workforce, and a shifting work environment—clearly indicates a rising demand for more meaningfulness in work—and other aspects of our lives. We'll talk a lot more about the various aspects of meaningfulness in this book, but let's explore other descriptors of how we see the corporation of the future.

The corporation of the future will be laser-focused on its

core business. Any services, functions, divisions, or structures not purely invested in fulfillment of the company's tight mission will not be part of the core corporation. To use scientific terms, the corporation of the future will be a nucleus. That's all. No extraneous or support organizations . . . just the nucleus. The people who work in the nucleus corporation will coordinate and manage the acquisition and application of outside resources to accomplish the work of the company. The focus will be very tight, with high levels of accountability accepted by each member of the team.

With this very clear understanding of the company's business focus, resources available, and results expected, there will be minimal need for a deep hierarchical structure of management. A very flat organization of collaborators will manage the work. These key people, each strongly empowered, will work closely together to guide both internal and external resources. The organization will be strongly decentralized, using technology-enhanced networking systems to communicate and share vital information.

With this kind of arrangement, employers will have a critical need to attract, optimize, and retain top talent. The kinds of people it will take to run tomorrow's businesses will be in short supply and high demand. This circumstance makes it vitally important to create, maintain, and promote a corporate culture that is highly supportive of high quality workers. With the intensity of the work to be done, much like the intensity we identify with the New York Stock Exchange trading floor, it is essential that obstacles to high performance be removed. The lean nature of the future corporation addresses this issue. And, under this kind of pressure, caring sincerely for the people who work with the company will be fundamental. Leaders will aggressively destroy obstacles and shred red tape wherever they find anything getting in the way of success. They'll encourage people to work *with* the company, not just *for* the company.

Resource Management

The team members of the nucleus corporation will manage a variety of resources to fulfill the company's mission. Probably the most critical—and volatile—resource will be the human resource. For many companies, the majority of people who work for the company will not be traditional full-time employees. They certainly will not be employees who expect to work their entire careers at that company to earn the gold watch and a rocking chair to see them through their final days.

The corporation of the future will be staffed with several categories of contingent workers: part-time employees, directly contracted individuals, people contracted through brokers, and temporary workers. Some of the so-called "permanent" workers will be leased employees, not even on the company's payroll. The variety of human resources suggests that nucleus corporation managers will be juggling options to connect the right type of resource to the right type of work.

Some workers will be engaged directly, some through var ious kinds of agencies—some of which will provide full benefit packages and maintain close relationships with their people. The workers' length and type of attachment to the core corporation will depend on the kind of work they do and the company's needs at the time. These relationships will be ever-changing in a flexible and responsive system that utilizes resources only when they are needed.

The corporation of the future will be heavily invested in the use of outsourced companies and services. Tasks and functions that are commonly regarded as part of the corporate structure today will not be part of the core, or nucleus, of tomorrow. They will gradually be spun off into outsource organizations, some actually operating within the environment of the host company. Others will be nearby, some may be across the country or on another continent, and some will be connected only through virtual relationships via the Internet or some evolution thereof.

Close relationships will develop between host (core) entities and their outsource networks.

Long-term agreements may guide their interactions, but we'll also see a lot of competitive bidding for work. The more solid alliances will be based on capacity and performance issues, of course. Beyond operational issues, shared values will increasingly determine which companies will work best together. Criteria used to select suppliers—and customers—will be some of the same qualities we relate as "meaningful" for employees in this book.

Strategic alliances will become increasingly important for the corporation of the future. These alliances will link vertical supply and demand chains, as well as reach into horizontal marketing machines. Organizations will seek—and find—all sorts of ways to build symbiotic relationships to maximize the utilization of resources and accumulated goodwill, while minimizing their own investment in any resources they don't need or use directly. Imagine the complicated webs that companies will weave to best share scarce resources.

The Culture

The culture of the successful corporation of the future will be exciting, fast-moving, and challenging. There will be an openness that fosters a high sense of camaraderie that will make work truly enjoyable. Attitudes will be positive, strongly influenced by enthusiastic leaders with a very clear sense of where they're going and how they'll get there. People will *want* to work for these leaders and these companies!

Risk-taking will be encouraged to respond to the ever-changing environments in which the company operates. And people working for core organizations will be cross-trained to handle a wide range of tasks inside and outside of their areas of specialty. Everyone will be concerned with the company's environments: market, supply, financial, labor, regulatory, and operations.

Life in the corporation of the future will be largely experiential. Depending on lessons learned in the past might be dangerous in the face of constant and rapid change. Whether operating in a local or global arena, every entity will build a heightened sensitivity to factors influencing the way they do business. The old adage of the butterfly flapping its wings in China affecting life on the other side of the world will be a reality.

Everyone working in the corporation of the future will be continually learning. Traditional training classes will be supplemented by on-the-job training, college and university education at undergraduate, graduate, and executive development levels, and ongoing research into what "the other guys" are doing. Given our freedom of communication and instantaneous media, most corporations will be like an open book. Secrets about how they're doing business—structure, relationships, and more will be relatively common knowledge . . . or at least readily available with a little bit of exploration.

The key to greatness will be how all the knowledge about what everyone else is doing is gathered, assimilated, and applied in each company. No one company cited in this book, for instance, is doing everything well. Each one does one thing or some things very well, but may not do other things as well as a company across town or across the country. We'll learn from each other, then create our own unique mix of how we will do things. That "mix" will determine our success in all the various arenas in which we operate.

Skills for the Future

We are often asked what skills will be most valuable—most needed—in the corporation of the future. Our answer includes noting the importance of all the skills we possess today. Technical and technological skills, in particular, will take on greater importance. We'll see growing needs for people who can understand and fix systems—from computer systems to product distribution systems to plumbing systems.

Visionary skills will be in demand. The ability to gather and absorb a wide range of input, then use that knowledge, understanding, and perspective to guide organizations into the future will be vital. Some will develop this capacity on a relatively short-term scale; others will look far ahead. Practically every company will have to move away from today's obsession with the next financial reporting period. Numbers and measurement will be important, of course, but smoothing the flow from month to month, from quarter to quarter, will be essential for highly profitable long-term performance.

The ability to organize will definitely be important in the corporation of the future. Everywhere you look there will be a need to organize something. Resources, work flow, marketing mix, financial opportunities, and much more will demand high levels of organization . . . and re-organization.

Persuasive skills will be used in all facets of the operation of the corporation of the future, internally and externally. Knowing how to present information and ideas in a way that others can understand and support a particular position will enable people to be considerably more effective. Salesmanship skills will be essential in many more interactions than we consider today, especially within the organization.

We hesitate to list "communication" skills. We hear that word so much from our corporate clients that we've often called "communication" the "c" word. However, the skills of listening, writing, reading, speaking, and describing will be invaluable. There will be precious little time to be misunderstood, only to have to make corrections later. Tight margins may well make miscommunication a fatal corporate disease. Human interaction will be significant, so the skills to enhance related activities will be central to the strength of the corporation of the future.

The ability to learn will empower people to grow in effectiveness, helping their companies achieve desired objectives.

Some of this skill is innate, but many people will acquire the ability to learn—and relate aspects of learning—in college and university environments. We believe the liberal arts education experience will prove to be the most valuable type of education for tomorrow's leaders.

The employees of the corporation of the future will be flexible, creative, and stimulated to make a positive difference in the world. They will seek balance, growth, and fulfillment in both life and workstyles. The corporation of the future must respond to those needs and desires, or they will find themselves hampered by a lack of qualified people to accomplish the organization's work.

Our next chapter begins our learning about the various aspects of meaningfulness that will be so important to employees of corporations in the future.

Table of Contents for *Lean & Meaningful*

Lean & Meaningful, Herman, Roger E. & Joyce L. Gioia, Oakhill Press, Greensboro, North Carolina, 390 pages, hardcover, 1998.

Appendix A

Behavioral Styles, Leadership Styles

For generations people have mused about what made people "tick." Why do some people behave one way, while other people behave differently under the same circumstances?

In the late 1890s Karl Jung suggested that human behavior could be classified into different categories, or types. He became known as the "Father of Type Psychology." His work was very helpful in understanding behavior.

In 1928, Dr. William Marston published ***Emotions of Normal People***. In a pioneering move, Marston mapped human behavior into four quadrants on a two-axis system. One axis measured *direct* versus *indirect* approach, while the other addressed *people* versus *task* orientation. This mapping was the seminal research and foundation for most of the study on needs-generated behavior.

A number of psychological tests and learning instruments have been developed over the years to help us understand and use this four-quadrant behavioral knowledge. The leader in the field of these materials is the Personal Profile System developed by Dr. John Geier.

The four primary behavioral styles, as shown in the Personal Profile and associated instruments are *dominant, influencer* or *interacting, steadiness,* and *conscientiousness* or *cautious*. Using the initials of the descriptors, the styles and the framework have become known as the "DiSC" approach.

Each of the styles is different from the others. Each is unique, with its own strengths. Each style of behavior, and each of us, is motivated by different needs. Our behavioral styles are unique, individually and in groups. No style can be characterized as being "better" than another.

The more we understand about human behavior, the more effective we can be in managing ourselves and in working with others. The more we understand and appreciate others, and what motivates them, the better we can work with them in a team environment, the better we can meet their needs, and the better chance we have of keeping them.

Before exploring the four primary styles of behavior, it's important to note that only about 15 percent of the population is recognized as a "pure type" Dominant, Influence, Steadiness, or Cautious. Research shows that about 85 percent of us are some mixture of the four primary styles, possessing the needs and outward behaviors of more than one of the primary styles.

Most of us use one of the styles as our primary behavior, with a second style as a secondary, or back-up, behavior. The more we can learn about how the styles interact, the stronger we will be in working with others.

Dominant

The first primary style we'll discuss is the Dominant type. Dominant people are characteristically determined and results-oriented. They can be demanding and directive as they exercise their tendency to take charge. Dominant people are risk-takers and innovators who enjoy challenges. They like variety in their lives, with the power and authority to get things done.

Freedom from controls and supervision is important for Dominant behavior types, as they seek a wide scope of operations. They like to get things done, to show their accomplishments. Dominants like quick, direct answers. Careful analysis and weighing of pros and cons is not characteristic of this style, and social graces may appear to be comparable to the proverbial bull in the china shop.

Influencer or Interacting

These folks are people-oriented. They love being with other people and are usually gregarious. They're positive, enthusiastic, and persuasive. Great talkers, Influencers enjoy entertaining people and helping others. We may see them as emotional and impulsive as they exercise their freedom of expression.

Influencers want freedom from outside controls and from the details of their work. They prefer to be the motivators, the initiators, the people who come up with great ideas and inspire others to follow them to fulfill those dreams. It is not characteristic of this style to concentrate on facts or task completion, to be well organized, or to be highly objective in decision making.

Steadiness

Our third behavior style is characterized by a high concern for getting tasks accomplished in a systematic, predictable pattern. They like security and stability and are seen as being very patient, loyal, and supportive. Steadiness people are usually very good listeners, excellent team players, and adept at solving problems in a deliberate and caring manner.

Specialists in their areas of endeavor, they appreciate sincere expressions of appreciation for their work. Their preference is to work with established procedures and guidelines, without abrupt changes. When change does have to occur, they are more supportive if they have input and if the changes are well-planned before implementation.

Conscientious or Cautious

People exhibiting the fourth style of behavior are highly oriented toward control, standard operating procedures, rules and regulations, and quality assurance. They are concerned with accuracy, details, critical thinking to research and analyze, and careful deliberation. Cautious people are usually diplomatic, but practically insist on compliance with recognized standards.

Anxious to see things done the right way, Cautious people are firm in their beliefs and rather set in their ways. They resist change—if it's worked well for 20 years, why change it? They prefer a sheltered environment and reassurances to being on the cutting edge of development where risk and creativity are the bywords.

With a deeper understanding of the needs-oriented behaviors and motivators, we can be much more effective leaders. Included in this behavioral knowledge is an appreciation of the goals and the fears of each style:

Primary Behavioral Style	Goal	Fear
dominant	directness	being taken advantage of
influencer	social recognition	social rejection
steadiness	traditional practices	loss of stability
cautious	proper way, self-discipline	criticism of work effort

Team effectiveness is dependent on the way the team members work together. Each person is motivated by his/her own needs, and brings that orientation to the team. Based on its composition, the team could be well-balanced in terms of the representation of the various behavior styles. If there are too many of one style and too few of another, relatively speaking, the team could be out of balance and therefore less effective.

Supervisors and managers, in their leadership roles, can achieve much higher levels of productivity, teamwork, satisfaction, and stability if they are attentive to the significance of behavioral styles. People relate differently to each other based on their styles and perspectives. Leaders who understand their own styles and the styles of each of their team members can be more attentive to meeting individual needs.

People with different behavioral styles approach conflict differently. Part of the leader's job is to resolve conflicts quickly, in ways that will be acceptable to all parties.

People will tend to remain as employees where their individuality is respected and appreciated. Much of this understanding and insight into how to deal with people flows from gaining and applying knowledge of behavioral styles.

These behavioral styles have been presented at a basic level to provide readers with a quick working knowledge and appreciation of the various approaches people have to their environments. Further information, learning instruments, and tools for analysis and application of behavioral knowledge are available from:

The Herman Group
3400 Willow Grove Court
Greensboro, NC 27410-8600
(336) 282-9370
FAX (336) 282-2003
info@herman.net

Leadership Styles

Quite a few studies of leadership styles have been done over the years. A number of helpful theories provide insight and understanding of the various perspectives on leadership. These theories are valuable information for managers to learn, since keeping good people often depends on using the right leadership style for the particular situation.

Local libraries are a good source of information for those interested in gaining further knowledge on this topic. Management and leadership textbooks provide good explanations of the various theories and their applications. College and university libraries are also good resources.

Several of the more familiar theories are the situational

leadership model developed by Paul Hersey and Kenneth Blanchard, the managerial grid developed by Robert Blake and Jane Mouton, and Theory X/Theory Y developed by Douglas McGregor.

Each of these theories looks at how leaders perform. The theoretical perspectives examine the degree of attention leaders give to task or directive behavior versus people or supportive behavior. There are, of course, positive and negative consequences of pursuing any leadership style, depending on one's perspective. Leadership is an art, not a science.

One point of emphasis prevalent today is to remain flexible and responsive to people. Leadership practices must be individualized; the way we work with one person may not be as effective with another member of our team. Our challenge as leaders is to provide the appropriate kind of leadership for each of our people so they can do their best, as individual performers, as members of work teams, and as employees of the entire organization.

Meeting this challenge is not easy to do, especially for managers who have not been schooled in the fine art of leadership. Understanding behavioral styles is an important area for training and development of managers. To be effective leaders able to keep good people and keep everyone highly productive in the 1990s and beyond, managers at all levels in all kinds of organizations must learn how to lead.

Supervisors lead team members at the operational level of the organization. Their need is to understand technical skills first, to be able to answer questions from subordinates. Second, they must develop a strong understanding of people and how to work with them. Supervisors get things done through other people, so the relationships have to be positive and productive.

Middle managers also need well-honed people skills, but are expected to perform with more of a conceptual orientation than technical. People at this level should be more concerned with the allocation of resources to accomplish the organization's goals and objectives. Procedures, systems, and interpretation of policies are part of their roles.

Senior managers of organizations will be stronger with technical and conceptual skills, their focus must be on the corporate mission, development and review of policies, and long-range planning. People skills continue to have importance, since most of what senior managers do involves heavy interpersonal communication.

People want to excel in their work. They want their organization to excel. To make this possible, the entire management team must lead with consistency and cohesiveness. No longer can the finger of blame be pointed only at labor; a significant part of the problem rests with management.

The opportunity for high achievement rests with management. If managers, as leaders, perform well for their employing organization, non-managerial employees will gladly follow them. If they are understood, appreciated, and treated appropriately, many good people will be happy to stay with one team for a long period of time.

Satisfaction and the resultant high productivity and stability come from the way we work with the various kinds of people on our teams, applying the right kind of leadership techniques to get things done.

Appendix B

Personal and Organizational Values

Appendix A explored needs-generated motivators to human behavior. The emotion-based "needs" perspective is only part of the picture. The second major internal motivator—for each of us—is our values or beliefs. Values are defined as the standards or principles we use to guide our decisions and actions. There is a direct connection or relationship between an individual's needs and that person's values or beliefs. Both of these internal drives shape one's performance.

A third driver is norms—those standards that are established by the society around us. The society could be our community, our family, or our employment environment. These influences on our behavior are external, rather than internal.

To understand this concept, you should begin with an exploration of the relationship between needs and values. Armed with this knowledge, you can then discuss the other life forces which initially and continually develop our values perspectives or belief positions.

Group I needs levels (physiological or survival and safety or security) tend to be accompanied by a values perspective with is *self*-oriented.

Group II needs levels (social and other esteem) are accompanied by an *other*-oriented perspective. Others provide the direction for the behavior or the decisions.

Group III needs levels (self-esteem and self-actualization) are generally accompanied by a perspective which places value on *integrating* self, others, and society.

Of course, the picture is not that simple. In addition to needs, other forces shape our values. Parenting shapes children's values. The psychological environment parents provide shapes children's values. However, if parenting does not meet a child's emotional, psychological, or physical safety needs, parental values programming is generally not successful.

Values are also shaped by schools, churches, media, and societal and cultural environments. Values shaping is also a function of demographics such as geographic location as well as the family's economic standing. Peers play an important role in the values-shaping process for young people.

The teenage years present a clear example of the relationship between needs and values. The young person is generally motivated by needs-generated social concerns. Physiological and security needs are largely taken care of by the parents.

Social needs and the related other-oriented valued perspectives are frequently evident in behavior which is group (peer) driven. Other influences, such as peer pressure, peer acceptance, and rules that flow from institutions like schools and churches motivate such teen behavior. Societal norms set standards of behavior.

A major milestone in the continuing development of personal values is the acceptance of responsibility. Generally, this shift occurs right after the teenage period, that is primarily focused on self and other's rights. Significant life experiences—personal crises, change in roles, institutional forces, or any combination will stimulate this change in perspective.

Here's an example for a deeper understanding of the relationship between needs and values. Paul, 27, an employee in your organization, is very responsibility-oriented. He is a good team player, loyal to his work group. He works hard. He values the respect of his peers and his manager. His day-to-day behavior and his decisions reflect these values. He comes in early and works late, as the workload dictates. These behaviors are not demanded by his superior; they are a result of Paul's own internal motivation.

Paul's apartment lease is not renewed. Apartment rentals have climbed steeply since he moved in several years ago. Then Paul's car is stolen. Insurance proceeds will not cover the purchase of a new or decent used automobile.

At this point, safety and security needs take on increasing importance for Paul. His behavior reflects an increasing *self* orientation. He may even raise a "what's-in-it-for-me" question when the team is assigned a project which will require extra work effort and time. Previously, his team orientation would have motivated him, without financial reward. Now, however, Paul is more needs-motivated.

Does that mean that the responsibility orientation to the team is gone? Has Paul ceased to value the respect of his peers or his manager? Of course not! Yet, his behavior may be much more self-oriented until his safety and security needs are once more satisfied.

There is an ongoing interaction between needs and values regardless of the needs level or the values orientation.

In another phase of values development, self-respect, responsibility to (and for) self becomes uppermost. The individual values integrating self with others, groups, and society. Responsibility at this phase is not to, or for, others. Responsibility is not to the rules of the group, team, organization, or traditional group.

Rather, responsibility is to examine the situation and determine the best course of action for *all* concerned. Therefore, a person motivated by this values perspective is more questioning than accepting. An individual with this values perspective does not value rules necessarily as the guidelines for decisions or actions. Rather, the individual values taking responsibility to personally think through the situation and, subsequently, decide upon the most appropriate decision for all concerned. Responsibility of this decision-making process is accepted by the individual. The individual also recognizes that accountability and responsibility go hand-in-hand.

This values perspective generally accompanies the individual who is motivated by self esteem and self actualization needs.

Organizational Values

Now, what does this values knowledge mean to organizations? Like individuals, organizations are needs-motivated. In fact, survival needs are most predominant in a young company. Safety and security needs, needs to establish financial stability, are met next. It is not until these are satisfied that the employer, or the employees, will be interested in social, procedural, structural, and developmental needs.

A company's founder establishes the firm's original operational values. The way employees and customers are valued, the basic assumptions which guide and structure a company, are a direct reflection of the founder and the company's continuing social forces.

Too frequently, the values which are to guide individual, much less organizational, behavior have never been identified nor clarified. An organizational mission or purpose, thai exceeds mere needs motivation, is nevei developed. Oı worse yet, a philosophy is espoused, but the actions of the organization are not congruent with the espoused philosophy.

Together, the organization's needs and values make up its norms. Norms are the written (or unwritten) rules, behavioral expectations, policies, and procedures (formal as well as informal). Individual performance and behavior that adapt to these norms usually meets with organizational approval and reward. Behavior which does not fit with the norms is not acceptable.

Organizational norms built merely upon needs motivation can not long or satisfactorily guide employee behavior. An organization's culture and norms must include the values which create an environment motivational to its employees. Without clear and identified values, it is impossible to build this motivational culture or develop these organizational norms.

Here's another specific example for consideration. In today's competitive business environment, customer service is frequently an organization's only competitive edge. Quality is no longer a motivatior for purchasing. It is simply expected. Quality does not attract customers. *Poor* quality, however, does cause an organization to lose customers. Price, another past competitive edge, is a competitive advantage no longer. The costs of products and services are generally quite similar. Service, then, is the value-added element which still creates the edge over one's competition.

Now, look at customer service that is driven by needs motivation alone. The motivation here for customer service does not come from customer or employee values. The objective is solely dollar income. It is not long before employees who are aware catch on. They are not valued. Policies, procedures, and the corporate structure do not reveal any real values for relationships with either customers or employees. Employees are not accorded the same treatment that they are expected (by norm expectations) to show the customer. All too soon, the customer catches on. It is difficult for an employee to treat customers with courtesy and respect when they, themselves, are given none.

Some organizations monitor customer service department telephone calls. What is the underlying assumption? What is the belief system that underlies this assumption? Clearly, the belief system is that employees are unwilling or unable to perform. They are not worthy of trust, certainly. Otherwise, their calls would not be monitored. Now, can you imagine employees whose organization is clearly expecting untrustworthiness, incompetence, unwillingness to not provide the expected behavior? Obviously, such an organization has never heard of expectation theory.

Only with a concise organizational mission/purpose built upon needs *and* values can a recognizable culture be developed. Clearly articulated mission or purpose statements can communicate to one and all what the organization stands for.

In the selection and hiring process, such clarity is invaluable. Turnover is extremely expensive, particularly at upper management levels. Yet, it is at these very levels that organizational and individual values become increasingly important and evident.

If you intend to *keep* good people, it is imperative that the organization's values be clear, be communicated well, and be reflected in decisions, norms, structures, policies, and procedures. Values conflicts between employees and the organization cause conflict and frustration, resulting in reduced productivity. The best employees will leave, rather than remain in such an comfortable situation.

Define what you believe in, and what your organization believes in. Share those beliefs with your people so there is a clear understanding of what is expected. If the values culture is strong enough, those who don't fit will leave quite willingly, often before you have an opportunity to make such a suggestion.

Appendix C

Self- Esteem in the Corporate Environment

An increasing number of people are becoming interested in self-esteem. The concept and the term are becoming popularized with our sharpening focus on the value of the individual.

Numerous consultants, authors, trainers, and professional speakers spread the word about the value of self-esteem. They approach it from a number of perspectives. Many of these exponents of self-esteem seek to motivate their audiences; others look for holistic approaches to the good life.

The late William J. McGrane, CPAE was a recognized national leader in the self-esteem field. Bill devoted much of his adult life to the study of the topic and its practical application in life. Director of The McGrane Self Esteem Institute in Cincinnati, Ohio, Bill spoke enthusiastically about how dedicated and enlightened leaders could build human self-esteem in organizational settings.

Being familiar with Bill's philosophies, I admire and respect his approach, depth, and sincerity. To share with you some insight into self-esteem and its place in the corporate world, I interviewed Bill when I wrote the first edition of ***Keeping Good People***. His words and thoughts are as meaningful today as they were then.

The balance of this appendix will be a sharing of Bill's comments. Rather than confusing you with the mix of questions, answers, and commentary, I will quote or paraphrase what Bill said so his thoughts may be experienced directly.

Let's begin with the premise that all human beings have been born with the birthright and the gift of high self-esteem. It is present within all of us, although many people have buried it away from their consciousness.

We seem to lose our awareness of our self-esteem over the years as we learn to value other measures of personal worth. As we shift our attention from genuine self-esteem, we tend to hurt and be hurt more easily. We don't have the inner resilience we need; we become more fragile.

As we realize we're missing something, we begin searching. We don't know quite what we're looking for, but we know there must be something more. In our materialistic society, we usually get caught up in the concern for self-image. It's a stage we go through and, unfortunately, many of us never quite come out of it.

Self-image is different from self-esteem. Self- image is comparison. If we run our company to compare one employee with the next, we are setting ourselves up to lose employees. Self-esteem says "I am valuable just because I exist." It's a self respect that we feel for ourselves; it has nothing to do with what we do or what we have.

That's tough for people to accept as reality. God set it up that way. He doesn't say we have to have anything or do anything to be loved by Him. Self-esteem is feared by a lot of people because it forces them to look inside. And that's difficult. People need to recognize that each of us has a uniqueness. When we value others because of their uniqueness, they will be encouraged to develop their competence and their self-esteem.

As we go through life, all of us make unwise choices. Our objective, as we grow and learn and strengthen our self-esteem, is to make fewer and fewer unwise choices. Once we realize this lesson, we become internally motivated to build our self-esteem. That exciting process is achieved through three steps.

To raise your self-esteem, you

1. review your personal history
2. re-program personal history as a result of the discoveries we make through unwise behavior
3. take action.

Our level of self-esteem is based on what we *do* after we've learned more about ourselves. Our sense of personal worth actually comes from what we do for others, more than what we do for ourselves. High self-esteem comes most to those who give of themselves to serve others, without any concern for reward or return. It's what I call personal tithing of one's talents.

True wealth comes from unselfish service. The concept of supporting others, of helping others grow and prosper, is a manifestation of genuine self-esteem. Managers who invest energy in supporting others, helping them realize their potential, are building their own self-esteem while enabling other people to build theirs.

Let's look at what happens in the corporate environment. In reality, we are able to keep people in a job even when the financial rewards may not be as high as the psychic rewards. In a money-oriented society, we wonder how this choice might be made.

To understand how self-esteem is applied wisely in organizations, let's look at the concept of bonding. I believe that the first year and half a human being is alive, the most precious gift we can give is the gift of bonding.

When bonding occurs, the child feels safe, secure, and comfortable. Those three words are critical if you're going to create an environment where people can thrive in an atmosphere of cooperation and trust.

Enlightened parents will leave the furniture where it is for at least the first three years so the child will sense stability and security. The child can count on being safe, secure, and comfortable every single day. An astonishing number of children today miss this vital bonding because both parents are working.

With both parents working, the child does not get the bonding because the parents need to work for family survival. There needs to be a balance. Many employers on the leading edge set aside a sufficient amount of space and create a daycare center inside the company.

Such a facility, on the company premises, allows for more bonding between parent and child. The parent can be with the child during lunch and perhaps during breaks. This opportunity for closeness and personal contact provides the child with a greater sense of being connected with the parent. The bonding deepens every day, but doesn't interfere with the flow of work or the continuity within the company. The parent forms a stronger bond with the company as a result of the company's support for the family bonding.

Unfortunately, childcare in proximity to work stations is not present to any great extent in companies today. It is part of our future, and caring employers should prepare to offer the service. There is a wonderful opportunity to support people, to hold good people, and to increase the psychic rewards.

Psychic rewards account for 95 percent of our desired income. Only 5 percent of our personal needs come as a result of financial reward. We have proven this ratio, and our news reports are full of stories validating this balance.

Psychic rewards recognize people for who they are, not for what they do. We are a society that values people for what they do and what they have. Yet, greed, power, and money have not brought fulfillment to people. Today we see this deficiency more and more, causing people to look for that elusive "something else."

The high-self esteem, value-driven, companies that will be most successful in the 1990s and beyond will be those organizations that model the behavior they want their employees to adopt. This strategy means our corporate leaders need to have high self-esteem, personally and organizationally. If we don't possess a certain feeling about ourselves, there's no way we can model that feeling for others.

Therefore, companies need to hire and manage people based on clear understandings of ethics, company policies, legitimate job descriptions, and vital job functions. These have to be reviewed constantly and re-affirmed. The people being led need to have considerable input into how their jobs are structured and how they are being measured.

Evaluations need to be done at the time of performance, not six months later. The "sandwich" approach to discipline is, quite frankly, outmoded and obsolete. Evaluations need to be given as *affirmations,* emphasizing the positive aspects and looking at how other aspects might be improved.

Managers need to accept the reality of the employees' existing skills, with a willingness to let the employees refine and strengthen those skills that need work. Note that the responsibility to improve is on the *employees.* Self-esteem is built by allowing people to take more responsibility for themselves.

Ideally, every employer would allocate a significant sum of money for each employee to invest in self-development each year. The employee would be trusted to select those learning experiences. The employee would have the freedom to make the choices about which learning they want to experience.

The growing employee would have the responsibility of gaining worthwhile knowledge, then sharing it with others. If we're going to create an atmosphere of trust, we'd better let the employee make the choices. Based on the choices the employee makes from year to year, the manager may be involved very little in structuring the learning.

I believe the more freedom we give to employees, the longer we are going to keep them. They feel needed, wanted, important, and valued. These are all basic areas of raising people's self-esteem. Unless we affirm people daily, we're missing an opportunity. Few people get affirmed daily. There are great voids of psychological emptiness to be filled. When we give people opportunities to self-actualize, then reinforce their achievements, they will stay with our firm for the intrinsic feelings that are so important to them.

Keeping good people does not take large amounts of money. It takes a personal investment. The organization's leaders, including the CEO, need to be visible to their people. The less visible they are, the more they set themselves up for high turnover Bonding, being with their people, needs to be their Number One issue—daily. People need to be affirmed daily.

Unfortunately, many people in senior management positions are from the "old school" that doesn't place such an importance on caring for the individual. When men dominated the workplace, things were different. They didn't experience strong bonding, as a rule, when they were children. So, they don't use bonding at work. It simply isn't there.

Today, and into the future, we will see how having more women in the workplace increases this concern for bonding. I believe that men are more concerned about things; women are more concerned about relationships. Both men and women need to be sensitive to this perspective and find the right balance. We can be highly productive with strong concern for each other, with bonding, with relationships.

We motivate people by valuing them. To the degree we value them, they will not steal, they will not manipulate, they'll act as if they own the company. It's good for employees to have some real personal ownership in the company. To the extent possible, particularly in public corporations, we should give employees the opportunity to buy stock in the company . . . to own a little piece.

When people buy into the organization, they have a higher level of commitment. Now they're concerned about the character of the company as a whole, in addition to their own character.

People perform better if character is encouraged, versus personality. The character of an individual, when developed, will be a high or low self-esteem. The character of the business will be determined by how employees act. If we act as if we own the company, keeping the concerns of others and of the whole above concerns for ourselves, our people *will* follow our lead.

"Intimacy" will be a byword of the 1990s, even though it still makes men uncomfortable. Paraphrasing, it could easily read, "into me see." To the degree that we allow others to see into us, to the degree that we encourage others to invest time with us as people, we will have relationships based on more than just business.

We should take time to get to know our employees, and help them get to know us. We must focus on the person, the family, outside interests, ideas, creativity, and similar concerns. Learn to value each other as human beings, not just as parts of the business.

I recommend people take 15-minute segments on some sort of regular basis to get to know each other. Character, self-esteem, relationships, are built through bonding. Managers need to invest the time to open up *as people* with their employees to establish and maintain long-term, mutually beneficial, relationships that are intimate . . . based on the level of intimacy that each person can have.

When people invest in this sharing, this knowing each other, this intimacy, in business organizations, the resultant relationships will produce a level of productivity beyond their wildest dreams.

We can't stop this process. We mustn't just support people for just one year, for instance, and that's it. Deliberate, daily, *constant* affirmations reinforce the belief system: Put the principles up on the wall for everyone to see them. Talk about them daily. Become more principle-directed, rather than needs-directed.

We need to help people understand, by talking about our

principles and acting according to those principles, what we stand for. As an example, can we say "no" to cheating somebody? Can we say "no" to stealing from somebody? Can we say "no" when somebody undercharges us? Can we say "no" when something simply isn't right?

When we direct our energies to helping others, to building character, we become much more powerful than if we are just helping ourselves. Self-esteem is considerably higher when we concentrate on serving others instead of serving ourselves. We feel better about what we are doing. We feel better about the organization we do it with. We *bond* with that organization because of the compatibility of our character.

That bonding, that reinforcement of self-esteem, holds people in the company. That bonding produces a feeling of being safe, secure, and comfortable. When people gain that feeling, they don't want to risk losing it by leaving the company to go somewhere else. They'll stay where they are valued for who they are.

People want to like where they work. They don't want to have a *thank-God-it's-Friday* attitude. They want to work where they have friends, where there are others who want to help the work become satisfying and fulfilling. They want to help the company be successful, so they can be successful, too.

People don't leave companies because of money, because of how much they got paid or didn't get paid. They leave because they didn't feel they were valuable, important, or needed enough. Once we know we're needed, we'll stay in that environment. Psychic income will always overpower money, even though people may say that's not true.

If a company pays its people and rewards them for their productivity, both psychically and financially, then they will stay there. There's no need for them to move elsewhere where they don't know what the atmosphere is going to be like.

People would rather remain where they have bonded, reinforcing those bonds, than take the risk of going somewhere else where they may not experience those feelings. Value people for who they are, and they will stay with you . . . happy and productive.

About the Author

Roger E. Herman is a Strategic Business Futurist concentrating on workforce and workplace issues. He studies trends in the field, exploring their implications. From his observations, he offers forecasts and practical advice on how to better lead, manage, and succeed in the turbulent environment of today's World of Work.

As a Certified Management Consultant, Roger advises a wide range of employer and industry clients in the United States and other countries. His firm's services include strategic design facilitation, staffing design, corporate culture assessment and change, executive briefings and coaching, and leadership development. Roger is a member of the board of directors of the Institute of Management Consultants (US), the pre-eminent global interdisciplinary organization of consultants to management.

A sought-after speaker on employee retention, the bigger picture of workforce stability, and the longer-range topics of trends and their influence, Roger addresses corporate and trade association audiences throughout the United States and in other countries. The National Speakers Association designated him a "Certified Speaking Professional" in 1989, positioning him among the top seven percent of professional speakers internationally. Clients engage Roger to deliver keynote addresses, to conduct seminars and workshops, and to facilitate retreats or strategic planning experiences.

Roger serves as contributing editor, workforce and workplace trends, for *The Futurist* magazine. He is frequently cited in business publications, trade magazines, human resource journals, and the popular press. His comments are heard regularly on radio, televisions, and Internet broadcasts.

As Senior Fellow of the Workforce Stability Institute, Roger engages in research and education in the fields of strategic staffing, recruiting, selection, hiring, orienting, training, compensating, optimizing, and retaining employees. He is co-editor with Joyce Gioia, CMC, of *Workforce Stability Alert,* a monthly newsletter published by the Institute. To support his continued learning, Roger is a member of the Society for Human Resource Management and the Human Resource Planning Society.

Roger is a graduate of Hiram College, a liberal arts college in Hiram, Ohio, where he majored in Sociology. He earned his masters degree (Public Administration) from The Ohio State University. During the Viet Nam era, Roger served as a Counterintelligence Special Agent.

Today he is Chief Executive Officer of The Herman Group, a firm of Certified Management Consultants formed in 1980. You can reach Roger directly by e-mail at roger@herman.net or by contacting

The Herman Group
3400 Willow Grove Court
Greensboro, NC 27410-8600
(336) 282-9370
FAX (336) 282-2003
www.herman.net

Oakhill Press

Oakhill Press is an independent publisher of business and self-help books. Our team of professionals assures that our products uphold our standards for high quality, readability, and usefulness. We are dedicated to helping leaders do a better job—in their business and in their personal lives.

Since the inception of Oakhill Press in 1988, we have endeavored to bring well-written books by knowledgeable people to readers who can benefit from them. The information and insight shared in our books is the result of years of experience combined with appropriate research. We value highly the letters, calls, and e-mail we receive praising our books.

Our authors are all management consultants and/or professional speakers. They are on the leading edge of their fields of expertise, strengthened by continual interaction with clients and audiences. Their thinking, speaking, and writing are stimulating, educational, and practical. We are pleased to serve as a vehicle for them to convey their thoughts to the world.

For further information on Oakhill Press publications, you are invited to visit our web site, www.oakhillpress.com. And, of course, you can give us a call at (800) 32-BOOKS. Thanks for giving us an opportunity to make a difference in your life.

The Workforce Stability Institute

The Workforce Stability Institute is an organization dedicated to research and education in the recruiting, optimizing, and retaining of workers in corporations, not-for-profits, and government entities. It was founded to assist organizational leaders in attaining greater workforce stability, thus allowing more revenue to flow to the bottom line.

The Institute monitors trends, corporate staffing and performance challenges, and responses to difficulties in maintaining a strong, productive workforce. Research is conducted at various levels of interest—global, industry, community, and individual organization. Results are typically published in reports or white papers, some of which are confidential at the request of the research sponsor.

Educational activities of the Institute include providing articles for publication, interviews with journalists—both print and broadcast, and conducting executive briefings on trends, conditions, and recommended strategies to achieve greater workforce stability. The Institute also sponsors publications and produces learning materials to assist corporate executives, managers, supervisors, and human resource professionals.

The Workforce Stability Institute maintains a Web site on the Internet (www.employee.org). A list serve is available as a public service. To access the list serve, send an inquiry by e-mail to webservices@employee.org.

From time to time, the Institute produces conferences and

workshops on workforce stability. These educational events are sponsored by corporations, trade associations, universities, or government organizations. Anyone interested in sponsoring or participating in such conferences is invited to contact the executive director of the Institute.

The Fellows of the Institute are consultants who specialize in various aspects of finding and keeping good employees. Each is a recognized and certified professional, respected for his or her contribution to the field. The author of this book is Senior Fellow of the Institute.

Workforce Stability Institute
3400 Willow Grove Court
Greensboro, North Carolina 27410-8600
(336) 282-1480 FAX 282-2003
www.employee.org
info@employee.org

Index

A

B

C

D

E

F

G

H

I

J

K

L

M

N

O

P

R

S

T

U

V

W